LA FRANCE GOURMANDE

Suddenly the air feels like September,
morning mist over the Dordogne valley
of scoop-sloped roofto
peek
the river is a shroud
salmon and swa
From
this
on a hill,
time when
crops of juicy
crisp
annual
field,
eagerly
the region's
vendors' tables
preserves, jams
garlic and jars of
FERMIER DU PERIGORD
FROMAGE DE CHEVRE
VALADOU
GAEC L.
PAVÉ DU LOT
FROMAGE DE CHEV
TISANALE
BUVEZ du VIN
et
vivez joyeux

Marolyn Charpentier

LA FRANCE GOURMANDE

A Food Lover's Guide to French Fairs and Festivals

PAVILION

DEDICATION
For Michel
The chef and driving force of *La France Gourmande*

First published in Great Britain in 2003 by
PAVILION BOOKS LIMITED
64 Brewery Road, London, N7 9NT
www.chrysalisbooks.co.uk
A member of **Chrysalis** Books plc

Text © Marolyn D. Charpentier, 2003
Photographs © Marolyn D. Charpentier, 2003, except those
detailed on page 256
Design and layout © Pavilion Books Ltd., 2003

Designed by Bernard Higton

A CIP catalogue record for this book is available
from the British Library

ISBN 1 86205 372 3

Set in Caslon Antique and Weiss
Colour origination by Classicscan in Singapore
Printed in Singapore by Imago Pte Ltd

1 2 3 4 5 6 7 8 9 10

This book can be ordered direct from the publisher.
Please contact the Marketing Department.
But try your bookshop first.

Contents

Introduction

To every season, a speciality...

Suddenly the air feels like September, the morning mist over the Dordogne Valley lets only tiny points of scoop-sloped rooftops peek through, and the river is a shrouded, fast-flowing home to salmon and swans. From our garden, from this hazy viewpoint on a hill, I watch the seasons change. It is a time when potagers and market gardens bear crops of juicy red tomatoes and round ripe crisp peppers, a time when annual harvest traditions in the field, the kitchen and in village squares roll round again.

For some twelve years, I have been surrounded by signs of seasonal change in one fascinating corner of Europe or another. My first home away from the American midwest was in Helsinki, where autumn winds swept in from the Gulf of Finland, ushering in short, dark days. Here, the annual October Herring Fair in the city harbour piqued my curiosity about the traditions of seasonal fairs. In the early 1990s, my husband and I found a stone cottage in Périgord, now our vantage-point to keep pace with *les quatre saisons*. Forays to food festivals in the southwest began as shopping adventures, but soon took on greater dimensions. I sought answers to questions about regional products – and found customs and traditions as well.

It was more than idle curiosity that drew us to Villefranche-du-Périgord for its annual chestnut and mushroom festival. The season, late October in 1993, promised baskets of the region's delicious chestnuts, and an inviting Sunday drive through autumn forests. In that first visit to a regional food festival, we found a normally drowsy village in the Périgord hills bustling with chestnut vendors, and alive with folkdancers in the town's historic bastide hall. The town's narrow streets were lined with stalls of golden pumpkins, shiny

apples, nut breads and mushroom tarts. It kindled our appetites, and during the following seasons we set out for *foires* and *fêtes gastronomiques* across the region – my theme for exploring the flavours of France.

Harvest time, I found, is not limited to late summer and autumn. In April, when asparagus bundles by the hundreds were lined up in crates, we enjoyed an asparagus festival in Gascony. June was the month to venture further afield, to Provence in southeastern France, to sample Banon's famous goat's cheese. With each *fête*, regional specialities we've tasted have been in the context of their season, fresh, on the spot. Watching parades of *confréries*, talking with winemakers and oyster farmers, I began to understand this gastronomic phenomenon that reaches deep into the French sense of communal celebration. With every *fête* and *foire*, I absorbed vivid images and flavours, took more photographs and jotted notes on our discoveries. These notes from my files led to *La France Gourmande*.

The traditions surrounding each *fête* are like little windows into the past, into the ways of the people and the land that nourishes their families. An evening melon fair in Provence, re-enacted with a parade of horse-drawn wagons loaded with baskets of the sweet ripe fruit, was one among many traditions we have been fortunate to witness. As I tasted cool slivers of melon in the July heat of Provence, I knew that it was well worth the long journey to be there.

Although they have certain features in common, a few differences exist between *fêtes* and *foires*. The origins of the *foire* lie solidly in commerce. They are still often expanded markets, attracting vendors of foods, crafts and tools from neighbouring regions. *Fêtes* more generally feature ceremony and pomp, with a mass in the village church, parades, a large meal and induction of new members into one or more brotherhoods (*confréries*). Themes for French *confréries* seem limitless:

chestnuts and mushrooms, cheese, wine, olive oil, apple tart and linden blossom are but a few examples. Frequently these societies are composed of men and women in a certain trade, producers or aficionados of a regional speciality. Not all members are producers (honorary members are commonly inducted), but may participate in the community and contribute support, helping to organize the *fête*, for example.

On the pages of *La France Gourmande*, personal encounters with *confréries*, *artisans du goût* and discoveries about their products are

recounted in three chapters for each month, each chapter focusing on one event. The selection was made to offer a sampling of the diverse gastronomic specialities that rural France celebrates through the year. In each chapter, I recount some of the events and flavourful details that await visitors with curious tastebuds. There are similarities along with the surprises, common denominators such as parades and vendors.

Many *fêtes* offer tastings, *dégustations*, in one form or another. A word of caution: as *dégustations* of nuts, honey, pastry, olives, cheese, spice bread, wine or sweet *apéritifs* are offered, beware the temptation to taste every tidbit. Fond as I may be of cheese or honey, after a sequence of sweet to salty, sharp to mild, one's palate becomes quite confused. By the time a nut wine or a good *vin rouge* is up for tasting, the nose and tongue have palled, disabled by a confusing parade of aromas and flavours.

Wine *fêtes* and *foires* are listed in the book's reference section. Personal suggestions for wine or cider with regional specialities tasted during the event are shared in most chapters as an integral pleasure of each gathering. Companion wines for recipes are noted as well. Is a meal available at every food fair? Often, but not always. In many cases, street foods offer

the true flavours of the region as well as the season, so just relax and have fun. For fine dining, there are usually restaurants in or near the host village. Large lunches or dinners catering for a crowd, usually under *fête* tents or in the local community hall, are optional, and places must be reserved in advance. Whether to join those seated at long tables for four to six courses is a matter of mood, season and budget, as much as appetite.

Les recettes: A note on recipes

For every *fête*, a recipe is included that brings a taste of the event to tables at home. Clearly, the ingredients for many of these are available during a short season, best sampled when at their peak. Shopping for vegetables, fish and fowl in the Périgord has taught me to cook from the market with ingredients in season. Timing applies to the day as well as the season: arrive early for the best selection and condition. Asparagus that has shrivelled in June's heat is no longer flavourful, imported strawberries have lost their sweetness, so they don't go into my basket. The recipes on the following pages follow this "in season" spirit, and will serve four unless noted otherwise.

On the whole, measurements are approximate, just as my neighbours, the butcher or our gourmet-grocers relay them. When I watched my stepson, a trained chef, measure sugar by the handful for a *sabayon*, there was clearly a limit to being "approximate" with the recipes, and so we measured. Readers will, I hope, feel free to use herbs they find available and to substitute ingredients – in season.

A few useful festival terms

animations	events, performances, contests
artisans du goût	craftspersons producing edible products like cheese, honey etc
bal	a dance, a ball
bandas	small brass bands common in southern France
buvette	stand selling soft drinks, snacks, perhaps beer or wine
chapiteau	large tent covering a fête, exposition or circus
chars, charettes	decorated floats
concours	contest
conférence	meeting on a subject; discussion
confrérie	brotherhood, pledged to support their product
corso	parade, festive procession
couvert	one place setting; plate, glass, knife, fork and spoon
défilé	procession
dégustation	tastings, samples to taste
département	administrative region, similar to a shire or state
dîner dansant	dinner dance
discrétion (à)	as you wish, serve yourself
fanfare	brass band
fête foraine	fun fair, carnival with rides and games
fête votive	religious fête on a patron saint's day, may be expanded into a larger event with a regional theme
goût	taste
inscriptions	reservations (for dinner or ball)
kermesse	a local fête sponsored by church or school
manège	a merry-go-round, rides to amuse children
messe solennelle	mass, read in the church
repas	meal
salle polyvalente or salle des fêtes	community hall
terroir	the soil, microclimate, the character of place and products reflecting this
tombola	drawing for prizes, a raffle for local specialities
vin d'honneur	honouring toast

Foire des Rois / Fair of the Three Kings and Foie Gras

Brive-la-Gaillarde/Corrèze, Limousin

Oysters and Champagne? *Foie gras* and Sauternes? The season of feasting in central France continues well past Christmas and New Year. Filled with a layer of almond paste, the buttery-rich *Galette des Rois* is the featured treat for Epiphany. The *Foire des Rois* (Fair of the Three Kings), also called the *Foire au Gras de Brive*, annually draws crowds to Brive-la-Gaillarde to celebrate winter's rich products.

Circling the city, a centre of communications and commerce on the edge of the Massif Central since Roman times, we follow a spiralling road into the heart of Brive. Bright orange tents and vendors' stalls stretch across the open market and into a contemporary hall. In diffused January sunlight, stalls display gleaming chestnuts and trays of perfect walnuts, fruit-filled pastries, hearty breads, winter pears and apples, and dense pumpkin cakes: indeed a visual feast! A tempting array of local bakers' breads and pastries star in this *Foire des Rois*. The centrepiece of each is a fresh pastry *Galette des Rois* with a golden paper crown adorning each flaky circle, and as the table empties, more are brought forward.

The *Galette des Rois* is surrounded by its own set of rituals. On a Sunday close to January the sixth, families and friends gather round to enjoy a *Galette* (made in two sizes, usually with a *frangipane* filling) together. Who will find the single *fève* and wear the golden paper crown? Tradition dictates that the round *feuilleté* cake for the Epiphany season should conceal a small prize, originally a simple bean, still called the *fève* no matter what the shape. A lucky finder will then be "'king" or "queen", wearing the crown for the day. The small figure that has replaced the bean is usually made of china, and has taken on limitless forms; it can be a tiny animal, fruit, or even a cartoon

The Foire des Rois at Brive celebrates winter's rich products.

character. During the winter months, local bakers also sell a version of the Couronne (a circular bread or cake). This, too, has a paper crown, but is made of sweet yeast dough topped with grains of pearl sugar.

The Foire des Rois is one of Brive's three winter fairs. The first, Foire Grasse, is in December. In January, the focus is clearly on flaky Galette des Rois and foie gras, while February's fair usually features primeurs (early spring vegetables) alongside foie gras. In all three, rich desserts of the season are in tantalizing abundance. Nut cakes and tarts take many forms, some baked in a pastry shell and glazed with chocolate, others topped with flaky crust. The selection includes delicious cakes dense with ground walnuts, as well as lighter ones made with chopped walnuts and apples. Golden Millassou is made with cooked pumpkin, eggs, milk and corn meal; as dense as a slab of polenta, or as custardy as a sweet flan, it is often studded with raisins and spiked with a dash of rum. A flat variation, Millas, is either served with a hearty stew or sugared as a simple dessert. Crêpes, sausages, quiche, grilled chestnuts, small nut cakes and assorted street food make delicious snacks or lunch for the visitors browsing the crowded aisles.

Shoppers throng to Brive's vast market place during the Foire des Rois to buy both starters and desserts for their on-going season of feasts. Long trestle-tables are set out in the market and large adjacent hall to sell dressed ducks and geese as well as fresh and preserved foie gras. Vendors from the Corrèze, the Lot and Périgord display pâtés, rillettes d'oie, mousse de foie gras and other delicacies, and are keen to discuss their products. Puzzled about a stack of duck carcasses, I ask a pink-cheeked, plump woman in a red lumber jacket what to do with them. She chuckles and replies: "La carcasse? Pour faire le potage, madame! We make soup with this, adding a few leeks and carrots." She reaches for a flattened carcass and points to the remaining meat: "but this paletot (overcoat) is even better roasted ... C'est délicieux, et économique!"

In the next aisle, I find an impeccable display of ducks. The vendor, a warm yellow scarf draped around his neck, is busy re-stocking a display of tinned duck products. He responds quickly when I ask about choosing a whole duck and its foie. "Choose a fresh foie gras de canard that springs back a bit to the touch, glistens and has no dark-ened edges. Many are creamy rose in colour, but variations on yellow to gold will depend on what the duck has been fed. Those in the Gers may be yellow in tone due to the corn that fattens them. In the

Foie gras en terrine / Foie gras terrine

Preparing *foie gras* at home is relatively simple, but delicate *foie* does need gentle handling. If it is too cold, it will be brittle and will crack. Capers or green peppercorns are traditional seasonings, to be layered in before baking if desired.

Ingredients
One 450 to 500 g/1 lb foie gras
  de canard
Fine sea salt, white pepper
28 ml/1 fl oz/2 tbsp Armagnac
(Slices of trimmed truffles
  optional)

Method

Clean and de-vein the interior of the *foie gras de canard* lobes with the point of a sharp knife, and peel off the fine outer membrane if still attached.

Place one lobe in a lidded terrine. Season, and add a dash of Armagnac. Slices of trimmed truffle may be layered in at this stage as well.

Press the other lobe on top, add another spoonful of Armagnac, and cover by wrapping the terrine in a tea towel. Let it rest in a cool place for a day or two.

When you are ready to cook the *foie*, bring it to room temperature before placing the terrine in a roasting pan filled with hot water reaching half way up the sides of the dish.

Heat the oven to 170°C/325°F/Gas Mark 3 and bake the terrine in its water bath for 20 to 30 minutes, depending on how pink you like the meat. Beads of yellow fat will form at the edges, a good sign that it is almost done. (The fat can be spread on toast later.) Take care, as a *foie d'oie* can dissolve into a puddle of golden fat if overdone.

When ready, lift the terrine from the roasting pan, let it cool gradually, and keep in a cool place for a few days to mature before eating.

To serve, lay a slice of *foie* on each plate and garnish with watercress or red *trevisa escarole*. Or, spread a slice of *foie gras* on a triangle of toast – a simple but delectable pleasure.

The classic, luxurious companion for *foie gras* is Sauternes, or aged sweet Monbazillac wine. A sweet Jurançon, or a late-harvest Gewürztraminer from Alsace are also festive options. The pleasure is not only sensual, but (dare I say?) chemical, as sugars in the sweet wine cut the rich oils and prepare the palette for the next bite.

Périgord and Corrèze, we feed a rosier variety of corn. This also produces a *magret*, a duck breast with fine texture and flavour."

In answer to my question about size, he continues: "A *foie gras* about the length and width of your hand weighs about 450 grams and will serve six as a starter. *Foie gras d'oie* (fattened goose liver), with its subtle flavour and silky texture, is twice the size and double the price of *foie de canard*. Geese are more difficult, more sensitive to maladies and they take more time – we must feed them five to seven times a day for a good *foie*. Also, the demand is not as great any more, as more people choose the economical and more pronounced flavour of duck *foie*." Rolling his brown eyes, a broad smile replaces his serious expression to conclude: "But remember, *foie gras d'oie*, like a good wine, has a longer finish on the palate."

A *fresh foie gras* should be kept chilled, and prepared within a week. Unless it is sealed in glass or tin, *foie mi-cuit* is perishable, best served within three weeks. A tin or jar marked *entier* indicates that the entire *foie* is preserved. This tinned *foie entier*, best when aged for six months to a year, is the closest to fresh *foie* on a scale of products that runs from pieces of *foie*, marked simply *foie gras*, to *bloc* and *parfait*, which are pieces or blends. Shoppers will also find *pâtés*, usually prepared with bacon or pork, and *galantines*. A *mousse de foie gras* is a whipped

A festive lunch at Chez Francis should really include foie gras.

foie, a delicious smooth purée. Completing the list, a *pâté de foie truffé* contains from one to three per cent truffles, perfect as a special gift or sumptuous entrée.

With my new-found knowledge on the intricacies of *foie gras*, I step back into the colourful bustle of the *Foire des Rois*. The *folklorique* after-noon continues as accordions, violas and fiddles mark the pace for dancers with the lilting strains of a gavotte. Broad-brimmed black hats and dark floral-patterned shawls whisk past the crowd, and I easily imagine the dancers' grandparents moving to the same melodies in a village *fête* a century ago.

Journée de la Truffe / Truffle Day
Uzès/Gard, Midi

In the winter air, a pungent, earthy aroma wafts through the cobbled streets and out to the ramparts of an ancient ducal city north of Nîmes. Uzès' annual *Journée de la Truffe*, held on the third Sunday in January, is a time to taste truffles at their most mature, their fullest flavour and aroma. The black diamond, *le diamant noir* of gastronomic legend and regal feasts, is in focus, in a setting as appealing as the *truffe* itself.

Uzès, the first French city to be honoured as a duchy in the eleventh century, bears traces of ancient grandeur in its convents, churches and private homes. Surrounding the broad place des Herbes, elegant façades of cream and ivory stone seem to radiate a mysterious light in spite of January's overcast days. A natural canopy of bare-branched linden trees adds a textural element to this backdrop for Uzès' colourful Saturday market and for the city's annual Truffle Day. Medieval arcades facing the square are lined with truffle-hunter's bounty, and shelter shoppers from seasonal rains.

Located in the uplands of the Midi, high in truffle-country hills, Uzès is close enough to Nîmes and Avignon to draw a good Sunday crowd, and hosts one of the few *foires* featuring truffles. The winter's brisk truffle trade is usually done in markets, held weekly for just a few hours when the fungus is abundant. Truffles from steep slopes in the scrub forests of the Gard and neighbouring *départements* of the Ardèche, as well as the Drôme and Vaucluse east of the Rhône, are brought to Uzès, carefully wrapped to conserve their all-important scent. Enveloped in checked cotton towels, they rest in baskets alongside single specimens displayed in rows on vendors' tables. A few *trufficulteurs* bring sturdy wicker hampers or cloth sacks holding truffles to be sold by the kilo. All on display are identified with a card certifying the variety and the region in which they were found or raised. These strict measures of identification have been necessary in recent years to protect consumers from illegal sales of cheaper Asian truffles. Observant *gendarmes* roam the crowd, watching as digital scales weigh each purchase. Depending on the size and the condition, prices can run to as much as six hundred francs per truffle. Prices fluctuate depending on supply, and tend to be higher in December when demand is greatest.

Why are they so expensive? Well, truffles are in demand, truffles are elusive and they take time to grow. Even secret, "dependable" truffle terrain may be void of the prized black gold some years, causing concern for both the farmer and the chef. From the first to the last frost, truffle hunters are busy hunting with trained dogs or pigs to sniff and snuffle them out across southern France and into Burgundy. The success of the season depends on rainfall, drought and other whims of nature. A *chêne truffier* (truffle oak) whose roots are riddled with tubers for decades, for example, may suddenly have a non-productive year. In spite of all the scientific and botanical studies written, the *coquetterie* of this strange and fickle fungus still enhances its value. So chefs know that it is best bought when it is in good supply, and they are always ready to pay the price. Some call the earthy richness a sublime taste, but for many it's a matter of scent over flavour, as I discover in Uzès.

Watching a young, lean *trufficulteur* from Richerenches in the Drôme as he sells a couple of perfect coal-black truffles, I notice that he has two price categories. I ask him about the difference between them. He gingerly lifts a perfect, round *truffe* with his fingertips and his dark eyes grow intense: "Look for perfection, *madame*, no lumps or knobs on the contours of the *truffe's* round surface, no yellowing or soft evidence of decay or worm holes, an even-textured uniformity." He leans forward, holding it up to my nose: *"Le parfum, madame."* Look for perfection, *madame*, remember perfection ... it rings in my ears. A trim, well-coiffed woman next to me places eighty euros on his counter, exclaiming in Parisian French: "I'll take it!" I step aside and note that all truffle transactions are in cash, always. No cheques are accepted, and forget about credit cards in payment for *gout et parfum*.

The *Journée de la Truffe* brings together vendors of many tempting specialities of the Midi and the Rhône Valley. In addition to cheese-

Le diamant noir of gastronomic legend...

makers with discs and logs of *chèvre* (goats' cheese) rolled and layered with chopped truffles, there are rich *pâtés* baked in flaky pastry – *pâté en croûte truffé*. Plump white *boudin blanc*, speckled with bits of truffle, are stacked on *charcuterie* stalls along with other sausages of the region, studded with pine nuts, exuding garlic or coated with the prickly wild herbs of the *garrigue*.

Areas of the Vaucluse, the Drôme, the Alpes-de-Haute-Provence and the Var now claim more than seventy per cent of French truffle production, taking the lead over the Périgord and the Charente. Of the thirty species of truffle, the *truffe noire du Périgord* is the most widely hunted and cultivated across southern France, its season running from late November through February. Weekly truffle markets are held in towns stretching across southern France from the Charente east through the Dordogne and Lot hills, the Midi and Rhône Valley to Provence's truffle-rich uplands. Many of these markets last only one hour, and are primarily for those buying truffles wholesale.

Omelette aux truffes / Truffle omelette

Ingredients
6 farm-fresh eggs that have been stored in a covered jar or bowl with 1 truffle for 4 days
A knob of butter for the pan
1 truffle, brushed clean, outer skin trimmed, one half sliced into fine strips
Salt and freshly ground black pepper

Method
Whisk the eggs in a large bowl, and add 1 tablespoon water.

Pour this mixture into a hot, buttered frying pan, lifting the edges to distribute the eggs evenly.

Cook on a medium-hot heat. When the edges crisp slightly (this should take no more than 3 minutes), lay the truffle strips across the centre of the omelette, add salt and pepper, and fold one side over the other. Cover for 1 to 2 minutes to puff up.

To serve, grate the remaining half truffle over the omelette.

A regional wine like Costières de Nîmes or Lirac would make the perfect partner.

On this January Sunday, I speak with a wizened hunter in a well-worn denim jacket who is ready to demonstrate truffle-hunting skills at appointed times during the afternoon. He is nudged by his small black terrier, an eager truffle hound. Each day from November to March, the *terrain truffier* must be searched with either his trained dog or pig. Like many farmers, he prefers dogs, as they are more agile on rugged slopes and do not eat the truffles as quickly as the pigs. (The pigs, notorious gourmands, are often muzzled.) He leans on a sturdy stick, then, pointing to its tip, explains: "We stir in the dry dead leaves, moving the pole in circles. This disturbs a fly whose egg-laying cycle is tied to the small black tuber, telling us where a truffle may be found just below the leaves." Like generations of farmers, his family has truffle ground on their land – a sideline for the winter months. However, he lifts his shoulders in a Gallic shrug, admitting that each season is different and that the truffle yield is *imprévisible*, unpredictable.

Once you have laid your hands on a truffle, you don't want to waste it, so a little care and attention is required to enjoy it at its best. To extend even one truffle's aroma, simply bury it in rice, or tuck it into a jar of eggs. A very fresh truffle can be kept wrapped in a damp tea towel, or in a covered glass jar or ceramic crock, but should be used within a week. Don't wrap it in plastic as, like most organic products, it will become mouldy. Before use, truffles must be thoroughly brushed to remove any grit lodged in the bumpy surfaces. Once peeled, truffle trimmings can be dropped into fresh olive oil. Strain the oil after one week, then enjoy a hint of truffle in winter salads or brushed on toasted bread. Truffle slices inserted under the skin of fowl the day before roasting lend delicate flavours to the meat. Tiny pieces, diced and layered between slices of goats' cheese, aged in a cool place for a few days, sends a simple *chèvre* to new realms of flavour. But a classic omelette, in its elegant simplicity, captures the aromas best of all.

Leaving the *fête*, truffles securely tucked in my basket, I look ahead to our indulgence in a little French finesse to share with friends. A festive sparkling wine – a Champagne from Les Riceys, or a *pétillant* Brouette from Bordeaux, perhaps, will accompany *les diamants noirs* from Uzès, sliced and wrapped in pastry on a base of *foie gras* – a delight, for all the senses.

Fête de St-Blaise et du Raisin / Annual Fair and Grape Festival

Valbonne/Alpes-Maritimes, Provence – Côte d'Azur

For a taste of Provençal traditions, a *fête* whose history stretches back five hundred years lures me south towards the scent-celebrated town of Grasse. With map in hand, I find Valbonne nestled in the steep hills above Cannes and Mougins. The foothills of the Alps rise to the east past Fréjus, a rim of snow blanketing the jagged horizon. Turning north at Cannes, a tangle of roads leads up through dense forests of tall pines, opening suddenly to a panorama overlooking Valbonne's dappled terracotta rooftops in the glorious Mediterannean light.

The *Fête de St-Blaise et du Raisin* fills the centre of Valbonne with festivities for two short winter days. Old proverbs in Occitan, the ancient language still spoken in southern France, claim that this day marks the middle of winter. In centuries past, on the Sunday closest to February the third, the peasant checked to make sure that his hay racks, bread-trough and salt-pork barrels were half full. If stocks were running low, he would anxiously anticipate selling his pig and chickens in March in order to be able to struggle through the last windy weeks before summer. The *fête* celebrates this point in the year, and to me it is a showcase of survival and ingenuity, alongside unusual gastronomic discoveries.

To find out more about the *fête*, and the ways of the people of Valbonne, we step inside its small museum, which adjoins the wing of the church of St-Blaise. A friendly guide leads us to an

The procession leads to the sunlit place des Arcades.

Valbonne is decked with bright mimosa branches for the fête.

old dovecote where two facing walls are lined with shelves of old handblown glass jars, once used to hold branches of grapes. She enthusiastically explains: "The *servan* grape is a survivor itself, preferring altitudes of 200 to 250 metres above sea level and the chalky clay soils found from Valbonne to Opio, Plascassier and as far as Biot. It kept very well and its golden colour and sweetness enhanced its value as a luxury table grape. Late in November, farmers would carefully sort out the best bunches, cutting branches long enough to support them. Five to eight branches would rest in a tall jar of water, with the grapes suspended over the rim and kept on shelves in a cool room for at least two months."

Her dark eyes dance behind thick glasses as she continues: "In some old stone houses the grapes were still sweet at Easter. One night, mid-winter, the farmer would saddle up a horse and strap on saddle-

The varied faces of Provence pass before us...

bags carrying the precious grapes, knowing a five-hour ride to Nice lay ahead. Travelling down the rocky ridges and trails to the coast, his load of grapes would arrive in time for fine coastal hotels to have fresh, sweet grapes on the table for lunch, when no other fresh fruit was available. When they returned," she nods to a tintype photo of a peasant and his horse, "the horses had stiff legs and had to be rubbed with a liniment of rosemary and peppermint oils." So the family survived, thanks to ingenuity and to this very special grape.

In Valbonne's old centre, narrow streets lead past shops to the central square which is surrounded by sheltered, arcaded passageways. From the shadows, I look up to brightly shuttered windows and step out into

A mime artist finds a sunny spot – for hours.

Valbonne's place des Arcades. The corners of a stage set up for musicians and speech-makers are decked with lemon-yellow mimosa branches and dark fronds of greenery. *Artisans du goût* arrange their *dégustations* to tempt the crowds; tubs of black olives shine next to scented hand-milled soaps, honey and spice bread, braids and clusters of garlic, fresh leafy vegetables and bright mounds of lemons. Rows of small cheeses are set next to heavy, firm *tommes* made of milk from goats and sheep grazing on the southern slopes of the Alps – tangy, crumbly bits are offered to taste. Freshly pressed, golden olive oils, herbs, sun-dried tomatoes, nougat and sweet dried fruit, wines from Bandol and Côtes de Provence, conserves and jams are all in good supply.

The *Fête de St-Blaise* coincides with the week of *Chandeleur*, observed on or near February the second. Northern France favours *galettes* or *crêpes* for *Chandeleur*, but in Provence, *navettes* are traditional. I stop to buy these biscuits, little oval shuttles brushed with orange-flower water, as well as *amaretti* rich with almonds, and round, moist chestnut *rocher*. Chestnuts from the mountains north of Valbonne roast on

Pissaladière / Onion, olive and anchovy tart

Ingredients
1 quantity basic bread dough (see
  August, chapter 1, page 141), which
  is enough to cover 2 rectangular
  25 cm x 35 cm/10 in x 14 in
  baking sheets
40 ml/1½ fl oz/3tbsp olive oil
1½ kg/2 lb 8oz mild onions,
  chopped
2 cloves garlic, chopped
1 bay leaf
1 tsp minced fresh thyme
Freshly ground black pepper
1 tsp salt
24 to 36 anchovy fillets
  (according to taste)
30 black olives, pitted, or as in
  the southeast — left unpitted
1 tbsp capers, drained

Method
First prepare the dough: working with oiled
hands, knead the dough, shape it into a ball,
cover and let rest for 1 hour. A simple pastry

crust is sometimes used instead.

In a heavy frying pan, heat 3 tablespoons of
oil, add the onions and garlic, and stir but do
not brown. Let this reduce, "melting" with the
herbs and seasoning — the mixture will
resemble a golden *confit* or jam. Cook this
gently for 30 minutes, then let it cool.

Roll out the dough to cover the baking sheets,
forming a lip around the edges. Spread the
onion *confit* over the bread dough base, then
add the anchovies evenly in an "X" pattern. Top
with the olives and capers, and adjust the edges.

Bake in a hot oven, 230°C/450°F/Gas
Mark 8, for 25
minutes, then lower
the temperature to
200°C/400°F/Gas
Mark 6 and cook for
another 10 minutes.
Spray-misting
during the first
20 minutes
gives a puffed,
crisp crust.

broad iron pans, sending their seared wintertime scent into the air. A
stall displaying a collection of jam and jelly, all with a floral base, is
tended by a slight, blonde teenager in a pink sweater and jeans. She
describes "Le Domaine de Manon", the family farm of three hectares
planted in rose bushes and jasmine. "We all collect the petals, then
my grandfather distils rose and jasmine essence," she says. "Our
family makes soaps, scented eau-de-toilette, and floral-infused jam
and jelly." She offers tiny spoonfuls of jasmine jelly, which seem
natural in a region renowned for aromatic plants. The floral aftertaste
is an unusual sensation, but then I've just tasted biscuits flavoured
with orange-flower essence, another floral-fragrant liaison of tastes.

Overlooking the place des Arcades, a sunny brasserie terrace is the perfect place to enjoy a savoury lunch of *pissaladière* and *daube aux olives*. *Poisson salé*, or *pissala*, means "salty fish" in the Nice dialect of Occitan, giving its name to this regional speciality. A *pichet* of the light red Côtes de Provence wine, made from Grenache blended with Cinsault, is a refreshing partner for these Provençal favourites.

On Sunday morning, church bells call townfolk to a solemn mass, ringing as they have on this day since the first *Fête de St-Blaise* in 1520. Concluding the ceremony, a parade emerges into the sunshine with the golden figure of St Blaise held high by two robed dignitaries in broad-brimmed black hats. Folkdancers follow, the men in brown cloaks, the women wearing long, print-lined capes and delicate lace bonnets. The faces of Provence pass before me under flower-trimmed arcs as they proceed to the square. The priest blesses the assembled crowd, the mayor's words of greeting follow. Then the music begins; a chorus singing in the local Occitan *patois* is joined by the tunes of a pipe and drum. In the afternoon, flower-decked floats and brass bands noisily romp through old Valbonne, each float filled with children tossing carnations and mimosa to the crowds. Reaching high, I catch a sprig of mimosa and tuck it in with my memories of the scents and images of the *Fête du St-Blaise*, mid-way through winter in this southern corner of Provence.

Sprigs of mimosa are traditionally thrown to the crowds during the Fête du St-Blaise.

L'Alicoque, Fête de l'Huile Nouvelle / Olive Oil Festival

Nyons/Drôme, northern Provence

Qui renonce à l'huile d'olive renonce au goût!
Whoever abandons olive oil gives up flavour!
  (Anonymous Occitan *dicton*, an old Provençal saying)

Clinging to rocky hillsides, gnarled and bent by fierce Mistral winds, olive trees have become an image synonymous with Provence. Both the oil and the life-sustaining fruit of the olive tree are mentioned in numerous proverbs and sayings, or *dictons*. So, when the the olive harvest is in and the first pressing of the oil is finished, ready for tasting, it is naturally cause for celebration.

The *Fête de l'Alicoque* takes its name from the ubiquitous clove of garlic, *ail* (an Occitan inversion changes the spelling to *ali*) which is rubbed on a chunk of bread, which in turn is drizzled with the fresh, fragrant oil. Hence *Alicoque*, the flavour of fresh oil – and this is what the fête is all about.

But the increasingly popular event also gives people an excuse to explore the surrounds of Nyons, in the neighbouring hills of the Drôme. For, where other regions have their wine or cheese routes marked, this Baronnies region, named after two baronnial seats at Le Buis and Nyons, has a *Route de l'Olivier en Baronnies*. A trip following this olive trail fits into the weekend, along with touring oil mills and hilltop villages – with stops for soap-shopping and olive oil tasting. Oil and olive products travel well; small pots of green or black *tapenade*, *anchoïade*, olive oils or olives can be easily packed to enjoy at home.

The popular olive spread for appetizers, *tapenade*, is made of chopped, crushed olives, blended with chopped capers,

The Tanche olive thrives at Nyons' high altitude.

anchovies, herbs and olive oil. *Tapenade* derives from *tapeno*, capers in Provençal. Two versions, either green olive *tapenade verte* or one with black olives, are made in Nyons. *Anchoïade* is a savoury spread made of anchovies and olive oil, and adds a Provençal touch to any lunch or *apéritif*. *Aïoli*, similar to a mayonnaise based on garlic, egg yolks and olive oil, gives its name to a traditional Provençal dish of vegetables, poached fish and potatoes. A contest for local cooks, the *concours d'aïoli et de tapenade*, for the best producer of each is held during *l'Alicoque*, usually on Saturday morning.

One hundred kilos of Nyons olives will produce twenty-five litres of sumptuous olive oil.

On this visit to Nyons the local cooperative (*Coopérative du Nyonsais*) on place Olivier de Serres is a great place to start. It is a one-stop shopper's source of specialities of the Drôme and is well stocked with wines from the region's vineyards, from Visan, Valréas and Vinsobres in the Vaucluse. What's more, the cooperative's director, M. Teulade, is a wonderful source of information on Nyons' olive oil production.

He pours *dégustations* of regional wines, including the fruity Côteaux des Baronnies rosé, and tells me all about Nyons' olive trade. "The Tanche is an olive that thrives in the Drôme's high altitude, rocky soil, with Mistral winds and hot summers, and yields abundantly. One hundred kilos of Nyons olives produce twenty-five litres of sparkling oil, or four to five kilos to one litre." Lifting a green-golden bottle from the shelf, he continues: "No heat is used, thus it is 'cold-pressed' to separate the olives' water content from the oil. No chemicals are used and no stabilizers added, and acidity is measured at less than one gram fruit acid per litre, which qualifies as *huile vierge extra*, extra-virgin." He points to the label on the bottle, and winds up with a word on *traçabilité*, a "quality control" procedure which, we will see, is taken up by winemakers, artisans and producers across France to ensure that defects can be traced back to their origin. "All parcels of olive trees are given numbers, so that any faults in the oil or olives can be traced to the source: we are responsible for upholding the quality of our *AOC* (*Appellation d'Origine Contrôlée*)." M. Teulade's keys jingle, ready to lock the co-op for lunchtime, so he wishes us *"Bon appétit!"*

Standards for an *AOC* rating are strict whatever the product, be it goats' cheese, wine or olive oil. In the case of Nyons olives, they must be the Tanche variety, grown in a specified area, harvested at a certain time in stated ways and must contain no chemical or preserving additives. South of Nyons, in Maussane-les-Alpilles, an AOC has also been granted for *Huile d'olives des Baux*, made from olives harvested and pressed a bit earlier. Each region sets its own regulations, preserving the quality and distinctive style of its product.

The mass of l'Alicoque, *Messe de l'huile nouvelle*, is a celebration with music and chorus, drawing young and old into Nyons' old stone church in the last rays of Saturday's light. Trumpets herald the processional for celebrants, the *confrérie* cloaked in green velvet and bearing olive branches. The region's bishop, himself a member of the *confrérie*, blesses the oil and reminds one and all that Noah's first sign of hope was an olive branch borne by a dove. The pale green leaves of the universal symbol of peace are held high before the congregation as hymns resound in the long, narrow sanctuary. Twilight has covered the valley by the time we all pour into the cobbled streets. Some will go on to the evening's banquet and award ceremonies, others will head home to prepare for Sunday, a full day of festivities,

Baskets in the market overflow
with delicious olive-studded
loaves of traditional bread.

including the special *Marché du Terroir*.

By eleven the next morning spirited Provençal pipes and drums can be heard approaching the place des Arcades. White bonnets of folkdancers bob in the bright February sunshine, skirts rustle in the brisk morning wind. The cold little Pontias, a local east wind, will whisk away any dry leaves before the sun reaches its noon position, I am assured by several vendors during the morning. Platforms for dancers and ceremonies are set up in the centre, edged by long tables for the *Alicoque* tasting. A huge vat of oil used to be enough, so each person would dip a piece of bread into it for a taste of the smooth, light *huile nouvelle*. In recent years, the tradition has been revised to serve greater numbers, setting long, white-covered tables around the square, for a collective tasting.

The *Confrérie des Chevaliers de l'Olivier* supplies each table with baskets of bread, dishes of olive oil, slices of garlic to rub on the bread and small spoons to drizzle the new oil. As I taste it (without the garlic to confuse my naïve tastebuds), I catch the aroma of freshly cut hay, followed by a mild, balanced, soft, herby but fruit-infused, smooth flavour. I taste and understand why the *millésime*, this year's flavourful oil, has been pronounced *un succès*.

Bells in the church tower ring noon. From the enthusiasm of the vendors and eager tasters it is clear that no one in Nyons is ready to abandon the olive or its oil ... still heeding the provençal *dicton*, prizing flavour.

Tapenade / Olive paste

Method
In a mortar, mash the garlic
and minced capers to make
a paste, then add the drained,
chopped anchovies and tuna (if using).

Mash, blend, rotate the pestle and mix in
the olives.

Add the thyme, lemon juice and pepper (no
salt), then the oil in drops to mix evenly. (You
can make tapenade in a food processor, but it
can become too smooth if you are not careful.)

To serve as an appetizer, simply spread over
toast and enjoy with a Coteaux des Baronnies
or white Viognier wine.

This versatile condiment enhances the flavour
of poached fish, such as turbot. Alternatively
omit the tuna and slip a layer of tapenade under
the skin of baked fowl.

Ingredients
2 or 3 plump cloves garlic,
  trimmed and finely chopped
100 g/3½ oz/5 tbsp each of
  capers and anchovies in oil
  (about 30)
1 tin shredded tuna, packed in oil
  (optional)
300 g/11 oz/1⅓ cup black olives,
  pitted and coarsely chopped
1 tsp fresh thyme, less if it is
  dried
28 ml/1 fl oz/2 tbsp lemon juice
Freshly ground black pepper
Extra virgin olive oil to blend
  the paste

Fête du Pain Chaud / Hot Bread Festival

Carestiemble/Côte-d'Armor, Brittany

The gold at the end of the rainbow for one intrepid bread-seeker is found in a village near the Channel coast of France. Hot, round crusty *Mirau* is the special bread sought by many who travel to tiny Carestiemble or neighbouring St-Brandan in search of this survivor of a long history of bread-baking in the Quintin region of Brittany. Tied to the church year, whether blustery or balmy, its spirit and enthusiasm create one of the warmest *fêtes* the winter holds.

"Sleepy" seems like an overstatement for this quiet village of grey granite houses, with no bakery, no shops, and a school no longer in use. The hamlet, less than five kilometres from the bustling textile town of Quintin (famed for its heavy linen and canvas for sailing ships), is now home to just a handful of families. But in the late eighteenth century, Carestiemble kept twenty-nine bakers busy with around twelve bakeries in operation. Bakers built their bread ovens in Carestiemble because it was in a neutral zone, exempt from a bread tax enforced at the time. Located near numerous flour mills, the village was an ideal spot for bakers and their families. Every week, wagonloads of bread were sent off to St-Brieuc, twenty kilometres north on the coast.

Today it is the reverse: once a year people come to the village for a day in the country, and to buy *pain chaud* at Carestiemble's annual *Fête du Pain Chaud*. This festival has evolved through the centuries, always holding the dense, hot *boules* as the main attraction. The tradition has brought Bretons back each year, driving from Dinan or Paimpol with families and friends in tow. During the weekends before and after Ash Wednesday, the doors of the grey stone school are open to visitors, and fires are lit in Carestiemble's two old bread ovens.

A baker lifts three loaves with one swoop of his wooden paddle.

Inside the old school, display panels document the central role played by *boulangers* in the community for three centuries. Hand-written correspondence, orders and price lists for flour shed light on life in times past. One item indicates that measurements used for flour around Quintin varied somewhat from those around St-Brieuc, until standardized measures were set early in the twentieth century.

I follow arrows painted on old boards, indicating *pain chaud*, around a corner and across the schoolyard to a sheltered spot. Back in the shadows, a baker in a woolly beige sweater lifts three loaves in one swoop out of two cavernous, tiled ovens, each holding a batch of thirty. His long bread paddle skilfully slides in to lift out only the loaves that are ready. He tests them with a knowing hand before slipping them into a tray for a cluster of eager customers waiting at a small trestle-table

Pain chaud is just around the corner.

covered in white. There is a brief pause before he gingerly shuffles out more *boules*, so I ask this rosy-cheeked gentleman in a tweed cap about his baking. M. Victor Turban, a retired baker, returns to this spot every year. "Yes, I stoke the wood ovens, keep a good tempera-ture and see that the *boules* are baked. It takes about an hour, but I move them around to bake evenly, gently ... *doucement*." When I ask about the secret recipe, his response is brief: "But ... I don't know it! M. Robert is the baker in St-Brandan who makes the bread and shapes the *boules* – he guards the secret, *le secret du pain Mirau*." More bread is ready, and he returns to the day's work.

Nibbling on hot, fresh bread doesn't exactly quicken the appetite, but a pause to sample a refreshing local cider, a Val de Rance – Cru Breton, is welcome. At the entry to the *fête* tent, a long table has opened bar service, busy by noon with men clustered around having a cider with old pals, *copains*. The barmen are busy with bottles of cider, juice, water and wine sold by the glass. As more people arrive, the accordion player warms up with some old, favourite Breton melodies. Lunch options this Sunday, prepared on the spot, are all popular, it is clear from the enthusiasm and rosy faces lining the long tables. For those wanting a complete Sunday dinner, a *repas* is served at one side of the tent: plates are heaped with *jambonneau*, the juicy cured fore or hind of a pork ham knuckle, potatoes, bread, a wrapped wedge of Camembert cheese and a dessert pastry. Others queue for a *crêpe* or *galette*. Some find a spot at one of the long tables, having put together their meal from offerings at hand, bringing succulent pork ribs from the vendor outside the tent door, adding a fresh, warm *boule* and a log of local *chèvre* cheese.

A battery of six *galette* makers at the far end of the tent draws me to watch the food-as-entertainment production of stacks of these

Galettes / Buckwheat crêpes

Makes about 10 galettes

Ingredients
100 g/3½ oz/ ¾ cup buckwheat (sarrasin) flour
100 g/3½ oz/ ¾ cup plain flour
1 tsp salt
1 egg
300 ml/11 fl oz/1⅓ cup warm water

High, even heat and a quick tilt of the pan produce thinner *galettes*. Add more liquid if the batter is too thick.

You will need a flat *crêpe* griddle and a cloth dipped into fat or oil to season the pan.

Method
In a deep bowl, mix the flours and salt, then make a well in the centre and stir in the egg and water, whisking until the batter is smooth. Let the batter rest for at least 30 minutes.

Dabbing the griddle's surface with fat every third *crêpe*, pour 3 tablespoons at a time onto the hot surface, and spread out. Turn as soon as tiny bubbles open on the surface, folding the *crêpe* in half over a spatula. Once the second side is nicely brown, slide off the pan and onto a warm plate. Cover the stack with foil until all the *crêpes* are made.

To serve, sprinkle with sugar or jam, wrap around grilled bacon or, as the Bretons do, fill with creamed seafood. Serve with cider, or a cup of tea.

The accordion player
warms up with some
old favourites.

enticing buckwheat *crêpes*, lighter than a pancake, fine as mesh veils. An undertone of conversation, strains of accordion music, and the aromas of hot *galettes* and fresh bread fill the air.

I have still to buy my *boules*, so I head towards Boulangerie Robert's stall, where they are heaped in basket-trays at a long table. They also sell fresh tempting *brioches*. When I purchase a *boule*, tiny, busy Elisabeth answers my questions as she fills another trayload: *"Sept mille, madame, peut-être plus,"* so in two weekends, 7,000 loaves are usually sold, or "perhaps more". Her long dark hair is pulled back from a small, serious face, intent on ensuring that the stall is never empty, the bread brought in from the bakery in nearby St-Brandan. I begin to see why the regional newspaper, *Ouest France*, has become an active sponsor of this unique event – this is where the people are.

If an outing to the Hot Bread Festival doesn't fit into a February travel schedule, all is not lost, for the famed *pain Mirau* is still baked in St-Brandan, east of Quintin, throughout the year (with the exception of August). In his *boulangerie*, Gérard Robert holds the secret of the true *pain Mirau*, handed on to him by Carestiemble's last baker, Yves Jago, in a relay of Breton tradition. The Boulangerie Robert is at the edge of St-Brandan on 1 rue du Manoir. Other bakeries in the region bake a *pain Mirau*, but the crumb and colour are not quite the same as the original.

As I leave the fair with a basket full of crusty *boules*, a newspaper report displayed with photos of an early *fête* in Carestiemble comes to mind:

"The Fête du Pain Chaud in this gentle country
once again respects a friendly tradition that is not ready to be lost."

Foire aux Vins d'Allier / Allier Wine Fair
St-Pourçain / Allier, Centre

North of Clermont-Ferrand, deep in the heart of *la France profonde*, lies one of the country's oldest, but least-known, wine regions. This is the Bourbonnais, an ancient land of kings and nobles – the house of Bourbon that put rulers on the thrones of both France and Spain. Once chosen for medieval royal tables, the wines of St-Pourçain are today relatively unknown outside their own region. However, today's winemakers are working hard to change this by improving their vinegrowing and winemaking methods, and their wines are once again finding a place in selected wine cellars across Europe.

The market town of St-Pourçain is set on the river Sioule, not far from the river Allier naming the *département*. It has long been a crossroads and stopping-off point for travellers wending their way through the hills from Lyons to Montluçon, or from Vichy northwards to Moulins and Paris. A story about a local innkeeper lives on in a lively group of men dressed in black with red hatbands and neckscarves, the *Compagnons de la Ficelle*. One member, M. Alain Stenger, a slight man with a trim grey moustache, recounts the history of *la Ficelle* to me. As he speaks, I notice a fine white cord knotted around his bright red neckscarf and a tiny pewter pitcher dangling on a ribbon around his neck. His tale explains it: "Many travellers stopped to enjoy the wine that Gaultier, a local tavernkeeper, kept pouring from his pitcher. Soon he had to devise a way to measure the quantity of wine each visitor consumed. A fine cord knotted to measure the wine level was slipped in, tied to the pitcher's handle, and from that day onwards, he had a clearer measure to charge each traveller more fairly." Not only did the fine white cord give rise to a brotherhood, but one of St-Pourçain's refreshing wines bears the name "La Ficelle". Tired, thirsty travellers still welcome a pause along this route, as M. Stenger adds, "La Ficelle is young and fresh, a wine to quench thirst, *un vin de soif.*" With that, assembling *compagnons* gather round with more stories to tell.

This weekend *foire* offers a chance to explore one of France's oldest winegrowing regions. Scenic and green, even in winter, its *Route des Vins* stretches south from Chemilly (below Moulins on the river Allier) to picturesque Chantelle along the Bouble and into the Sioule Valley. St-Pourçain, on the banks of the Sioule, is located almost mid-route, and is the centre of winemaking activity. Cold winters on this edge of the Massif Central's northern tip would not seem hospitable for growing grapes, but those on the hillsides around St-Pourçain have been coaxed into producing excellent wines. At this time of year vinegrowers are busy pruning vines to prepare them for growth, their small white vans parked in lanes along our route.

Enthusiastic winemakers celebrate their production late in February each year with a *Foire aux Vins,* which coincides with the annual livestock fair. The *foire* is held in a large community hall facing the sunny market place, and at the entrance a table sells tasting glasses for twenty francs, the "entry ticket". The full range of St-Pourçain

Clockwise from top left: impressive towers mark St-Pourçain's old quarter; a friendly vendor in the market; the story-tellers of the compagnons.

wines lines the auditorium – winemakers represented here are independent growers as well as those involved in the region's state-of-the-art wine cooperative – but no other *vignoble* or wine-making area is invited to participate.

Within its official description as a VDQS (*Vin Délimité de Qualité Supérieure*) winemakers can grow several varieties of grapes, to bottle as single varietals, or as blends. The soils range from granite to clay, sand to pebbly flint or limestone, each adding its own influence to the final balance of the wine's structure, nose and flavour. Pinot Noir, a dominant variety in wines made across the centre of France, is today becoming more common in the Allier and Puy-de-Dôme as well, though it is more difficult to grow successfully in the damp region of the Allier. Reds are made with this *cépage* alone or blended with Gamay for colour and fruity freshness. Pinot Noir is sometimes given a quick pressing to make a silvery, surprising *Vin Gris,* with the

Poulet au St-Pourçain / Chicken in red wine

St-Pourçain is known for its hearty *Coq au vin d'Allier*, rooster simmered in red Allier wine. This variation on the classic dish uses a large chicken as it is more readily available than the authentic rooster. It can be marinated in the wine overnight if desired and is best cooked a day ahead, instead of the three days needed to tenderize the rooster.

Ingredients
One 1½–2 kg/3–4 lb large, free-range chicken, cut in quarters or eighths
Salt and freshly ground black pepper
2 tsp thyme
Whole cloves
75 ml/2½ fl oz/4½ tbsp fat or oil
30 g/1 oz/2 tbsp shallots, peeled and sliced
2 slices bacon, chopped
60 ml/2 fl oz/¼ cup Cognac or eau de vie
225 g/8 oz/1 cup fresh mushrooms, cleaned, trimmed and sliced
500 ml/18 fl oz/2¼ cups medium-bodied red wine
Chopped flat-leaf parsley for garnish

Method
Pat the chicken dry, season it, sprinkle it with the thyme, and insert one clove into each piece. Heat 50g/3 tablespoons of hot fat in a deep braising pan. Brown the chicken (do not crowd the pan), add the shallots with the bacon pieces and cook, stirring, for 5 minutes.

Next pour in the Cognac, heat and ignite it, tilting the pan as the flames die back. Stir in the mushrooms and cook until well browned.

Add wine to cover, then let it simmer on very low heat for 40 to 60 minutes – test with a fork; do not overcook.

Once the chicken is cooked, let it cool, and keep in a cool place overnight to allow the flavours to develop.

Before serving, skim off any surface fat, remove the chicken pieces, and simmer the sauce to reduce it, whisking all the time. Return the chicken to the sauce and reheat gently.

To serve, top with chopped parsley.

Potatoes cooked with leeks, whipped with crème fraîche and a twist of nutmeg go well with this hearty winter dish. An hour before dining, decant a red St-Pourçain wine.

lightest colour and just a hint of berries. White wines have evolved towards Chardonnay, with smaller amounts of Sauvignon Blanc and the regional grapes Tressalier and Sacy still being grown for many of St-Pourcain's popular dry white wines. Tressalier is also a good base for sparkling wine.

During a *dégustation* of his flavourful Domaine de Bellevue 1998 red wine, winegrower Jean-Louis Petillat explains: "We're gradually concentrating on better grapes, making better wines. My great-grandfather farmed here on three hectares, which my father and I have gradually increased to eighteen. Some vines were here in grandfather's time, but he also raised cattle and grains. Now we've devoted our land solely to vines." When I ask if they plan to expand what appears to be a successful enterprise, his response is sensible: "We can't – no – St-Pourçain is a *vignoble dit de droit de plantation limité*, by the European Union. There are parameters we must stay within. I see it as a positive limitation, so we focus on making better wines. Ours is a family effort, and except for help from wine-school interns who work with us, we must manage it ourselves." Nodding to his two daughters, helping with tasting glasses, he adds: "future *vigneronnes.*"

A vendor teases us to taste hot beignets aux pommes.

At the foot of the steps leading to the *foire*, a *beignet* vendor teases us to taste *beignets aux pommes*, round and puffy apple fritters sprinkled with sugar. He dangles the tempting, hot samples under our noses. Munching on these I continue round the stalls, past jams and honeys to sweeten any *petit déjeuner*, tiny home-made *cornichons* – the pickles that garnish every *pâté* – eggs and fresh fowl ready for the roasting pan or soup pot. Warming soups and energy-filled potato *gâteaux* and *tourtes* will be made from the vegetables piled on vendors' stands. It is a classic French market-day tableau, with St-Pourçain's huge grey abbey church of Ste-Croix as the backdrop.

Leaving the *foire*, we drive past hillsides of vineyards, both old twisted trunks and staked new, young vines. A haze of winter sun slants across the landscape dotted with dramatic silhouettes of ancient châteaux and Romanesque chapels, crumbling walls and medieval towers. While amused by the *compagnons'* tales of the past, at the same time the *foire* has given us a glimpse into the future of wine-making in the heart of the Bourbonnais.

Foire du Printemps et aux Bestiaux / Spring Livestock Fair

Le Buisson/Dordogne, Périgord

March blows in with unpredictable weather – *les giboulés de Mars* keep us all guessing whether a sunny morning will be swiftly swept away with gusty winds and showers – or perhaps the reverse! Sunny daffodils wave in farmyard gardens, sparks of rose and purple prim-roses line pathways and riverbanks, and the days of Lent (*Carême*) begin. It is a month of carnivals, but in fact few gastronomic festivals dot the calendar. In many towns and villages, the annual spring fair held in March takes the form of a *Foire aux Bestiaux* with its array of regional produce vendors. The need to restock herds and flocks for the coming season brings people together. It is time to buy and sell calves, chickens and beef cattle, as well as plant sets and vegetables, tools and fishing tackle.

One of my favourite fairs, a vignette of local livestock events held from one end of the French mainland to the other, takes place in Le Buisson. It captures perfectly the spirit of a small *Foire aux Bestiaux*, reflecting long-valued commerce and traditions. The origins of these *foires* can be traced back to the Middle Ages, when annual fairs were declared by the ruling lord or baron of the region, their dates set down in the town charter. Frequently the charter also defined what could be traded or sold, stating which livestock would be brought to market: sheep in one season, for example, cattle in another.

Surrounded by the commotion of Le Buisson's spring *Foire aux Bestiaux* on a bright, windy Friday, we stand on a street corner with the town's mayor. M. Ducat's handshake is brisk, his dark hair slicked back, and his step determined. "It [the *foire*] is always on the feast of St Vivien in March and St Firmin in October, *toujours, toujours*," he explains. Lifting off his dark glasses he continues: "About twenty-five

Clockwise from top left: early flowering tulips, stoneware crocks and dark willow baskets are spread before the eager shoppers.

years ago, we revived the old traditional March *foire*, interrupted by many years of war and reconstruction. It still serves as a market for young animals, prize veal, beef and fowl, and ..." he waves towards the crowded streets of Le Buisson, "... you'll find lots of regional specialities!"

Le Buisson is in the heart of the ancient region of Périgord, a large part of which is now the administrative *département* of the Dordogne. This sleepy market town lies about mid-way between the larger, historic trading centres of Sarlat and Bergerac. The classic, square train station is a cross-roads for rail traffic to Périgueux and Toulouse. In the centre of town, a round, narrow stone tower rises ahead, like a pivot point, and marks the "entry" to the town's market day and *foire*. Distant sounds of braying donkeys and bleating sheep become louder. My step quickens along a street lined with stalls, their trays of apples, bunches of tiny rosy radishes, dressed chickens and ducks, flats of fresh spinach and braids of garlic, all sheltered under colourful orange or blue umbrellas.

This is the season for *Merveilles*, or "Little Marvels", the little light-as-air pastry twists sold in markets during Carnival, a season stretching through *Carême* – the entire Lenten season and Easter. Regional adaptations of the universal *beignet*, a deep-fried twist or pastry puff, are found in markets and bakeries from one end of southern France to the other. Whether called a *Ganse* near Nice, *Oreillette* in Provence, or a *Bugne* near Lyon and the southern Alps, they all represent a crispy little delight. Many are cut with a crimped edge, as though snipped with pinking shears. In Périgord, *Merveilles* are crisp, dusted with powdered sugar ... perfect strolling-through-the-fair food.

I slow down to admire a white china plate in the shape of a reclining duck, holding bite-size samples of *foie gras*, *pâté* and *rillettes de canard*. When the

A white china plate displays samples of pâté de foie gras.

Delicious gâteaux aux pommes are simply sugar-dusted.

vendor of Delbos Foie Gras invites me to a *dégustation*, it is easy to accept a smooth mouthful, one of the glories of the southwest. Because tinned *foie gras de canard* improves with time, the *foie gras* or *confit de canard* sealed in November should be very good in the spring – and even better in another six months. Duck preserved in seemingly limitless ways, and the use of garlic, are basic elements of the region's cuisine that run deep into this *terroir*, the land and its climate.

Baskets are stacked in the next stall, their open, dark willow forms casting linear shadows on the street. Some are freshly made, the willow still an olive tone edged with burnished red on the supple stems. Spring is the prime season to find Périgourdin baskets, as they have been made during long winter evenings, and by the time March arrives a fresh assortment is ready for sale. An open, oval shape is traditional. The smallest are just big enough for a few fresh eggs. Medium-sized shopping baskets are nested inside broad working baskets capacious enough to hold a load of laundry, or wood for winter fires.

A tiny blonde woman, busy stocking her assortment of raspberry vinegars, looks up as I ask about the colourful products she carefully sets in place. Mme. Dutertry's range of berry products is ambitious for a small family-run business: raspberry syrup for cordials and desserts, jams and preserves, beautiful rosy vinegar, and special little pots of

raspberry mustard. She suggests a use for the vinegar: "You might like this: toss strips of preserved – or even rare – grilled duck breast (*magret*) in a vinaigrette made with two tablespoons of raspberry vinegar, a pinch of fine sea salt, gradually drizzling in five table-spoons of hazelnut oil. A strip or two of cooked bacon, *ventrèche fumée*, can add flavour, and you can garnish it with toasted walnut halves – this is a favourite in the southwest." This is not the first, nor the last time that a vendor offers us tips and helpful *astuces*.

Cadouin's abbey provides a tranquil setting for a gentle stroll after lunch.

Moving right along towards the farm animals that are the focus of this event, I pass a row of heavy tractors, harvesting machines and lighter garden-tillers, an integral part of most rural fairs. A row of tawny brown Limousin calves reminds me of signs posted along the region's roads announcing *Le Pays du veau sous la mère*: this is the land of milk-fed veal. Huge, creamy Blanc d'Aquitaine bulls are waiting to be judged, surrounded by men in long blue jackets and high, mud-splashed boots.

Le Buisson, derived from an old Occitan word for wood or bush, has long been a part of the Cadouin *commune*, a short six-kilometre drive away. A table is reserved for us in L'Abbaye, the restaurant facing the enormous, flat façade of Cadouin's historic church. The dark, textured beams overhead, the sandy tones of the stone walls, and a large fireplace at the end of the restaurant's dining room set us in the mood for a leisurely Périgourdin lunch. Aromas of garlic soup drift my way as *Tourain blanchi* is ladled into bowls at surrounding tables. Across the southwest, every area seems to have its own variation on the *Tourain* (and its various spellings) theme: some are made with onions in Gironde and Gascony, or with tomatoes near Toulouse. In most cases it is a light soup, leaving room for richer

courses to follow. Today's menu features veal with *cèpes*, entrecôte of beef, pike-perch in red wine, all to be paired with wines from Bergerac's many vineyards: hearty Pécharmant reds, sweet whites from Saussignac and Monbazillac, and complex red wines of Côtes de Bergerac.

After lunch we amble out into the sunny afternoon for a visit to the cloisters of Cadouin's Cistercian Abbey, an enclosed garden edged by golden stone columns dating from the twelfth to the fifteenth century. Each column's capital is carved with peering faces, bible stories and fantastic beasts. Later, watching the awards ceremony in Le Buisson, I'm prompted to compare the intertwining forms, the beasts and faces carved in stone, with the people and their traditions, still woven into the seasons and the land in this corner of Périgord. Whether they bring three calves or a truckload of cattle, the spring *foire* is still a meeting place to sell, swap, and to share news, preparing for warmer days and the work that lies ahead.

Tourain or *tourin* / Garlic soup

Ingredients
14 ml / ½ fl oz / 1 tbsp walnut oil or
  duck fat
5 cloves garlic, peeled, degermed
  and chopped
28 ml / 1 fl oz / 2 tbsp flour
1½ litres / 3 pints / 7–8 cups water
  or light chicken stock, heated to
  boiling
3 eggs, separated
14 ml / ½ fl oz / 1 tbsp vinegar
Salt and white pepper

Method
Heat the fat in a deep soup pot, add the garlic and cook gently, making sure it does not brown. Sprinkle in the flour, stir, and gradually add 1 litre/1 pint/5 cups of the hot water or stock. Cook for 20 minutes on a low heat, then whisk in the egg whites, but don't allow the mixture to boil.

In a separate bowl, whisk the yolks with a dash of vinegar, and add this to the soup at the last minute before seasoning to taste. Serve in hot soup plates.

Traditionally, 2 slices of day-old bread laid in the plates quickly softened and thickened the garlic broth. Serve with a white wine from the Montravel vineyards in the Bergerac region.

Foire Internationale aux Fromages et aux Vins/ Cheese and Wine Fair

Coulommiers/Seine-et-Marne, Île-de-France

For many, one's first taste of France might be a sip of good Bordeaux, or a sliver of Brie – a brief encounter at a wine tasting or buffet supper where a warm room assures that the wine is *bien chambré* (at room temperature) and the cheese begins to "relax". For a cheese-lover, it is a fleeting moment, but one inscribed in a memory of flavours. When I discovered that an entire family of Brie existed, the region moved to the top of my list of gastronomic destinations. Now, it is time for some destination shopping, and I am ready to taste Bries from Meaux, Melun and Coulommiers.

We set out toward the land of Brie, *le Pays Briard* on the eastern edge of the Île-de-France, just close enough to be a day trip from Paris. Our route takes us into open country, past heaps of round, just-dug sugar beets stacked on the edges of fields. The river Seine defines Brie's southern limits, while the Marne snakes along its northern border. Turreted corners of farms walled in brown fieldstone conceal manors built during centuries of wealth and power, marking a land-scape of wheat and dairy *richesse*. For centuries, Coulommiers has served as a major market for the Brie region's fine cheeses.

The *Foire Internationale aux Fromages et aux Vins* (always held during *Rameaux*, the weekend of Palm Sunday) takes place on the edge of the city, near the Cultural Centre Halls, *La Sucrerie* (the sugar factory). As we arrive, a fanfare of trumpets leads a parade of regional officials, *confréries* and organizers. Judges have finished their work of tasting, deciding and declaring the "best Brie", so they, too, join in the procession. Flat Brie-like hats of the *Confrérie du Brie de Meaux* bob along above the cream or purple robes of many cheese brotherhoods. There will be three days of *dégustation*, cheese promotion and meeting

Above: a subtle earthiness develops in Faugères.
Below: Brie aged on barley-straw mats.

the public. By noon on the Friday before Palm Sunday when the tent doors are opened, two hundred makers of cheese, bread, sausages and wines have set up *dégustations* for thousands of visitors. Other events during Coulommiers' spring *foire* include the *Grande Exposition d'Animaux*, which opens on Saturday morning. In the evening, attention turns to the *Grande Soirée de Gala*, a grand dinner. Doors remain open on Sunday and Monday for the *Foire aux Fromages et aux Vins*.

I'm amused by the Brie-topped hats of two *confrères du Brie*, and follow them to their stall to find out more, and perhaps sample some Brie. They explain: "There have been two distinct Brie AOCs, *Brie de Meaux* and *Brie de Melun*, for about twenty years. Regulations are strict and the zones clearly outlined for dairies and cheesemakers producing Brie, defining a smaller region for *Brie de Melun*, and a larger one for *Brie de Meaux*. Raw cow's milk must be used for both to merit the label." They show me a small scoop, a *pelle*, used to add renneted milk to moulds for the Meaux, and point to straw mats used to age the cheese. "After two months on barley straw mats, a subtle earthiness develops in the flavour," one adds, "but this practice appears to be changing to meet EU hygiene regulations." The slender, brown-haired man continues with details: "A *Brie de Meaux* is about forty centimetres or sixteen inches wide, and it is a large and rather slim disc, which needs careful handling while draining and rubbing it with dry salt, then again while it is ripened. During the eight weeks it is aged, it must be in the hands of an *affineur* in the area specified in the AOC." The two *confrères* are devoted Brie-men, and I watch as they slice, serve and sell long slivers of Brie, smiling as many wandering tasters-of-tidbits become customers, and half-Bries are slipped into their satchels.

Affineurs play an important role in producing Brie, working to ripen the cheese. They must work within the AOC geographic limitations, and must receive the fresh cheese one week after it is moulded. They are then responsible for turning the fresh cheeses several times every day, then weekly, and monitoring temperatures and humidity at all stages. Close controls are kept on these broad, white discs resting on straw pallets for about eight weeks before delivery to shops, restaurants and market dealers. This ensures the consumer will receive a properly aged Brie at its optimum flavour. When ready, the cheese's powdery crust will take on a few reddish-brown points, as though woven under the snowy cover. When cut, its pale straw-toned interior should be even in texture with perhaps a few tiny bubbles. This refined and balanced cheese was reportedly the favourite of Charlemagne, and has been called both the "King of Cheeses" and the "Cheese of Kings".

Hunting for more Brie, I find the rest of the family, made by local artisans or dairies, including *Brie de Montereau*, *de Nangis* and *de Provins*. Another, *Brie de Coulommiers*, a somewhat smaller disc, is said to be the original Brie. It is no longer made on small farms in the region, but in small dairies. The delicate, slightly musty *Coulommiers* is not quite as widely known, though it is the pride of enthusiastic specialist dairies and *affineurs* who offer samples during the four days of the *Foire aux Fromages*. One difference between the fine-textured *Brie de Coulommiers* and the thicker, smaller *Coulommiers* cheese is the inner *âme*, or heart, of the smaller cheese that remains firm but is surrounded by a soft edge under its white crust.

Two devoted Brie men offer advice on the art of cheesemaking.

Gratin printanière au Brie / Vegetable casserole with Brie

Ingredients

Select 600 g/approximately 1lb
spring vegetables such as new
carrots, tiny turnips, new
potatoes or earliest courgettes
28 ml/1 fl oz/2 tbsp butter
28 ml/1 fl oz/2 tbsp flour
225 ml/8 fl oz/1 cup milk
56 ml/2 fl oz/4 tbsp white wine
or sherry
Celery salt, white pepper and
freshly grated nutmeg
50 g/2 oz Brie, trimmed and cut
in matchstick-strips to arrange
on top of the casserole
Fine white breadcrumbs
Paprika

You will need a 20 cm/8 in wide by
8 cm/3 in deep casserole dish, buttered.

Method

Preheat the oven to 190°C/375°F/Gas Mark 5.

Trim, peel and thickly slice the vegetables. Steam them for 8–10 minutes and drain, reserving 1 cup of cooking water to thin the sauce if necessary. Arrange them in the casserole dish.

In a saucepan, melt the butter but do not brown it, then sprinkle in the flour and let it bubble before whisking in the milk gradually.

Once all the milk has been incorporated, add the wine and seasonings. Simmer for a few minutes, stirring to avoid scorching.

Once the sauce has thickened, pour it over the vegetables and top with Brie strips in a lattice pattern. Scatter lightly with breadcrumbs, dot with butter and add a sprinkling of paprika. Bake for 25 minutes until golden. Brown under the grill.

Serve with an endive and orange salad seasoned with chives, and enjoy with glasses of crisp, white Sancerre.

How do I select a good cheese? Brie is best when pale yellow, and not too dark or firm. It should be supple – does it spring back a bit when you touch it? – and aromatic. *Brie de Melun* smells a bit more savoury, as it is actually slightly saltier. *Brie de Coulommiers'* aroma is delicate, exuding a hint of fresh mushrooms. A whiff of *Brie de Meaux* suggests freshly cut hay- or barley-straw. Tastes will vary, but a sweet note lingers.

Tasting cheese at Coulommiers' *foire* is a challenge, for you must progress from subtle to stronger flavours, otherwise a delicate cheese at the end of the sequence doesn't stand a chance! So, I begin with Camembert from Normandy, a fine, raw-milk farm-made example that is just beginning to bulge and turn *onctueux*, soft and creamy. The wood-banded box of this rich, round cheese fits in the palm of my hand, and inside, its paper-wrapping can be lifted after a light press of the thumb to test resilience, to sniff the aroma. Both Brie and Camembert are made with cow's milk, but their own microclimates ultimately affect the flavour: Camembert is closer to the sea, Brie closer to the Seine.

Next, I stop to sample a rich Boursault, made north of Paris, in the category of double- and triple-cream cheeses, with a taste that turns either sweet or slightly tangy. Then a herby Boursin ... which should have been sampled at the beginning of the tasting. I feel dwarfed by huge wheels of mountain cheeses (who lifts these into place?), flanked by stacks of crusty country bread, from *flûtes* to boulder-sized oval *pain de campagne*. Some bakers have installed wood-fired ovens, assuring tempting aromas along with plenty of fresh baguettes in tall wicker baskets. Thus, the French basics are abundant: cheese, bread and wine.

Before we leave Coulommiers, one last item on my list leads to an *épicerie*, a little grocer's shop, to find a pot of aged, mellow and grainy *Moutarde de Meaux* in its squat, red-sealed stoneware crock. Made nearby in Meaux, *moutarde à l'ancienne* is a rustic blend of whole and crushed mustard seeds. This old-fashioned mustard is capable of turning a simple pork chop or rabbit stew into a culinary triumph.

Which wine partner would you choose to sip with a fine Brie? Saumur, a fruity, medium-bodied red from the Loire, suits its delicate character. For a festive alternative, consider a glass of Champagne – Epernay is not far from the *Pays Briard*.

March

Foire au Jambon de Bayonne / Ham Fair

Bayonne/Pyrénées-Atlantiques, Pays Basque

The vibrant colours and piquant flavours of the Basque country lure me south for a spring weekend. In this southwestern toe of the French *hexagone*, we'll enjoy sea and mountain panoramas, and encounters with friendly people. Driving south to the coast is always like going towards a different world. Roads follow an arrow-straight path through the grand forests of the Landes, where towns are few and far between.

Visual keys to cultural changes appear gradually in rural buildings. Low, off-centred rooftops set in the flatness of the Landes evolve towards a steeper, even and symmetrical pitch as we approach the foothills of the Pyrénées. Fat, truncated letters on signs announce towns, merchants, hotels – all in cherry red. The Basque country, whatever the season, is the realm of an ancient language, a region whose people carry a sense of confidence in their ways, their sports and in their robust cooking. And robust it is, a cuisine of fish stews, tender mountain lamb, and spicy air-dried ham.

Approaching the centre of Bayonne, we descend towards rivers running to the sea – the serpentine, canal-like Nive flows into the mightier river Adour, which bisects the city. A canal running directly to the coast from this inland port was opened in 1578, and served as a link for communication, commerce and defence between France and Spain through the ages.

For five centuries, the celebrated *Jambon de Bayonne* has been the *raison d'être* for this spring gathering of products and people. Every year for three days before Easter, air-dried hams are in ample supply, regional food specialities are on hand to be sampled, and local person-alities parade through the city's steep streets led by enthusiastic

Above: the hills of the Basque country. Below: the famous Bayonne hams.

A Basque vendor has ham ready for dégustation.

confréries. The centre of this commotion is a vast green-and-white-striped tent a few steps from Bayonne's market *halle*, set on the quay of the steely grey river Nive.

We are all here for the ham, and stepping inside the tent doors, it is everywhere: pendulous rosy, peppered hams dangling from hooks or stacked like cord-wood on vendors' stalls. Near the entry, I turn to take a photo of two sturdy young *charcutiers* in blue-checked shirts and black berets. As the shyer cousin slices samples, the animated extrovert explains: "There are only three *producteur* families for Ibaïona hams. Its fine texture is due to the pig itself, the *grand blanc*, a *cochon gourmand* who likes sweet grasses, corn and chestnuts." I listen while the sample sliver dissolves on my tongue in nutty, salty richness – with a hint of chestnuts. Then I envisage happy pigs roaming in open woodlands, and move on to find a salter, a *salaisonneur*, who is essential in curing this savoury ham. An IGP (Indication Géographique Protégée) defines the zone, methods of production as well as the seasoning for ham carrying the Jambon de Bayonne label.

A greying, serious *salaisonneur* with wide-set dark eyes and a black beret set back on his silvery head offers a slice of ham. He describes his work and the process of bringing an air-dried ham to market. "Consider the time it takes to raise a *porc Basque*," he says. "Time is a key element, though this adds to its higher price. The variety that I season takes longer to bring to maturity." The morsel of his prize-winning ham is spicier and more chewy than my first sample, its texture delicious. "The salting and seasoning to cure these fresh hams is done in two stages. First, a mix of dry salts rubbed into the hams cures them for eight to ten weeks. Underground salt deposits between nearby Briscous and Mouguerres are our best salts for curing. Then each ham is rubbed with a blend of garlic, the region's *piment d'Espelette* and salt before being hung in a protective white cloth sack to season. Every *salaisonneur* has his own, guarded recipe – always a secret." This *salaisonneur* relies on scent to determine when a ham is sufficiently seasoned, while other seasoners use a long pointed bone-probe to test the interior of each, their *savoir faire* handed down through the generations.

Whether or not there is a *foire*, Saturday morning is the time to visit Bayonne's central market. Vendors line the quay of the Nive outside the long, covered market hall, their tables heaped with crinkly-edged frisée lettuce,

Stop for chocolates before walking up to Cathédrale Ste-Marie.

Pipérade / Tomato and pepper dish

Lunch in a neighbourhood café, the Bar du Marché, stirs me to find a recipe for a snappy *pipérade*, a regional favourite that has as many variations as there are cooks. The basic *mélange* of peppers (both green and red) and mild onions can be used as the base for braised *Poulet Basquaise* (quartered chicken in a spicy sauce), or mixed with eggs – as in this version.

Ingredients
28 ml / 1 fl oz / 2 tbsp olive oil
1 large yellow or white mild onion, trimmed and cut into cubes
3 cloves garlic, trimmed and chopped
4 peppers, green and red (pointed pimento peppers if available), sliced in strips
1 kg / 2 lbs plum tomatoes peeled, seeded and quartered
4 paper-thin slices of country ham, such as Jambon de Bayonne
6 fresh, free-range eggs, whisked
Sea salt
1 tsp piment d'Espelette, or less to taste

Method
Heat the oil in a broad, heavy frying pan, add the onion and cook until transparent. Add the garlic and pepper strips, stir to cook evenly, then add the tomatoes and simmer for 10 minutes. At this point, the *pipérade* can be used with braised chicken or grilled fish.

Place the *pipérade* in a warm dish, then heat the ham on both sides in the frying pan. Next pour the beaten eggs into the hot pan, lifting to cook under the ham. Add the *pipérade*, give it a little stir, season, and cover for 3 minutes to heat through before serving. In the Basque country, the eggs are very soft and almost soupy when served.

An Irouléguy red wine, with a lightly spicy aftertaste, is a good wine partner.

plump, scrubbed radishes and shiny spring onions. Small pouches of shelled white beans nestle between bouquets of red and blue-violet anemones on one stand, baskets of fresh eggs and dressed free-range chickens at the next. Inside the hall, I come to a halt in awe of the *fromagère*'s stacked towers of ivory mountain cheeses. Sheeps' milk cheeses with marvellous names – *Ossu-Iraty*, black-waxed *Etorki* and *Ardi-Gasna* from large dairies, and *Cayolar* or *Abbaye de Belloc* from smaller farms – are here to tempt us. I opt for a wedge of firm cheese, with plans to grate it over steamed fresh asparagus wrapped in paper-thin slices of *Jambon de Bayonne*, to be run under the grill before serving to friends for a spring lunch at home. After a stop to buy the region's white Tarbes beans for a cassoulet and jars of pink *piment d'Espelette* to tide me over until Espelette's own pepper fair late in October, my shopping is finished – for the moment. Anticipation of an autumn jaunt to the Pays Basque whets my appetite for another, later season of flavours.

A French band plays Dixieland.

Just outside the *foire* tent, an English Dixieland band kitted out in straw boaters and green shirts swings from one old favourite tune to another. With a swift banjo riff, a French band joins in, leading to a spirited informal "event". Nearby cafés fill with a growing audience, and I'm lucky to find a table the size of a postage stamp. There's time for an after-market pause to enjoy the music and a refreshing Basque cider, before a walk uphill to find the parade route.

In the winding, cobbled streets of Grand Bayonne I pass shop windows of renowned *chocolatiers* – now daintily decorated for Easter. An overhead banner announces the forthcoming Chocolate Festival in May, an event that brings a host of international chocolate-lovers and chefs to the city. For aficionados of dark chocolate, a weekend in Bayonne could easily be spent haunting Cazenave, the elegant *salon de thé* whose piping hot chocolate can be relished whatever the time of day. The windows of *chocolatier* Darantz lure me inside for sweets spiced with cinnamon and studded with almonds. An after-lunch bite of *chocolat amer à l'orange* fuels an uphill trek to watch the parade near the elaborate, multi-spired Cathédrale Ste-Marie. A marching band in blue leads silver- and green-robed *confréries* in the lively Easter Saturday parade of the *Confrérie du Jambon de Bayonne*, all keeping pace with the trumpeting refrains of "Ain't She Sweet".

Fête de l'Huître / Oyster Festival
Sarzeau/Morbihan, Brittany

Welcome to the realm of the oyster, a route along the southern coast of Brittany that winds past windmills and leads to the sea. As we skirt the town of La Roche-St-Bernard, northwest of Nantes, round blue signs begin to announce the briny treasures of these sheltered coastal waters. Just as there are Wine Routes and Cheese Routes in other parts of France, the oyster farmers along Brittany's coast have posted signs indicating an Oyster Route. Those of us in search of this slippery, delicious mollusc find Sarzeau at the centre of it all, situated on the long finger of land that is the Rhuys peninsula. Here, shallow inlets of the Gulf of Morbihan have been "farmed" by generations of oyster-men, whose pride in producing quality oysters equals a collective enthusiasm for their enduring cultural traditions. Evidence of this Breton spirit abounds during Sarzeau's April Oyster Festival weekend, when all shapes and sizes of shellfish fill stalls in the town's old centre.

Locals tell us how the air, sea and land influence the size and flavour of oysters. The word *terroir* comes up again and again, a term used by agronomists, vintners, asparagus growers, chefs and oyster farmers. At first I thought it simply meant the nature of the soil and subsoil in vineyards. Then I heard it used by a chicken farmer in the Bresse and understood that climate is an aspect of *terroir's* many meanings. It is clear that the *terroir* umbrella stretches over the coves of coastal waters and indicates what the oysters feed on – as well as the climate and temperature of the water. All of these elements lend nuances of algae, salt and differences in textures to the famed Breton oysters.

Brittany has twelve varieties of *grand cru* oysters, each with its own qualities. The most abundant in Sarzeau's market are *huîtres du golfe*, the cupped, oval oysters of the Gulf of Morbihan. *Belons* of

Shallow inlets of the Gulf have been farmed by generations of oystermen.

Immaculately attired piping sailors lead the way in their parade uniforms.

l'Aven-Belon (further north on the coast), distinctively round and flat, are more fragile to produce and are known for their delicate, nutty quality. Regarded as the prince of oysters, *Belons* are *grasses*, rich, appreciated for their special thick consistency and taste. Along the southern coast, the delicious oysters of Quiberon, Penerf and Carnac are available in local shops and markets. Further north, oysters from Le Croisic, Rade de Brest, Rivière de Tréguier, Morlaix-Penzé and Nacre des Abers find their way to markets in Rennes and major northern cities.

The oysters farmed along the coast, kept in estuaries and coves, are regularly moved to densely-packed "parks". Some are selected to be fattened for a month in *clairs*, in more open water, allowing room to mature and develop flavour. A *fine de claire* has had an extra month to develop a green "beard" and more briny flavour – called by many *la reine*, the queen of the oyster realm. *Plates* are flat oysters, one of two types farmed in France; the other is the deeper *creuse* variety.

Through the winter and early spring, almost every village in any region of France seems to have Sunday morning oyster vendors on busy corners. In Sarzeau, oysters are literally on the doorstep, and the classic French Sunday lunch can easily

Precisely timed as a light rain starts to fall, pom-pom girls lift their umbrellas.

begin with a plate of six or twelve *fines claires*. Simply cleaned, opened, and set on plates, oysters are usually eaten raw accompanied by thin slices of rye bread and butter. To pique their fresh flavour, lemon juice or a dash of vinegar mixed with chopped shallots is spooned onto each glistening oval. A sip of oyster liquor straight from the shell ends the ritual, followed by a palate-cleansing sip of dry white wine, such as a Muscadet.

Sunday in Sarzeau, the *fête* begins with a special shellfish market. Long seafood wagons and small oyster stalls overflow with a colourful jumble of shells and antennae. Lobsters, crayfish and sea eels wiggle in tubs, and the claws of spider-crabs (*araignées-de-mer*) poke out in all directions next to a tray of small, delicate scallops (*pétoncles*). Shrimps are weighed up for quick lunches, their sizes running from plump *gambas* to little greys, *petites grises* the size of your smallest fingernail.

Nestled next to the imposing stone church, vendors offer *dégustations* along with repartee. A red-jacketed oysterman shows me how to open a *creuse* oyster: he slips an oyster-blade into the tip just where the muscle holds the shells tightly, and says: "If it is hard to open, you know it's fresh – the muscle is still protecting the oyster!"

With a quick-prying twist, a white, pearly inner shell displays the mollusc, and it is lifted out for me to taste. "Our oysters from Penerf have an *iodée* quality – like the sea air. How do you like it?" *C'est bon!*

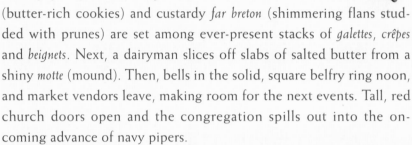

I admire pastries in a baker's display of Brittany's buttery pastry-bread, *kouign' amann*. Flat discs of *sablées* (butter-rich cookies) and custardy *far breton* (shimmering flans studded with prunes) are set among ever-present stacks of *galettes*, *crêpes* and *beignets*. Next, a dairyman slices off slabs of salted butter from a shiny *motte* (mound). Then, bells in the solid, square belfry ring noon, and market vendors leave, making room for the next events. Tall, red church doors open and the congregation spills out into the oncoming advance of navy pipers.

Piping sailors lead the way in parade uniforms, complete with white spats. Breton bagpipes, piccolos, flutes and pipes harmonize and alternate, as snare drums set the cadence. The fixed element in festive processions arrives next: the local brass band, playing pop tunes as they march up to the church. Trumpeters are followed by rows of long-limbed pom-pom girls, kept in line by their leader's shrill whistle. Red and white pom-poms rustle from shoulder to hip in brisk flourishes, and they all lift red, white and blue umbrellas in precision as light rain begins to fall.

High, eerie sounds of more bagpipes approaching are underscored by thumping rhythms of Celtic drums. In a rousing advance, a handful of bagpipers in traditional Breton vests join the young sailors, echoing the same familiar melodies. The spirit of the moment suggests such passion for their music that it might continue all afternoon – whatever the weather. But suddenly the music subsides and everyone takes shelter around the square for a glass of cider before the oyster-shelling contest begins.

A platform, ready for the shelling contest, is set in the square between the town hall and Sarzeau's grey church. Winners of the preliminaries through the week are non-professionals, competing without assistants. A young Alsatian vintner swiftly clocks thirty oysters, shelled in one minute and fifty seconds. He steps forward to applause, accepts a trophy from the mayor, and qualifies for the national oyster-shelling finals. At last, shellers, pipers, vendors and visitors are ready for a long Sunday lunch.

The *Fête de l'Huître* concludes, and at the end of the day, a few daylight hours remain for a stroll along a country lane toward the Kerguet château, east of Sarzeau. Evening clouds lift before sunset as I walk past a rainbow of rose, coral and white azaleas in bloom against grey stone walls. Behind me, cottage shutters being closed for the night click shut, and in the distance... could that be a bagpipe still playing?

Velouté d'huîtres / Creamy oyster soup

Method

Simmer the fish stock, fish and celery together in a saucepan for 20 minutes then season. Stir in the cream.

Remove from the heat, and add the oysters to poach them gently for 2 minutes. Then pour everything into a blender, whizz it to liquify, and pour it back into the soup pot to reheat very gently. Add a drop of lemon juice, and season to taste.

Serve in warm bowls, adding a dot of butter to each serving.

Light white wines, a Chenin Blanc from Anjou, for example, or a Muscadet, suit the *velouté* nicely.

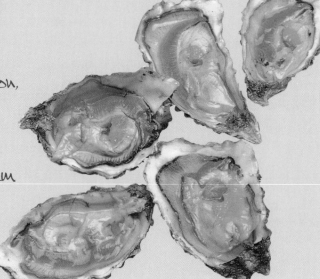

Ingredients
500 ml / 18 fl oz / 2¼ cups fish stock
15 g / ½ oz / 1 tbsp smoked salmon, cut into strips
1 branch celery, chopped for the stock
Fine sea salt, white pepper
15 ml / ½ fl oz / 1 tbsp sour cream
2 dozen oysters, opened and reserved
½ lemon – or less
40 g / 1½ oz / 2½ tbsp salted butter

Fête de l'Asperge / Asparagus Festival

Fargues-sur-Ourbise/Lot-et-Garonne, Gascony

A spring weekend in Gascony sounds inviting, but isn't it off-season? Isn't the fertile, rolling farmland of the southwest more colourful in summer when sunflowers stretch for as far as the eye can see? Then, too, Gascony's gastronomic wonderland is a rich platter of flavours when the legendary winter *foie gras* markets are bustling with shoppers, and during the holidays when travellers join the crowds. Whether it is off-season, or on, a spirited spring *fête* one April Sunday lures us south to a tiny *bourg* claiming the title *Capitale de l'Asperge*.

Through pink clouds of fruit trees in bloom, our route descends towards Agen where it crosses two historic waterways – the Garonne river and the *Canal latéral*. At this northern edge of Gascony, the terrain opens up to sweeping expanses of brilliant yellow *colza*, or rapeseed fields. Country roads straighten out, lined with the burnished greens of plane trees in bud. There's a sense of surprise and urgency in the air: asparagus is at its peak for a short season, just from April the fifteenth to the end of May. In Fargues-sur-Ourbise, the asparagus growers' timing is perfect for this tender member of the lily family – their *fête* is always held on the third Sunday in April.

We approach the eastern edge of the vast forests of the Landes, where the tall pines grow denser, still allowing light to play on spiny golden branches of gorse glowing on the forest floor. At a crossroads – the village of Fargues-sur-Ourbise – cars are parked between the

A tiny bourg claims the title Capitale de l'Asperge.

dappled trunks of trees. Walking towards the church, I pass a striking white-on-white display of *glycine blanche* branches

Spring in Gascony brings a sweeping expanse of lush new greenery.

and tendrils of white wisteria trained across the entire façade of a white stucco house. This faces a grey stone chapel surrounded by thick, lichen-encrusted stone walls. Just behind the chapel, we find the fair in full swing, around a community centre and stretching across a shaded field to the wooded edge of town.

Asparagus growers' stalls are set in a horseshoe shape in the field. Business is brisk before noon on this April Sunday. People toting sacks and broad trays of fresh asparagus pass us on their way out... to freeze, preserve, or cook them for Sunday lunch. A young blond man in a grey poplin jacket steps forward to discuss his display of elegant white and violet-tipped asparagus. Benoit Cugnière has the healthy glow of someone who spends the day outdoors. He reaches for a bundle of *asperges blanches*, long the pale, white favourite in France, and explains: "These are actually the same asparagus, but they grow so fast that if they are missed in the morning cutting, in a few hours, *voilà! l'asperge violette*." The creamy stalk is tipped with a pinky-violet tone, and both the white and violet asparagus are bundled in thinner or thicker varieties. "We have five different varieties, some fatter and others with finer stems, growing on four hectares of sandy flat land," he continues, lifting a bottle of white Buzet from his Clos Lauran display. "The asparagus fields give way to our slopes, clay and rocky soil where we've planted vines; twenty hectares within the AOC Buzet. The *terroir*, the soil's minerals as well as the climate here, produces asparagus – and grapes – with special qualities."

Growing asparagus is said to be relatively easy, though M. Cugnière points out a few brown blemishes on the stalk due to a touch of frost. A root takes about four years to become established and to bear well in their sandy, well-drained soil. It needs sunlight and protection from any spring frost that might dip below minus five degrees centigrade. Regular doses of rich organic fertilizer feed the asparagus, which is a *gourmande*... always hungry. In this area of the southwest, asparagus grown under protective translucent tunnels is ready as early as mid-March, though the season is over by the end of June. During this time, Aquitaine growers produce seven thousand tons a year, a tripling in ten years – truly a fast-growth "industry".

How do the French eat asparagus? Tradition dictates that the pared spears should be steamed for about ten minutes, drained and served at room temperature with a herb-lemon vinaigrette, or a froth of whipped hollandaise. When I first saw people eating asparagus with their fingers, I watched the ritual with great interest. Taking one spear at its base, it is dipped into a little pool of *sauce vinaigrette*. Then the asparagus is nibbled from the tip down the stem as far as threads will allow and pulled between one's front teeth before disposing of the tougher threads at the stem end. Usually this is done at home, *en famille*, but sometimes asparagus is heartily eaten in this mode in country restaurants as well.

Before noon, Fargues' community centre has filled for a *vin d'honneur* ceremony, the crowd applauding the family asparagus stall that has won the "best display" award. The mayor, regional elected officials and organizers are on the stage at one end of the hall; each in turn offers encouraging words. A dark-haired man in a suit and tie reviews figures, citing how asparagus production benefits the region, employing four thousand seasonal workers in the Lot-et-Garonne and the Landes *départements*. Another steps forward to congratulate the teacher who coordinated a drawing exhibition on the asparagus theme, involving schools in two towns. We study the children's drawings, illustrating asparagus invaders, asparagus in outer space and asparagus growing underground – all vivid images drawn by seven- and eight-year-olds. The speakers continue; the last, a small, round gentleman in a checked jacket, sums up the event: "These *fêtes* emphasize our work for quality, and in this region we have a diverse range of excellent products ... that will assure our future, our economic future. Now, let's go taste it all!"

As church bells ring out *midi*, our thoughts turn to lunch, which is right at hand. A crew of servers has laid places at long tables under a white tent where a stylish, energetic woman has enthusiastically engineered the day's catered lunch. She pauses for a moment to review the menu for me. "We begin with a *salade Gascogne*, with slivers of duck *magret* and *foie gras* garnished with asparagus ... of course, today it's our special feature," she explains. "Then, a choice of *confit de canard* (a preserved leg or breast of duck) or entrecôte of beef served with a gratin of potatoes and asparagus, followed by cheese. The first of the season's local strawberries, or flaky apple *tourtière* are the dessert choices." With Buzet wine and coffee, the meal is fifteen euros. She remarks that over the last couple of years, most people reserve places several hours in advance. Wishing me *bon appétit*, she returns to her crew and the lunch service.

Later in the afternoon, after I have tasted bites of *foie gras* and *rillettes de canard*, sampled Buzet wines, munched slices of crisp apples, and sipped smooth, liquid-amber Armagnac, I return to the community hall to watch an asparagus-bundling contest. The crowd cheers for Rose, a stout red-head in a navy blue jogging suit, as she sets seven bundles in a row in just two minutes, estimating the weight of each close to a kilo, a job she obviously knows well.

Last on the day's menu is the chef's round-table discussion and tasting. Trays of bite-size squares, layered terrines, tiny cream puffs, all prepared according to winning recipes, are arranged alongside small plates and spoons on white-covered tables. Elegant bottles of Buzet wines are lined up to complement the samples. Six well-known regional chefs who have an alliance called the *"Saveurs et Traditions des Cuisiniers Lot-et-Garonnais"* take their places at a round table on the hall's stage. They have not only given their Sunday to the *fête*, but each has prepared one of

the winning recipes in a nationwide asparagus-recipe contest. A wine specialist, Jacques Réjalot, is on hand to advise on the wines to serve with each preparation. The recipes are diverse, making

Asperges en tout simplicité / Simplest asparagus

Time and again, the chefs' advice is: keep it simple. The freshest asparagus needs only minimum preparation – but perfect timing is crucial when cooking. Sort asparagus into even lengths, paring white or violet stems up to the first leaf-triangle. Handle them carefully, as the tips may snap off. More fibrous late-season stalks can be used for vegetable stock (which can be used in hollandaise sauce). White asparagus needs to cook for a few minutes longer than green.

Ingredients
1 kg/2 lbs fresh asparagus, stems pared, tied in bundles of 6
14 ml/ ½ fl oz/1 tbsp lemon juice
A pinch of sea salt
1 tsp Dijon mustard
40 ml/1½ fl oz/3 tbsp best extra virgin olive oil
Fresh chervil (if available)

Method
Heat a large pot of boiling, salted water, submerge the bundles of asparagus and cook for 5 to 10 minutes.

Make the lemon vinaigrette: season the lemon juice with the salt and mustard then whisk in the oil gradually before adding the chopped chervil.

Test the asparagus with a knife point. When tender, lift the bundles out and drain. Snip off the string, arrange on plates and dress with the vinaigrette and leafy chervil.

Serve at room temperature, with glasses of cool white Buzet wine.

wine-matching tricky. To balance asparagus's natural acidity, the serious M. Réjalot suggests: "Choose a fuller white, a Muscadet or a Sauvignon with some age to bring out the best, the fullest flavour. The *amertume* or light bitterness in asparagus, and its frequent preparation with cream sauces, also pose pairing challenges." This event wraps up the *fête*, with citations to contest winners and a jovial give-and-take of opinions and wine recommendations.

Fargues-sur-Ourbise, the sleepy crossroads village, changes very little from year to year, but the producers of asparagus, Buzet wines, *foie gras* and Armagnac appear in greater number for each *fête*, their displays put together with more humour, spirit and finish. For local colour and the freshest, finest asparagus, it is indeed worth the journey to Gascony off-season, but definitely in-season for *l'asperge*.

April

Fête de la Chèvre / Goat Festival
Aubazine / Corrèze, Limousin

Searching for a *fête* that lies off the beaten track, I'm led to a niche in the Corrèze forest that feels centuries away. It is a village that once was a pause on a pilgrimage trail for Cistercian monks whose routes led through the Massif Central's wild forests to the immense, welcoming abbey then known as Obazine. To locate Aubazine, as it is known today, I scan the route to Tulle just east of Brive-la-Gaillarde, a road that leads into denser pine forests. At the crossroads of Gare d'Aubazine, a turn onto smaller lanes takes us across the rushing Corrèze river, swollen with spring rains. Continuing on ever-narrower roads, through groves of chestnut trees and managed pine woods, we wind our way uphill into this calm village, arriving the day before its annual *fête*. Aubazine's dramatic setting on a steep-sided promontory surveys two valleys. Forested hillsides are chiselled away by dark red granite cliffs, a rocky site in a region well suited to nimble goats.

Many *chèvre* fairs dot the calendar of the French year, from the Loire to the Rhône Valley, from the Ardèche to the hills of Charente. Further south, in the Banon uplands of Provence, a June fair features goats' milk cheese in all its smooth and tangy variations, but Aubazine's celebration focuses on the goats as well. We step into the bakery shop, a fine old grey granite house on the square facing the village fountain. I am eager to meet the organizer, the president of the fair's committee, M. Charageat, who is also the village baker. He emerges through a bead curtain behind the counter, all in white to the tip of his clogs. A trimmed white beard circles the lower half of his round face, and he smiles as he speaks about the *Fête de la Chèvre*: "We've kept as close as possible to the spirit of the centuries-old,

The Fête de la Chèvre is close in spirit to the centuries-old St George fair.

annual St-George fair, making room for regional products alongside the animals. Families enjoy it, and many Brivistes (people from Brive-la-Gaillarde) return every year to spend a day in the country and to have lunch together. It is still held on the Sunday closest to April the twenty-third, St George's Day."

When I ask about the products we might find, he answers: "A bit of everything! Aubazine no longer has a weekly market, so this is an important event for us. It has grown to include over one hundred vendors. You'll find honey and nut specialities, many *chèvre* cheeses, foie gras, sausages, wines and always some surprises. There are calves, goats and sheep to be judged, ponies, too – some will be sold." With Charageat's enthusiastic preview, we expect to find something for everyone. He bids us a warm goodbye and disappears through the bead curtain, back into the bakery, to make more nut bread for the *fête*.

Goats are celebrated throughout France for their cheese, which has a very distinctive, tangy taste.

I stand facing the huge twelfth-century church that dominates this clearing in the forest, an enormous structure built on a site dedicated to the monk St Etienne. Inside, candles light tiny recesses of chapel-bays, but in the south transept, high narrow windows surround the tomb of St Etienne. Pale light enters through the windows' grey interlace pattern, falling on the saint's tomb, itself a masterpiece of carved relief from the Gothic era. Still on pilgrimage trails, the church and its abbey are now the home of an active religious community.

The morning of the *fête* dawns white, as a coverlet of ground fog suspended over nearby valleys rises across the church square. Vendors set up tents and stalls around the fountain, filling the village with trays of cheese, plates of *chèvre* pastries and planks loaded with honeys and jams. Hoses are connected to the fountain spigot to pipe in a supply of red wine to refresh the day's visitors and vendors. Long links of sausage are snipped apart, ready for the grills. Stalls selling bedding plants – the earliest leek and tomato sets that will grow in local potagers – are arranged in leafy displays. Against the church wall, a colourful mound of squash and vegetables is piled up by a vendor of pumpkin jams and pickles. Apples on another stall are displayed with fresh yellow sprays of broom, brighter as a few sunbeams pierce the morning's clouds. Above it all, a banner proclaims in bold red letters: *Fête de la Chèvre!*

On the edge of the village, goats and sheep have been unloaded from small vans to be penned against a long granite wall. I watch a short, dark-haired woman in a red sweater as she grooms her goats. Reprimanding a brown alpine goat, "Bambi", who nudges the others, she proudly holds up a little brown kid to show me. "They have a lot of character, goats do – *ils ont du caractère, c'est sûr!*" she says. Goats are clearly in the majority, and their musky scent is in the air as I work my way through the crowd and around pink-faced *rouge de Limousin* sheep, toward horses and ponies and on to the *volailles*. The *Association d'Aviculture et de Colombiculture du Pays de Brive* has assembled a colourful collection of feathered creatures large and small, including doves, pigeons, ducks, chickens, guinea fowl and geese.

Pausing a moment, I notice mature black and brown goats tended by a lean man with a narrow, wind-tanned face. His olive corduroy cap rests at a tilt, and a black cotton herder's jacket covers a warm brown sweater. He squints at my questions, smiles and offers: "This is a good Alpine cross, madame ... want to buy a goat?" I respond that it would nibble the green beans in my *potager*, but he persists: "Oh, but it's so good to have a goat, such a clever animal." I decline and move on, watching a little pure white goat climb over the nanny's back. From a corner I hear: "Six hundred francs for a good kid!"

It is easier, much easier, to resist buying a goat than to resist the cheeses at this diverse *foire*, especially when tastings are offered. *Chèvre* takes a variety of forms here, as it does in other goat-rearing regions of France. Fresh to well-aged cheeses are attractively displayed in trays full of leaf-shaped *feuilles de limousin*, set next to large, firm, Gouda-like *tommes de chèvre*. Soft, fresh *faisselle*, the just-drained cheese with minute button-like imprints still visible, is the mildest of *chèvres*. Cylindrical *bûche* or logs are popular, as are the small discs, *cabécou*. Fresh *cabécou* are often served grilled or toasted on salad as an *entrée*, but when aged are more likely to appear on cheese platters before, or as, dessert. Aubazine's *fête* also attracts sellers of rich cows' milk cheeses from neighbouring Auvergne and Cantal. Stacked cylinders of blue-veined *fourme d'Ambert* and grey-crusted, perfectly *affinée* (matured) *St-Nectaire fermier* extend the tempting selection. Loaves of rye and nut bread, the

Chèvre aux endives / Cheese-filled endive

Each region of France has its ways with fresh goats' cheese, a versatile basic ingredient to whip with garlic and fresh herbs, or to drizzle with honey and decorate with fresh berries in season. In the spring, while endives are still at their best, try a simple *chèvre* canapé or *entrée*...

Ingredients
150 g/5½ oz fresh chèvre cheese, mixed with 2 chopped cloves garlic
1 tbsp each of chopped fresh tarragon, chervil and chives
40 ml/1½ fl oz/3 tbsp crème fraîche
500 g/18 oz Belgian endive (not curly endive), bitter ends trimmed out, leaves separated

Method
Mix the cheese with the herbs. Add spoonfuls of crème fraîche as needed to spread.

Lay the endive leaves on a serving plate and spread the chèvre mixture at the base of each leaf. Garnish with toast rounds and wands of fresh herbs.

This is also delicious spread inside a crêpe folded around steamed asparagus spears.

A crisp, dry white wine such as Montravel from the Bergerac area suits both the tangy chèvre and the endives.

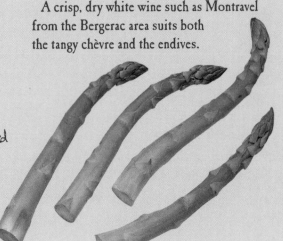

natural foil for firm or creamy cheeses, are sold from a kiosk in front of M. Charageat's bakery. Walnuts and chestnuts poke their way into many Corrèze breads and pastries, but my surprise was to find them in nut wines and liqueurs, too. Rich and slightly sweet, nut wines are popular as an *apéritif*, but can also accompany the cheese course.

After lunch, a walk uphill from Aubazine takes me along a path where I tread on a crunchy carpet of last season's fallen chestnuts that snap underfoot. I turn to look down over the town's fish-scale slate rooftops and the solid forms of granite houses hugging the hillside. With a change in the wind, a few strains of accordion music drift upward and I hasten my pace to return to the church square. Then, taking a whiff of the fresh spring air, I know: the goats are having their day.

May

Fête de l'Agneau/Lamb Festival
Pauillac/Gironde, Médoc, Southwest

In the fine soft morning light of the first of May, vendors of tiny bouquets of lily-of-the-valley (*muguet*) announce spring in all corners of France. We pass them at intersections in villages and towns on our route from Bordeaux to Pauillac and stop at a dusty crossing in the vineyards near Beychevelle. A girl tends the family *muguet* stand, simply a shallow green bucket with yellow streamers on the handle. Giving a nosegay of these fragrant flowers as a *porte-bonheur*, to bring good luck, is an ancient custom marking the return of spring on the first of May. In some regions, I'm told that offering *muguet* is a gesture of respect, a practice whose origins are lost in the mists of time. After a cheerful exchange of *"Bon weekend!"*, fragrant flowers in hand, we soon arrive in Pauillac, on the banks of the Gironde estuary.

Pauillac is a harbour town that grew with the booming eighteenth- and nineteenth-century wine trade, thanks to its proximity to the Gironde, the confluence of the Garonne and Dordogne rivers which flows past Bordeaux and Pauillac, and out to the Atlantic at Royan. To remind people of its important past as a port, two majestic sailing ships of the French Navy are docked at Pauillac's pier during the festival weekend. From the boulevard on the broad, calm estuary, we climb a steep, cobbled street leading to Pauillac's stark, grey, quarried stone church.

Above: the charming harbour at Pauillac
Below: After the transhumance parade the sheep are driven to the safety of a fenced enclosure.

Noises of an approaching crowd can be heard by the time I find a place in the shade of the church: bleating sheep, the rattle of snare drums and general commotion. A flock of Lacaune sheep (raised for both their excellent milk and their fine meat) lead the morning

parade escorted by a small, vigilant sheepdog. Children on brightly decorated bicycles wheel into the place de l'Eglise, a wide intersection that leads to the church door. Town dignitaries and the *fête* committee follow in a loose procession. A band brings up the rear and locals follow, keeping step with the fanfare and taking part in this ritual re-enactment of a *transhumance*.

Welcoming speeches by Pauillac's mayor and the fair's chairman are amplified to the small crowd and to people leaning to listen and watch from their balconies. On a long table decorated with small cotton sheep and meadow flowers, *apéritifs* of wine-based fruit punch, bottles of water and fruit juices are set out. When the speakers have finished, I watch the crowd milling around the refreshments table, a diverse mix of local folk, shepherds from other regions who have come to participate, children petting the sheep and day visitors. In the midst of all this, a small black dog lies flat on the ground, but not resting, his eyes fixed on the flock, always on duty.

Where there are sheep, there must be sheepdogs. As the fair opens, sheepdog trials begin in fields on the edge of town, run in the morning and again on Saturday afternoon. The test for these dogs is spread over broad pastures on the edge of the estuary, and entails driving the sheep through a narrow passage and rounding them up to be driven from a dry river bed to an open field. Having never seen dogs

Sheepdog trials are an integral part of the Lamb Fair.

"work" sheep before, I watch with fascination. Moving silently, rounding up any stragglers, the sheepdog disappears for a moment. However, its presence is evident in the direction the flock takes, moving as a drifting unit of creamy-grey fleece until they all arrive in the pen or shelter. The energy and intelligence of the alert little black-and-white Border Collies put them high on many a shepherd's list of working dogs, and today they are the award-winners in the trials. By Saturday evening, judges have conferred and a crowd again gathers in front of Pauillac's church for the awards ceremony,

A bergerie shelters Pauillac sheep from the rain.

applauding each winning shepherd and his or her dog as their trophy is presented. From this preliminary *Concours Inter-Races de Travail sur Troupeau*, winners go on to the French national competition later in the season.

Afternoon events run the gamut from demonstrations of sheep-shearing and ewe-milking to a hike, a *rallye pédestre*. This appeals to many as it is also a *rallye dégustation* of fifteen kilometres, stopping for wine-tastings in Pauillac vineyards. The surrounding Médoc villages of Artigues, Le Pouyalet and St-Lambert help to plan the rally, and other *fête* events.

Across a grassy bank on the harbour boulevard, Saturday's *transhumance* flock of sheep spend the weekend in a sheltered and fenced area, a *bergerie*. An attending shepherd answers questions from visitors, so we join the crowd. When he has finished with a cluster of children who gingerly pat the soft, timid lambs, I ask a few questions about the *transhumance*. The tall, ruddy-cheeked man scratches his dark head, re-adjusts his black beret, leans his staff against the pen-rail and smiles at this entry-question to a long conversation. "My home is in the Pyrénées, where my sheep and I spend the summer in mountain pastures. In autumn, the sheep are brought to vineyards on the Gironde estuary and along the Garonne River. It's not just that the winters are milder, but the sheep serve more than one purpose. They not only provide fertilizer for the vineyards, but sheep are natural weed-nibblers, so no herbicides are needed to keep weeds down among the vines." The system clearly works to the advantage of both the vinegrowers and sheep farmers. Lambs are born late in January and are raised on ewes' milk for seventy-five days. With the *transhumance* in May, the ewes return to the Pyrenean pastures for the summer, where their milk is made into firm mountain cheeses, the ample wheels of *brebis* of the Basque country.

Agneau en croûte / Lamb in a herb crust

To replay the flavours found in Pauillac, try rolling a leg of lamb in a herb-crumb crust with almonds to seal in the juices. Serves 6 to 8.

Ingredients
56 ml/2 fl oz/4 tbsp/¼ cup olive oil
1 leg of lamb, no more than 2 kg/ 4½ lbs
Sea salt and freshly ground black pepper
1 egg beaten with 2 tbsp Dijon mustard
160 ml/6 fl oz/8 tbsp cream
110 ml/4 oz/½ cup crushed almonds
90 g/3 oz/5 tbsp fine breadcrumbs mixed with chopped thyme and sage

Method
Preheat the oven to 210°C/425°F/Gas Mark 7.

Heat the oil in a frying pan and brown the leg of lamb on all sides. Transfer it to a roasting pan and season with sea salt and pepper.

Make the crust by mixing all the other ingredients together. Spread this paste over the lamb and bake for 45 to 60 minutes, depending on preference.

Before serving, let the lamb rest for 10 minutes on a warm platter. Serve with colourful, steamed spring vegetables and a fine Pauillac wine, decanted earlier.

Later, as daylight fades, the flashing lights and sounds of fun-fair rides and games create a carnival atmosphere, and the band warms up for a *soirée dansante* in Pauillac's *Salle des Fêtes*. Special menus for long, leisurely dinners in restaurants facing the estuary pique my appetite: roasted lamb, *agneau garni printanier* (with spring vegetables), grilled chops or lamb braised with garlic; *agneau* is firmly in the dining spotlight.

The fine wines of this eastern niche of the Médoc are better known by their prestigious château labels. Top of the range are the *premiers crus* including Latour, Lafite and Mouton-Rothschild. However, a number of *cru bourgeois* are excellent and worth sampling with a *côte d'agneau*. Or, try one of the grand château's second wines (not inexpensive) to bring depth and fullness to a succulent bite of pink *agneau rôti*.

After dinner, taking a breath of cool air, we stroll along the harbour. The lights of sailing ships are reflected on the calm estuary waters, and a spring moon ascends into a clear sky ... all signs that we'll have a fine second day in Pauillac.

On Sunday morning, the old lamps, platters and dusty pitchers of a flea market fill the main streets in Pauillac's town centre, stretching out to Quai A. Pichon facing the harbour. Ever on the trail of interesting odd crockery or tools, I watch for a good *"friperie"* section, displaying turn-of-the-century table linen. Often the *brocantes* and *vide-grenier* (clean out the attic) are on the periphery of a *fête*, but in Pauillac, keen collectors and weekenders amble and browse in the town's narrow streets.

Other events, from ice-sculpture to cooking competitions, take place this morning in the large modern, wood-framed sheltered market, where the butcher, Bernard Ardouin, is doing a brisk business in lamb chops. I have the chance to speak with M. Claude Dubédat, a sheep farmer who presides over the producers' organization *"Ovin Gironde"*. To my question about salt marsh lamb, the esteemed *pré-salé*, he responds promptly: "No, *agneau pré-salé* is raised on the salt marshes of Normandy's coast near Mont-St-Michel. *Agneau de Pauillac* is milk-fed lamb, prized for its pale colour and tenderness. Lamb bearing the Pauillac label is raised in a defined region, must be no more than eleven to fifteen kilos in (carcass) weight, of very light colour (almost white, as it is primarily milk-fed), and no older than seventy-five days. The lambs stay in shelters, and the ewes graze in meadows and vineyards." With this succinct explanation he rushes off to a forum, a discussion that is next on Sunday's schedule of events.

Later, as we board the last ferry to Blaye, just across the Gironde, I recall the shepherd's explanation of the *transhumance* and marvel at the symbiosis of a system that has long served many *producteurs*. Drifting across the water, the green pastures and vineyards of the Médoc disappear behind us in a haze of May's filtered sunshine.

Fête de la Fraise/Strawberry Festival

Beaulieu-sur-Dordogne/Corrèze, Limousin

I discovered the picturesque river town of Beaulieu-sur-Dordogne on a return trip from a week hiking in the Auvergne to trace the river's sinuous course. The Dordogne has watered farms and floated timber to the sea. It has served as a traffic lane for hams, cheese, wine and coal from the mountains of the Auvergne to Bordeaux and on to ports around the world. A Benedictine monastery founded in the ninth century on this bend in the river was at the heart of village life, and welcomed pilgrims through the twelfth century, an expansive time in its building and influence. In our era, the abbey of Eglise St-Pierre has become a mecca for followers of European art history, bringing another flow of pilgrims to see this example of the Clunaic style, a treasure of High Romanesque sculpture. The magnificent south portal, a tympanum carved to depict the Last Judgement, has at its centre the figure of Christ, with hands outstretched as in benediction. Flanked by rows of figures that seem engaged in some vital discussion, the majestic Christ figure is heralded by trumpeting angels.

In Beaulieu, the stormy years of the thirteenth century during the Hundred Years' War saw shifting powers and allegiances; the town suffered greatly under English conquest. Through centuries of hardship, pestilence and plague, Beaulieu and its abbey endured further damage under the French during the troubled years of the Wars of

At this bend in the Dordogne, a Benedictine monastery has welcomed
pilgrims for centuries.

Religion. Today, in more peaceful times, nut and fruit orchards thrive in the moist climate, while cattle graze placidly on rich grasses. The southern corner of Corrèze stretches into the northern hills of the ancient region of Quercy.

Beaulieu's central square is garlanded with strings of strawberry flags on this sunny, cool Saturday afternoon. Its warm sandstone houses capped with brown-tinged red tiled roofs give the town a southern air in comparison to upland Corrèze villages built of grey granite. Window boxes around the square are freshly planted with cascading pink geraniums, and huge strawberry posters attached to lamp posts announce the annual *fête*. Inside the *"info"* office, a guide shows us a series of exhibits documenting the early days of the strawberry, a fairly recent development in the town's history. "The French strawberry was actually developed in Brittany by a certain M. Frezier, who crossed plants from Chile and from Virginia in the United States." Then her story takes a dramatic turn: "Major changes occurred over one hundred years ago, when the phylloxera epidemic devastated vineyards in the Limousin and southern Corrèze. Later in the nineteenth century, a number of crops were introduced to rebuild the rural economy. Tobacco and strawberries were planted and took hold, doing well on the slopes of these green Corrèze hills. Local production dates to 1945, after World War II, when strawberries became an important crop. The 1950s and 1960s were peak decades for berry growers until Spanish and Italian strawberries flooded local markets. That was a very hard time for us."

Sunday, the day of the *Fête de la Fraise*, dawns bright and fresh. We stop for coffee in a corner café, watching as the town swings into festival mode. Early shoppers disappear down a narrow street, then reappear with broad smiles and trays full of the ruby fruit, heading for the kitchen and the preserving kettle, the freezer, or the pastry tins to enjoy the season's best. Before I even see the bright red banner over the street, I know that this is the place to be, in front of the town hall, surrounded by berry sellers. Vendors with trays (*plateaux*) or boxes (*barquettes*) of berries fill the small place de la Mairie.

Fifteen producers in the Beaulieu region have set up colourful displays, each decorated with branches, berries and spring flowers. Beside one stall, two small children are eating berries from one *barquette*, the pink juice running

Barquettes of brilliant red berries fill Beaulieu's place de la Mairie.

Vendors will suggest their favourite way of preparing these luscious berries.

down their chins. I ask their father about the varieties he grows, and he responds quietly: "Gariguette is well known across the southwest as a *primeur*, an early berry, and along with Elsanta and Belrubi leads the list of spring varieties. Into the summer, our crops of Seascape and Mara des Bois are ready for market, and Mara may continue in a good season into autumn." When I ask if he grows only berries, he answers: "Oh no, to survive we need a seasonal balance, so I grow tobacco, and corn for my pigs as well – I have some open terrain. My brother raises chickens and has some woodlands, so he sells wood after his berry crops are finished. Our families work together – the berry balances the year of work and income." Before I buy a basket of choice strawberries, he leans over to wipe the berry-stained faces of his two little curly-heads.

Advice on keeping them is offered: "They shouldn't be kept against or in plastic (with no air, mould will form), but in a cool, dark place. Remember, *madame*, the true *goût* doesn't come through when served too cold." And finally: "*Faites attention!* Strawberries don't keep well in stormy weather."

Glancing up at the sky again, a few clouds are moving in, so I stand forewarned. On our way back to the square, I ask a few producers about their favourite ways of serving berries. A voluble woman with hair as wiry as a Brillo pad suggests: "Cut them in two the night before serving, then sprinkle with a bit of sugar and macerate in a bowl of good red wine to keep their aroma ... *ça conserve leur parfum!*" The next, suggested by a stout woman who clearly enjoys cakes, is to slice berries on *quatre-quarts*, the French pound cake, and top with *crème chantilly*. "*C'est un régal, madame!*" Prime-season berries are indeed a treat.

Fraises au sabayon de menthe/Strawberries in a lemon and mint custard

While I like serving berries simply, a more refined dessert can be made for special occasions, adding the whipped cream just before serving.

Ingredients
3 egg yolks
80 g/3 oz/ ½ cup caster sugar
60 ml/2½ fl oz/ ¼ cup slightly
  sweet white wine
½ tsp grated lemon zest
56 ml/2 fl oz/4 tbsp whipping
  cream (whipped, unsweetened),
  optional
½ kg/1 lb strawberries
2 tbsp fresh mint leaves, chopped
  fine, plus 4 leaves to garnish

Method
In the top pan of a double-boiler (over, but not touching boiling water) whisk the egg yolks, adding the sugar gradually, and continue to whisk until the mixture becomes light and airy.

When it forms a ribbon as the whisk is lifted, pour in the wine, in a steady stream. Increase the heat a little, constantly whisking for about 20 minutes as it foams and thickens; never let it boil.

Once the sabayon has thickened, add the lemon zest and taste: it should not taste of raw eggs.

Let the custard cool for 10 minutes before carefully folding in the whipped cream to add volume.

Pour into *parfait* or Champagne glasses filled with stemmed strawberries. Top with a strawberry and a sprig of mint.

To serve this as a gratin, omit the cream, pour the sabayon over the berries in a shallow baking dish, and brown under a hot grill.

Serve with a chilled Monbazillac wine.

In the central square, banners and garlands of bright paper berries wave over the crowds arriving for Sunday's festivities, all under a cornflower blue sky. Soon, a stream of brass bands begins to weave through the old streets before eleven bells have sounded in the church belfry, when they retire for an informal performance in a friendly café. Over one hundred volunteers have worked through the year to put this well-organized event in motion, making allowances for zany street theatre and *bandas*. Above the crowd, I spot an organ-grinder drawing a little parade of his own: following the marching band, he leads clowns and street musicians to the place du Champ-de-Mars, where aisles of regional products create a *fête* market called *Salon des Métiers de Bouche*.

Assorted sausages, home-made jams, organic fruits and vegetables, *pâtés* and *rillettes* (to sample, creating thirst), cheese from the Cantal, and nut-studded sweets fill the stalls. But drinks dominate the displays: beer from St-Martial and the region's Côteaux de Glanes – the light, fresh, country wines made in upper Quercy near Bretenoux. Inspired by the hotel's dessert list, our picnic wine inventory is expanded with a collection of rosy-red Glanes … to splash over berries. Simplicity is my rule with berries in any season – add just a sprinkling of sugar or a dash of wine to bring out the flavours. Layering stemmed fresh mint (at its mildest in the spring) between berries and whipped cream creates a seasonal form of gilding of the lily.

In the afternoon, the crowd will be served portions of a glistening red *tarte aux fraises géante*. When we arrived during the intense hours of its construction on Saturday, I watched many hands arranging sections of pastry, adding a strawberry jam glaze, and fitting a sea of strawberries over the top. The giant tart holds 800 kilograms/1,800 pounds of fruit and measures eight metres/twenty-six feet in diameter.

A late afternoon stroll through the historic quarters of Beaulieu takes us past a Romanesque church, the Chapel of the Penitents, rising out of the rocky river bank. As we pass, a bell rings the hour, sounding out across the sparkling river. The Dordogne flows on, as it has through time, round the bend, past historic, bustling Beaulieu-sur-Dordogne.

May

Fête de la Cerise / Cherry Festival
Céret/Pyrénées-Orientales, French Catalonia

Whitsuntide, the long Pentecost weekend in late spring, is cherry time. Fruit harvests are under way in French Catalonia as we ease our way south along the Mediterranean coast, turning inland from the port town of Collioure. Driving west, the massive Canigou's snowy mountain peak dominates every turn. It is a relief to move away from the incessant *tramontane*, the wind that whips through vineyards and fishing fleets of the Roussillon. Barely a linden leaf stirs over the boulevards of old Céret, a tranquil town that has drawn artists and writers to its centre for over a century. The site for this annual fruit festival could hardly be more dramatic, dominated as it is on one side by the immense Canigou mountain, and on the other by the the breathtaking Albères range which drops to the Perthus pass.

Always held during Pentecost, the *fête* celebrates ripe, juicy cherries. People of all ages flock to Céret, musicians stroll past cafés in Renaissance costumes and vendors offer sweet and savoury *dégustations* as this fruit-growing region turns to festival mode, for a spring *foire* with local colour and international flavour.

Official opening ceremonies for Céret's *fête* take place on Saturday afternoon on the historic pont du Diable, a remarkable fourteenth-century bridge with a single arched span forty-five metres across, and twenty-two metres above a gorge. A parade from the old bridge into the centre of town is led by *bandas* of drums and trumpets, and then the cherry-pickers start to have fun with a range of cherry-related contests. The first *concours*, for the fastest cherry pitter, is soon under way as each contestant is covered with a black plastic sheet. Cherry-pitters young and old are seated in a row, timed, and cheered on by siblings or grandchildren. Photographers adjust their cameras to fastest speed to record the blur of action in these preliminaries, whose winners proceed to the *finale* on Sunday afternoon.

Next is the cherry-spitting contest, assigned to a roped area on a shady boulevard. The media is here to cover all angles as cherry-spitters are interviewed on the radio, and for the evening television news. Will someone beat last year's record distance of nine metres? In other parts of town, more contests are under way, one for cooking with cherries, another for the biggest cherry *clafoutis*, open to all. Outside a café, a face-painter has set up shop, and children sit very still while tiny red cherries, leaves and swirls are painted on their cheeks.

Our next stop along the central avenue d'Espagne is the Museum of Contemporary Art, housing a collection of Picasso ceramics and work of French artists of the 1960s. The "Céret School" of artists that gathered and worked in this Catalan town in the early twentieth century included the Cubists Braque, Juan Gris and Picasso, poet and painter Max Jacob and the painter Soutine, among others. Shady squares, old narrow streets, the sound of fountains, clean air, a mountain setting ... it is not difficult to see what drew this creative crowd to Céret.

As the afternoon temperature rises, everyone seeks a spot in the shade to listen to the group *Las Tunas de Salamanque*. Nine Spanish law students on a lark, these strolling musicians ramble between squares and cafés. They could have stepped out of a Velázquez painting, dressed in Renaissance red and black velvet, black breeches, red jackets and starched frilly white shirts. Playing traditional mandolins, pipes and guitars, they continue to harmonize with every stop for another *cerveza* (beer).

The more serious business of judging the entries in the cherry-growers' competition continues in a specially designated area near the *Syndicat d'Initiative* (tourism office). Out of fifty varieties grown in France, fifteen are produced in the Languedoc-Roussillon, and make up eighty per cent of total French cherry production. The judges will be marking examples of each. The southeast and Rhône-Alpes is France's next largest cherry-growing region, with the Gard a major

Las Tunas de Salamanque are as colourful as a Velázquez painting.

site for cherry orchards. Other regions celebrate the season – one of the best known is Ixtassous' Black Cherry Festival in the Pays Basque, held in June. But at Pentecost, everyone looks to Céret for the nation's earliest, sweetest cherries.

When they are ripe, many hands work fast to sort the fruit (all cherries are hand-sorted), which is then rushed to Perpignan to catch the last train north to Paris and Strasbourg, so that the cherries will be glistening in market stalls the next day. The *very* first cherries picked in Céret are always ceremoniously sent to the President, an event regularly reported in the media.

A grower whose weathered hands showed evidence of many cherry seasons admits to us: "The cherries are actually *better* a bit riper ... a few days later. Forty days pass between the blossoms (the trees are

A young vendor assures us she helps with cherry-picking.

among the first fruit trees to bloom in March, or at the latest in April) and the picking of the cherries." He scratches his grizzled chin and continues: "Depending on the year, some varieties are ready as early as Easter." By the first week in May, the Burlat variety has ripened. This dark, sweet cherry comprises eighty per cent of Pyrénées-Orientales' crop, and is destined for conserves, the sweets industry and for fruit markets around Europe.

Waiting for the announcement by the judges, the cherry-grower continues: "The Burlat is our biggest crop, *elle est sucrée et très juteuse* – sweet and juicy. But it is a little fragile, it doesn't store very long. Eight to ten days after Burlat, Bigarreau Rouge is ready and this goes to be preserved and bottled. Then follow dark Bigarreau Noir, and Bigales with its broad, rosy top." I scan the display for other cherries in season, which include Moreau, Coralise, Garnet, Brooks and Stark Hardy Géante, the last making up ten per cent of production. Lighter-coloured varieties such as Van, and the golden-blushing, pink-topped Rainier, fill market stalls later. Napoléon, a golden, firm-fleshed cherry with wonderful flavour, is also grown. "The season is very concentrated for us," he admits, and returns to lean against a post, ready to hear the results of the competition for the best cherries.

On Sunday there's a special morning market. Small stands decorated with cherry branches offer the fruit for sale by the kilo along Céret's main street, which is garlanded with red-and-yellow-striped flags – the colours of Occitania, the south. On several stalls, the youngest in the family help replace baskets or *barquettes*, small boxes, as the tables clear and more cherries are needed. I choose a small open box of glossy cherries, their stems intact. In the cherry-grower's absence, the vendor in charge is a little girl with freckles sprinkled

Clafoutis aux cerises et amandes / Cherry almond pudding

Alongside cherries, almonds are another regional speciality, grown near Perpignan. They add a crisp touch to the traditional *clafoutis aux cerises*.

Ingredients
345 g/11 oz/1⅓ cups whole milk, simmered with 1 split vanilla pod
28 g/1 oz/2 tbsp butter
3 eggs
60 g/2 oz/¼ cup sugar
70 g/2½ oz/5 tbsp flour
A pinch of salt and ground nutmeg
30 g/1 oz/4 tbsp ground almonds
14 ml/1 tbsp kirsch or eau-de-vie
500 g/1 lb fresh, sweet cherries, washed and pitted
90 g/3 oz/6 tbsp flaked almonds

Method
Preheat the oven to 180°C/350°F/Gas Mark 4.

Simmer the milk and vanilla pod and add 1 tablespoon of the butter. Remove from the heat to infuse.

Whisk the eggs, one at a time, with the sugar in a large bowl. If late-season, tarter cherries are used, more sugar may be required. As the eggs become foamy and light, sprinkle in the flour, salt, nutmeg and ground almonds and mix well.

Lift the vanilla pod out of the milk and whisk the milk and kirsch into the batter.

Next prepare the moulds: butter 4 to 6 ramekins or 10cm/4in brioche moulds, place on a large baking sheet and distribute the cherries evenly between them all. Fill each two-thirds full with batter and sprinkle with flaked almonds.

Bake for about 20 minutes, until the clafoutis are puffed and golden. Cool and unmould.

Serve with tiny glasses of sweet Maury wine.

across her nose. She assures me that she helps pick the cherries, alongside her cousins and friends.

Music is in the air again as a band strikes up familiar tunes on avenue d'Espagne. Dancers of all ages lift their hands together, moving to the rhythm of the Catalan *sardane*. No costumes or special hats are worn for this impromptu, free-spirited gathering of friends in the traditional circle dance of Catalonia. I step back with other bystanders as, one by one, dancers join the *sardane's* ever-larger circle, in the spirit of the *Fête de la Cerise*.

Fête Gourmande / Food-Lovers' Festival

St-Paul-Trois-Châteaux/Drôme, southern Rhône Valley

When friends say they're coming to Provence, I often wonder: which Provence? From coastal Provence, Marseilles and the marshes of the Camargue, we drive north into a different world, approaching the Drôme Provençale and the Rhône Valley's expanses of vineyards and orchards. The Drôme is itself like Janus with two faces, one with wooded, steep slopes rising into the Dauphiné and the Alps. The other face is bright, a broad dish of valley land rimmed by stony, craggy cliffs reflecting sunlight and funneling Mistral winds. Entering the Tricastin, driving north from Bollène past shimmering silken fields of lavender and vineyards edged with roses just in bloom, I am surrounded by an expansive open landscape, a face of Provence turned towards the sun.

This portion of the broad Rhône Valley, cut and flattened as the river flows south from Lyons, crosses the Tricastin plain (named after a Gaullish tribe whose land the Romans conquered). St-Paul-Trois-Châteaux's location as the capital of the Tricastin, on the lower edge of the ancient Dauphiné, is almost midway between Orange and Montélimar. To me, the Tricastin is a gateway to, and from, Provence. Looking west across the Rhône, the wild and rugged forests of the Ardèche supply an energy-boosting cuisine rich in chestnuts, pork, fruit and honey, while further north, vineyards and orchards carpet the landscape to Valence. As dense in history as in gastronomy, the route just south of St-Paul-Trois-Châteaux towards Orange follows Gallo-Roman roads under ancient arches, past columns and amphitheatres that have weathered centuries.

Like so many Provençal towns, the oldest quarter of sun-bleached grey stone buildings rests on top of a wind-swept hill, with meander-

Tricastin, the gateway to Provence, has an abundance of lavender in June.

ing streets cascading down from the church in three directions. Fresh geraniums (being watered as you walk under them early in the morning) tumble from summer's *jardinières* on wrought iron balconies. Vendors along side streets have settled into their folding chairs, their displays in place, and in an open square close to the town's centre, artisans are adjusting broad, sheltering orange umbrellas as the sun shifts. At the summit of the town, we step inside the cool space of the *Maison de la Truffe et du Tricastin*.

Three things have put Tricastin on gastronomic maps: truffles from its hills, wines from this windy stretch along the Rhône, the Côteaux du Tricastin, and tender lamb, *agneaux de Tricastin*. It is a small region covering forty square kilometres north of Bollène, but from November through February, both Richerenches, about fifteen kilometres east into the hills, and St-Paul are major centres for truffles, *tuber melanosporum vittadini, truffes de Tricastin*. Richerenches celebrates a Truffle Mass late in January, and St-Paul holds a truffle *fête* the second Sunday in February. Near the truffle exhibition, the Maison shop's shelves are stocked with truffles in tiny bottles, tins of *foie gras truffé* and racks of elegantly labelled wines from Tricastin vineyards.

Outside again, we return to the square to begin our food-lovers' foray. The Château la Croix, Côteaux du Tricastin banner behind winemaker Monsieur P. Daniel attracts us to the stall for a *dégustation*, and a chance to satisfy my curiosity about the region's red wines. The tall, greying vintner smiles and offers a sample of his Grenache Noire-dominant blend. Though not as dense in dark cherry notes as Côtes-du-Rhône-Villages, this Tricastin red is similarly fruity and delicious. Packing up three bottles of Château la Croix, he confirms: "Reds make up ninety-five per cent of our production and much is shipped abroad. In fact, many French wine-lovers haven't tasted Tricastin!" Their loss, I remark, and imagine the perfection of a simple, elegant truffle omelette and a glass of his Côteaux du Tricastin. "Don't keep it more than three years – this isn't a *vin de garde*," he warns as we leave. No problem, it may not last past the truffle season – this year.

This is a *fête* for all the senses – the scent of lavender is in the air. An old lavender-distilling wagon, an *alambic*, has been set up and the lavender perfume intensifies as the day's heat surrounds us. The healing, versatile herb is displayed in many forms: lavender essence and oils, ribbon-tied sachets in Provençal prints, oval soaps, long wands to nest with linens, *Eau de Lavande*, and lavender *pastille*, sweets to soothe the throat. The vendor, a young man with tousled brown hair, explains the flower's finer points. "True lavender is very subtle," he begins, holding a long, single, budding violet-tinged flower under my nose. "This, *Lavandula*

angustifolia, grows at high altitudes and gives its delicate, clean scent to perfumes. It does well on the high plateaux from Sault towards the Lurs mountains, and around Grasse in the Alpes-Maritimes. Lavender has calming properties – one drop on your pillow may help you sleep, but a larger dose of, say, three drops can stir up more energy, so be careful how it is used." Then another stem, with a few branches holding more flowers, is drawn past my nose. Stronger, it is scented with lavender scent, but with an edge of camphor. "Now, take a deep breath of *lavandin, madame*, this is the variety that you use to discourage moths, and it gives its scent to household products. All lavender has natural antiseptic, cleansing qualities." We thank him for all the *bons conseils*, and continue the day's discoveries.

On one narrow street we pass a display of wooden toys, on the next I admire perfectly formed *chèvre* cheeses from Taulignan, higher in the Drôme hills. Across the aisle, rows of glistening candied fruit, sticky with sugar but balanced in flavour are displayed ... whole Reine Claude plums, perfect ruby cherries from Apt's orchards in the Luberon,

translucent green wands of *angélique* and bits of candied violets. There are also perfectly formed miniature marzipan shapes of tiny apricots, aubergines, ears of corn and avocados. I succumb, and bring home a collection of these hand-made almond paste fantasies, sweets for any season.

A seller of *Nougat de Montélimar* tempts us with an almond-crunchy morsel. His enthusiasm is contagious, his white cap at a tilt. "We are very careful in choosing the ingredients – only the best lavender honey is used – an important twenty-eight per cent of the *pâte*, the mixture. Egg whites, and then almonds are stirred in with a smaller amount of pistachios," he explains. "Do you like the softer or the crisper kind? You see, there are two types. Also, try the dark nougat." Almonds snap between my teeth, melting in a sweet mouthful, so I point to the soft nougat sample, with "umm", as the answer. The Latin name for nut cake, *nux gatum*, evolved into *nougat* in Provençal, as it is in French. This speciality dates back to the seventeeth century when a local agronomist planted almond trees from Greece on his land. For the traditional thirteen desserts served in Provence homes on Christmas Eve, both are always offered.

Perfectly formed miniature apricots, aubergines and even watermelons are creatively made from almond paste.

By the time the ceremonies of the *Fête Gourmande* begin, the sun is directly overhead. The parade approaches, a series of trumpeting *bandas*, then accordion players with spirited dancers, followed by the dignified *confrérie*. Walking together at a measured pace, the *confrères* in blue satin-robes proceed to the platform, the golden braid on their capes sparkling in the sun. Feathery plumes on their hats add a seventeenth-century air to the pageant that *confréries* have a way of making official, and whimsical.

On the platform, a moustachioed *confrère des Vins du Tricastin* steps forward to begin the day's speeches. Words of welcome are not enough – he has composed a poem, delivered with theatrical gestures, constantly twirling the fine tips of his white moustache. A

hand rises emphatically into the air to proclaim the glories of the guest from the Haute-Savoie, St-Paul-en-Chablais (each year, a guest town or region whose name is also St-Paul is invited to participate in the *fête* – in France there are sixty-three towns named St-Paul!): their wine and hams, cheeses and fruits of the mountains. We join the crowd, applauding this *confrère's* performance, as soft, high melodies of alpine horns sound an interlude in the *animations folkloriques*. At the edge of the stage, folkdancers gather and the accordion player's fingers race through reels and gavottes.

The face of June in the Drôme, when the gleaming surfaces of lavender fields soften the landscape, is a pause between spring's sharp Mistral winds and the enveloping heat of summer. It is a transitory time in Provence, the best moment to be seized, *carpe diem* ... catching the essence of a season in its prime.

Aïoli / Garlic mayonnaise

A visit to this region of the Midi calls for a taste of the pungent garlic-infused mayonnaise called *aïoli*, a speciality that sums up the flavours and scents of the south. Traditionally, *aïoli* is the centrepiece on a platter of poached cod and mussels with steamed potatoes and green beans, served as standard Friday fare during the Lenten season. Toast rounds spread with *aïoli* float on the popular fish stew, a *bourride*. June's fresh, juicy garlic easily crushes to flavour this blend of *ail* (garlic) and *oli* (oil).

Ingredients
4 to 6 cloves fresh garlic, peeled and chopped
1 tsp sea salt
2 raw egg yolks, plus 1 hard-boiled yolk (sieved)
280 ml/10 fl oz/1¼ cup best extra virgin olive oil

Method
Have all tools and ingredients at room temperature. In a mortar or heavy bowl, crush the garlic with the salt to achieve a paste, and blend in the raw egg yolks with a spoon until thick.

Then whisk in a very thin stream of olive oil until you have a smooth, glistening emulsion. Add the sieved hard-boiled yolk; adjust salt as required.

Snipped fresh basil leaves can be stirred into this savoury mayonnaise, adding a Provençal touch to steamed artichokes or a platter of cold sliced roast veal or chicken. Coteaux du Tricastin rosé wine completes a simple, delicious summer lunch.

Fête du Fromage / Goats' Cheese Fair

Banon / Alpes-de-Haute-Provence, northeastern Provence

Banon's stone church surveys fields of
lavender and stony pastures.

Sometimes the sun is with us in Provence. I had hoped it would be for Banon's *Fête du Fromage*, but no, it looks like a steady all-day rain. Driving to the *fête*, the road winds east through the Luberon Valley from Apt in the Vaucluse, up into the hills approaching Banon. We roll past grey-green olive trees in bloom, misty fields of *lavandin* and Côtes-du-Luberon vineyards, rising towards the edge of the Albion plateau, into drier, rockier terrain. It is land well suited to nimble goats, lavender and olive trees. The village of Banon, built into the rocky foothills of Montagne de Lure, is crowned by a grey stone church that surveys the open, stony pasture, the *garrigue*.

Recalling previous visits in warmer days, I imagined pulling into the dusty centre of the village where a lazy brown dog would surely be sleeping in the street. But today the Cheese Fair's bustling activities discourage idle old dogs, who amble off to find calmer corners. The hubbub of the day begins as trucks deliver cheese, platforms are set up for musicians, and a pen is roped off for pony rides. We are here for the busiest day of the year in little Banon.

A special *chèvre*, Banon's creamy, distinctive goats' cheese, wrapped in a chestnut leaf and tied with a thin raffia string, is the focus of this

Chestnut leaves impart a special character as Banon ages.

foire. As well as being traditional, the leaf and natural string are the Banon cheesemakers' practical touch to both protect and flavour the cheese. Vendors set their displays in order, and we watch as the circular emblem for the *National Site of Taste* hung above Joel Corbon's stall is adjusted. With this last touch, he is ready for customers ... and a few questions. When asked whether Banon is ever made from *lait de brebis*, ewes' milk, the serious, dark-eyed goat farmer replies: "Yes, but then it is not called by the same name, not officially included in the AOC specifying Banon as a goats' milk cheese. Some cheesemakers do make a ewes' milk, leaf-wrapped cheese, and label it as *brebis*. For us, *chèvre* is a seasonal cheese, the best made from April until November as the goats feed on spring and summer's wild herbs in the pastures and the *garrigue*. During the winter, when the nanny-goats are 'kidding', fresh *chèvre* is not made, but for an occasional taste we preserve some in olive oil. My three children love it, *ils l'adorent!*" His serious expression lightens and the furrow in his brow disappears.

The days are long for cheesemakers like Joel Corbon. The goats must be milked at six o'clock in the morning, and the milk preserved right away. The cream is skimmed off after the milk has settled for twenty-four hours, is put into perforated (*faisselle*) cups to drain, kept cool to dry for two or three weeks, then wrapped in chestnut leaves to age. "Those wrapped in green leaves have not cured as long," explains M. Corbon. "They'll be milder. Some is sold fresh, some will be brushed with fruit brandies: plum or pear *eau-de-vie*. Alternatively, leaves can be dipped in salt water." On an earlier visit to his stand, I bought a delicious fresh sweet goats' cheese, *caillé frais*.

The leaves used for wrapping Banon *chèvre* are a subject in themselves. "In the past," continues M. Corbon, "they used whatever was in season, whatever was at hand, including grape or plane tree leaves, chestnut leaves, to keep the flies off and to make it easier to tuck the cheese into baskets and pockets. To meet AOC regulations now, we must use chestnut leaves, which give the cheese a special flavour as it ages and the leaves turn brown. The aroma is a bit 'goaty', but complex, and the creamy texture brings people back for more."

Joel Corbon leads his goats to their garrigue pasture.

Customers approach, indeed coming back for more.

A signature is scrawled in white on a bright red awning facing the *foire*: Chez Melchio! A few sausages are sold just outside the door, but we enter to see what other spicy goodness lies inside this *charcuterie-épicerie*. M. Melchio, a slight, animated man, is behind the counter, and he peeks at us through a curtain of dangling thin sausages strung over rods, ready to clip off links to order. People follow us in, shopping baskets ready to tuck in parcels of cheese, vegetables and, of course, sausages. Pine nut, peppery, garlicky, *pur porc*, *sarriette* (wild savory, see page 110), herbed sausages all lend their scents to the air of this long, narrow grocery store, a one-stop shop for paper goods, fishing flies, dish soap, cooking supplies, cheese and spicy sausages. During the winter, M. Melchio stocks broad flat sheets of cod, *morue salée*, hung, ready to be cut and sent home for a Friday *Aïoli*. Pine nuts are abundant in this region, so a packet or two go into my basket along with Melchio's chewy fennel and *sarriette* sausages. Wild herbs of the region season sausages and *chèvre* cheeses. I ask M. Melchio about *sarriette* especially, as it seems to show up in all good things Provençal. He explains: "Wild savory, *sarriette*, likes our stony, dry climate – it grows everywhere, so when the goats eat it and then we roll the chèvre in the fresh or dried herb, you get a good dose of the country whenever you take a bite." Thyme, called *serpolet* when it grows wild in the *garrigue*, is part of the popular seasoning blend of "*herbes de Provence*" which includes sage (*sauge*) and bay (*laurier*) leaf as well.

Chèvre à l'huile épicée / Goats' cheese in spiced oil

Careful selection is crucial if you want to keep *chèvre* for a week or two, as this recipe will allow. Choose *cabécou* or discs of *chèvre* that have a slightly firm edge (*demi-sec*), not the softer ones. Use any fresh, seasonal herbs. A fine, fruity, extra virgin olive oil is best for preserving.

Method
Simply fill a sterilized jar with layers of *chèvre*, herbs and spices, and fill with oil. Close the jar tight and keep in a cool, dark place for up to 2 weeks.

Serve with a fresh salad and a white Côtes du Luberon.

Ingredients
Enough discs of chèvre to fill a
  1 litre/36 fl oz/4½ cup jar
Fresh herbs: 2 bay leaves, a branch
  of fresh savory, rosemary,
  tarragon, thyme
Spices: 2 peppercorns, 1 dried red
  pepper, 1 clove garlic, sliced
Extra virgin olive oil (enough to
  cover the chèvre in the jar)

Tiny figures, Santons de Provence, decorate a cheesemaker's display.

Noon bells ring at the top of Banon's hilltop *clocher*, sounding out time for lunch, and our table in the Hôtel des Voyageurs dining room is ready. Today's menu features *chèvre* in every course. First, a warm round *feuilleté de chèvre* – a creamy *chèvre* in the flakiest pastry casing imaginable – is served garnished with sharp rocket salad greens. A small pitcher of the house Côtes du Luberon arrives alongside *poulet farci de chèvre aux herbes* with a baked tomato, a formed flan of courgettes and crisp, round frites. Fresh *chèvre* mixed with *serpolet* and sage has been slipped under the skin of the plump chicken, melting as it bakes. A sweet rendition on the day's theme wraps up lunch: fresh *chèvre* whipped with sugar into a mousse, set on a *couche*, or layer, of thick, red, fresh-fruit *coulis*.

After lunch we are ready to explore more products of the Alpes-de-Haute-Provence. Under a large white banner, lavender, nougat and spelt are spread on a cicada-print cloth. For centuries spelt has been cultivated in Provence (and throughout Tuscany) and is a staple of soups and stews of the south.

On Monday, the *Fête du Fromage* has come and gone, and we set out on the high road along the Albion plateau to Sault. Sunday's rain has left puddles in the rough, pebbly pasture where brown and white goats browse. Clouds lift to let brilliant shafts of sunlight beam down on the hills – a stark and beautiful scene. The goats in the *garrigue* don't notice, they're too busy nibbling June's fresh *herbes de Provence*.

Festival du Casse-Croûte et des Goudots Gourmands / Snack Fair

Aurillac/Cantal, southern Auvergne

A *fête* devoted to *what?* Snacks. Friends were sceptical when we raved about a summer festival in the Cantal devoted to snacks, but as I described the event, it became evident that there was a cultural difference here. "Snacks" may need some translation. This is not an event celebrating a quick Mars bar munched on the run, or a sip of soda while waiting for the bus. In the Auvergne, *casse-croûte* – "breaking the crust" in direct translation – usually suggests a snack on, or with, bread in some form. Cracking off a piece of crust from a crisp baguette, spreading fresh butter on a slice of country rye and layering on a paper-thin slice of mountain air-cured ham, or a *tartine* of freshly halved baguette buttered and slathered with wild blueberry jam, all qualify. Pancakes, too, including the rye-flour, yeast-raised *bourriole*, are regarded as a snack, especially in the Auvergne, where the *casse-croûte* is an important part of life ... and where we are headed.

A web of roads lined in green on the map indicate that whichever route we take to Aurillac, the panoramas will be spectacular. Solid brown, quarried-granite barns, their shiny grey-slate roofs cut in a scalloped fish-scale pattern, and thick, square *pigeonniers* (dovecotes) punctuate the forests and fields. Our approach, driving north from Figeac in the eastern Lot, is scenic and serpentine, wiggling along the river Cère. Ahead, the southern Cantal mountains rise north of Aurillac, a town founded in ancient times as *Aureliacum*, the domain of a wealthy Gallo-Roman, Aurelius.

Two questions are rustling in my mind as I arrive. First, what is a *goudot* – is it a snack? I have heard that a golden *goudot* will be awarded to someone, so it must be important. Second, what does the regional potato and cheese speciality *aligot* taste like, and how is it made?

Fresh, crusty loaves are ready for a hearty casse-croûte - which is a valued part of life in Cantal.

On this Saturday morning, *goudot* is the subject of a radio programme presented by gastronome and critic Jean-Luc Petitrenaud and broadcast live from the Aurillac fair. On the platform, a black string tie looped at the neck of his white shirt, Petitrenaud holds up a golden pot and explains: "In the gold rush days along the Jordanne river, gold panners from Aurillac used this round pot, a *goudot*, to hold

their *pépites*, gold nuggets. *Goudot* thus has become synonymous with people from the town, extended to refer to those who enjoy *la bonne table* with copious servings.

Aurillac's vast Saturday market is a flurry of colourful activity, and a lively meeting point for the townfolk.

Now, I am surrounded by *goudots*, by cattle farmers, gentian-gatherers and cheesemakers ... all who enjoy the best of country fare!" He turns and introduces his guests, who explain the origins of the event. Originally two separate events, the *Goudots Gourmands* and the *Fête du Casse-Croûte* merged in the early 1990s to become **a** a larger festival, attracting diverse *artisans du goût* from a distance to sell their edible specialities.

Aurillac's old quarter, built in dark grey-brown quarried granite, is currently being restored and pedestrianised. Shop-lined streets lead up and down the hill into the old quarter. Overhead, in front of windows curtained with Aurillac's own lace, pink and purple geraniums spike the dark, narrow alleys with colour. We pause in a café for a glass of Côtes d'Auvergne from Marcillac, enjoying a sip of surprisingly full, red wine. It exceeds a simple description of "light and lively", so I decide to seek out a Côtes d'Auvergne winemaker at the *fête*. Festival events are set up in a newer section of town, in a contemporary outdoor theatre and a park. An enormous chestnut-red Salers steer is being led to the edge of this temporary pasture, and more follow. Men in black broad-brimmed hats, checked shirts and red neckscarves warn me to watch my step: *"Attention où vous marchez, madame!"*

Salers is the name of a town, a breed of cattle, and a cheese featured in Aurillac's *fête*. Cylinders of large, firm and uniform Salers cheese are stacked on a stall; the nutty aroma of this sliced cheese stops me in my tracks. It resembles Cheddar in texture, but its pale, creamy-ivory colour and density set Salers, the farm-made cousin of Cantal cheese, apart. The curly-haired vendor, in his heavy cotton Auvergnat smock, hefts another forty-kilo (eighty-pound) Salers cheese onto the tasting counter. He explains: "This is a pressed cheese, not cooked, made with the milk of our mountain-grazing Salers cows from early May to the end of October." His brother, he reports, is in the mountains now for the summer cheesemaking, living in the family's stone house, a *buron*. The outer crust of his cheese looks more like an old brown pitted rock, but when I taste it the texture is soft, the taste long-lasting and rich, with a buttery aftertaste. I try another cheese, this time a Cantal with a smoother rind, sweeter taste and a pleasantly salty quality. "This Cantal is made in a dairy *co-opérative* in our town, *not* in a *buron*," adds the cheesemaker.

At last I find my opportunity to learn all about the regional speciality, *aligot*. Under a large tent, a man and woman in white T-shirts stir up a batch of this stick-to-your-ribs Auvergne dish, prepared on the spot. A large aluminum pan is set on a broad hot-plate, and as the potatoes soften and become a purée, the man stirs slowly with a long-handled wooden spoon. His petite partner stands on tip-toe, adding chunks of white cheese – fresh *tomme de Laguiole* (pronounced *Laiyol*) from a (bottomless?) carton. As the fresh cheese melts and becomes dense and stringy, the man's muscles begin to ripple, his brow furrows. He is in the thick of it, and the whole pan begins to shift and slide on the burner. When the *aligot* is ready, the plastic plates and forks she has set out are in hand, and the first in line are served. I watch the scoop-lift-swoop delivery of one serving from pot to plate ... if I ever thought serving spaghetti was tricky, I hadn't yet tried to scoop *aligot*!

There is a secret ingredient in *aligot*. The minced bits of garlic that pop between my teeth in the first bite are like tiny pearls packed with flavour, and are essential in this Auvergne classic. Garlic from Billom, east of Clermont-Ferrand, is favoured in the Auvergne, and the cheese is local, too. Fresh, formed cheeses are best for *aligot*, such as the famed white, fresh *tomme de Laguiole* made in and around the town of Aubrac.

Saturday afternoon's parade through the old quarter of Aurillac eventually winds up at the *fête* grounds where the parade cattle are led to grassy pens and the *confrères* and *chevaliers* wait in groups. The most colourful of assemblies I have seen, *le Rassemblement International des Confréries* gathers for introduction ceremonies. Many bakers join the procession, carrying baskets of bread, their long golden chains hung around their necks glimmering as the sun catches their *confrérie's* medallion embossed with sheaves of wheat. Others in long robes and plush velvet hats bear their emblem banners high. Some take it all in fun, like the *Confrérie de la Tête de Veau* dressed in pasture-green capes with symbolic clover edging, hats shaped like flapping calves' ears and snouts tied over their noses. Cattle farmers have pride of place in the line-up, the *Confrérie de la Vache Sacrée de Salers*, the Holy Cow Brotherhood of Salers, leading the way.

On Sunday morning, I hear the soft bleating of sheep as we return to the festival grounds, where a shady area has been roped off for farmyard animals. Families bring small children here to pet the ponies, sheep, goats and rabbits. More events (including pig races) fill a day of on-going *dégustations* of cheese, sausage, gentian liqueur, wine and fruit. Folkdancers from Alsace begin to polka in the centre

Aligot / Potato and cheese purée

Freshly made *tomme* is the best cheese to use in this Auvergnat speciality. In France, *tome* or *tomme* is a formed cheese, as is a *fourme*, round and tall, and heavy. This recipe serves six.

Ingredients
1 kg/2 lbs floury potatoes, peeled, cubed and cooked until tender, then drained and mashed

500 g/1 lb tomme de Laguiole (a mild, young Cantal could also be used, grated)

Sea salt, freshly ground white pepper

225 g/8 oz/1 cup crème fraîche or sour cream

60 g/2 oz/4 tbsp butter

2-4 cloves garlic, chopped very finely

Method
Beat the mashed potatoes over a very low heat with a wooden spoon, then add the cheese and season to taste. Stir steadily, then fold in the crème fraîche and the butter and garlic. When the texture becomes "stringy" it is ready to serve. Less cheese may be used, but do not leave out the garlic.

An easy Auvergnat dinner features *aligot* with rainbow trout, sautéed with bacon, crisply done, taking less than an hour from pan to table.

A country wine, Côtes d'Auvergne, for example, or a light, red Gamay, is well suited to a *casse-croûte* pause, and to dinner as well.

of the festival square, while *crêpe* and sausage sellers heat their portable griddles. A stall selling fresh *flognarde*, a custardy flan-like pudding, still warm and moist with pears or apples, provides a mid-morning *gourmandise*, eaten on a park bench. Banners over Aurillac's festival promise *"Casse-Croûte Non-stop"*: to each her own *gourmandise*, to each his own *casse-croûte*!

July

Foire aux Melons / Melon Fair
Cavaillon/Vaucluse, Provence

The quest for a perfect melon, a fruit that condenses the warmth and colours of Provence, leads us to Cavaillon. This sunny land of arid terrain is a region of hard-working farmers who have coaxed orchards and vineyards to produce olives and grapes on rugged, terraced hillsides, and fruit in richer valley lands. It is a region of seasonal abundance wrought over the centuries by generations of farming families. Approaching Cavaillon from Avignon, a diverse landscape whizzes past us – orchards protected by tall cypress wind-breaks and open fields ribbed with protective plastic tunnels, small farms and solid, simple houses whose blue shutters are closed against July's intense sun. As each cicada-chirping kilometre passes, skirting the dramatic, white-stone edges of the Alpilles mountain chain, we approach the large market town of Cavaillon. It is set in a broad valley, watered by the river Durance flowing on to the Rhône below Avignon. Orchards and melon fields stretch out far to the south, while to the southeast the blue ridges of the Luberon range loom against the sky. The plateau of the Vaucluse rises abruptly to the north and east, forming an impressive stony backdrop for a colourful July *foire* celebrating the region's famed, fragrant melons.

The melon in focus, *Cucumis melo*, is an aromatic fruit with a pungent but fresh scent that perks up appetites slumping during the heat of midday, rehydrating the spirit as well as the body. It is not native to the south of France, but has evolved from a much rougher, but sweet, Italian melon from Cantalupo, grown in Europe since the Romans introduced it from the Middle East. The sweet melons first cultivated near Cavaillon were primarily winter melons, ripened off the vine for nobles' banquet tables. In the nineteenth century, cantaloupes gained

Clockwise from top: sundial on an ancient Cavaillon wall; the ever-present sunflower; sun-ripened canteloupe melons at the Melon Fair.

ground and became a major fruit crop in the Durance Valley. The small, smooth-skinned, pale green-and-ivory variety that was grown extensively in France's Charente region was cultivated in the 1920s when Cavaillon producers expanded their melon fields. By the 1960s, their portion of French melon production approached eighty per cent. Since then, melons of the Charente, Quercy and other parts of the southwest have rolled into markets in increasing volumes, challenging production in Provence.

Cavaillon is a city of surprises in its corners and courtyards, a town of numerous museums and exhibitions. The city library holds the complete manuscripts of nineteenth-century author Alexandre Dumas, a renowned gourmet. The author of *The Three Musketeers* was so fond of Cavaillon's melons that he donated his four hundred literary works to the city – his literary legacy in exchange for a dozen melons, delivered to him each year of his life.

On Saturday morning as the *foire* is getting under way, I find my way along shop-lined streets, up cours Bournissac towards the Colline St-Jacques, the impressive cliffs that rise sharply behind the southeast edge of Cavaillon. Colourful stalls fill the place du Clos, some decorated with the season's first sunflowers, others with melon vines, all well-stocked with crates and baskets of fresh melons on soft excelsior straw. An array of apples and melons, perfect red, golden and ivory-green fruit, draws me to Mme. Bertrand's display, and her welcome is hearty: "A sample of melon, fresh from fields this morning, *madame?*" Her round, sun-tanned arms and cheeks speak of hours in the fields, her hazel eyes sparkle as she describes her family's fruit production. The melon sliver that melts like honey on my tongue is cool, but not cold.

She offers me guidance on choosing a melon: *"Faites attention, madame* ... look carefully, if it is too pale it will not be sweet. Count the green stripes that mark wedges, the best melons should have ten. The melon should feel heavy in your hand and the colour should still be creamy with streaks of green. If the stem end, the *pédoncule*, wiggles loose easily, sniff. That fruity *parfum* will let you know it is ready – catch the scent ... very pungent? Eat it today, don't wait." She leans over and touches my arm, as if to confide: "... best to choose a melon the day you serve it." Soon, two perfect melons are cushioned in my basket and good advice rings in my ears. It takes a while for the nose to learn; I watch French shoppers sniff up to five melons before choosing the perfect one.

By eleven o'clock, it is time to watch one of several performances during the weekend by a spirited, professional troop of Italian flag-throwers. Stepping out of a Renaissance painting, dressed in burgundy and cream velvet, *Les Lanceurs de Drapeaux de Volterra* toss and twirl huge flags in precision,

Stirring melon confiture.

synchronized in a fast-paced choreography. These western valleys of Vaucluse once belonged to a larger province reaching into Tuscany's hills, to the northern duchies of Italy whose terrain bears such a strong resemblance to this part of the country. During the centuries of Roman rule, Cavaillon was an *oppidum*, a fortified camp. The lithe, fast-stepping Italian flag-throwers conclude their spellbinding performance in front of a first-century Roman *arc de triomphe* on place François Tourel, the white rocky wall of the Colline St-Jacques as their backdrop.

The order of the *Confrérie des Chevaliers de l'Ordre du Melon de Cavaillon* presides at this event, awarding prizes to winners of a nationwide cooking contest for recipes using melon. Of the previous year's winning dishes, crayfish and melon aspic with Parma ham, and a chilled soup, gazpacho of melons, head the list. In pursuit of other variations on the day's theme, I explore the local *épiceries* and *boutiques*, including the gourmet grocery Le Clos Gourmand, facing place du Clos. In the window is a fancy bottle of melon liqueur, *apéritif à la pulpe de melon*, which is delicious when used as the base for an unusual summer Kir, topped up with sparkling wine or Champagne. Drop in a melon ball and garnish with a mint leaf, for the finishing touch. Alternatively, pour a dash over fruit salad or lemon sorbet for dessert.

As the last light of day fades, the annual pageant begins, tying past to present in Cavaillon. At the turn of the twentieth century,

Soupe de melon aux épices et fruits rouges/
Spiced melon and fruit soup

Should you start dinner with melon or save it for dessert? Why not for both? This cool, spiced soup could be used for either course.

Method

In a saucepan, mix the sugar with boiling water to make a syrup and bring to the boil. Add the vanilla and the orange and lemon zest and boil until the syrup thickens.

When thick, remove from the heat and add the herbs and the juice of the orange and lemon. Leave to infuse overnight then chill.

To serve, remove the herbs, distribute the melon and fruit in soup plates and pour the spiced syrup over the top. If served as dessert, add a scoop of lemon, rosemary or lavender sorbet.

Ingredients
200 g/7 oz/1 scant cup caster
  sugar
450 ml/16 fl oz/2 cups water
1 vanilla pod, split with a knife
  point
1 orange and 1 lemon, washed,
  dried and peeled, and juice and
  zest reserved
Fresh rosemary (and optional:
  2 stems liquorice (réglisse),
  sold in Provence markets)
3 large melons, trimmed and
  seeds removed, flesh
  scooped into melon balls
300 g/11 oz/1½ cups mixed
  red fruit in season
  (cherries, raspberries,
  redcurrants)

Cavaillon's night market began at sundown, and melons were sold through the night's cool hours when the fragile fruit would travel more safely. Now, melon farmers and families in old carts and wagons line up for the evening's parade. In the lead, a small cart drawn by a brown donkey holds just one basket of ripe melons, set behind the smiling driver in a broad-brimmed black hat. Next in line, a longer wagon loaded with more melons carries a family: little boys in print vests and their sisters (in white caps tied under small chins) wave at friends along the boulevard. About ten o'clock, all eyes are trained on the Colline St-Jacques, and as the twinkling lights of lanterns appear, the "hermit" from the hermitage on the hill descends followed by others. Bells ring from the hilltop chapel, and a choir begins to sing old Provençal songs.

What's in store for us on Sunday in Provence's centre of melon culture? Overnight, the place du Clos has been transformed and is filled with vendors and *artisans* in Provençal dress. The skills of a spinner, carder, blacksmith, soapmaker, laundress and *confiture*-maker are demonstrated with ease, tools in hand, working as they would in days gone by. A thin, greying woman in a traditional print skirt and apron is intent on her work, stitching white thread on to white cloth, nimble fingers flying to finish a white *piqué* baby cap. Next to her is a neatly folded collection of Provençal quilts and *boutis*, the finely stitched coverlets that fill a home's *armoire à linge*, the household linen closet. Wood smoke is in the air, mixed with the sweet smells of jam simmering in a huge copper cauldron over an open fire. A large woman stirs the bubbling pot, as chunks of melon appear, suspended in the thick orange mass. She looks up when I ask about jam-making: *"Je la remue pour qu'elle ne brûle pas* – I stir it so it doesn't scorch and stick." Her cotton blouse clings to her broad back – it's a hot job on a July day, but the melons will not wait. We continue past a shoemaker, charcoal-makers and other trades of years past, *les temps d'antan*.

The droning buzz of *cigales*, the cicadas, resonates above the hum of voices and traffic all day on Sunday. This sound of summer in Provence persists as background music, but in the foreground of my memories, the people stand in high relief against their melon fields. Families still harvest Cavaillon's melons, taking the dust and heat in their stride as they gently tuck the grey-green globes into baskets of fine straw to bring to the *foire*, the eagerly awaited melon market.

Festival des Crus de la Vallée du Rhône / Rhône Wine Fest

Vacqueyras/Vaucluse, Provence

Bright blue skies over the jagged Dentelles' mountain skyline promise a fine weekend for an especially festive French day. The *Fête Nationale, Quatorze-Juillet,* celebrates the birth of the French Republic in a colourful, popular Provençal wine fair *bien arrosé* (awash) with the region's wines. Local winemakers have staged this festival for over twenty-five years and in 1990, when Vacqueyras' AOC was announced, the fair expanded to include other wines of the Rhône, turning it into a four-day event. Each year another region of France is invited to participate, so the wines of Alsace, the Savoie or other *vignobles* might also be sampled, along with their regional specialities.

Our route from the ancient city of Orange to Vacqueyras weaves through the eastern edge of the southern Rhône Valley, past undulating rows of grapevines. They sweep upwards, scaling bushy slopes to sheer white cliffs, topped by a lacy rim of rock, the Dentelles de Montmirail. These sharp rock formations edge a natural amphitheatre for Côtes du Rhône vineyards.

On the fourteenth of July, cours Strassart, a sleepy *platane*-shaded street skirting Vacqueyras' thick medieval town walls, is quickly being transformed into an open-air banquet. Long white tables are laid for the *Grand Repas Compagnard,* a sumptuous lunch. An arched entry gate in the medieval walls, the Porte Basse, is the passageway to the *fête.* Here, tickets are sold for the *repas,* tasting glasses are purchased, and people sign up for a *rallye découverte* ("discovery rally") the following morning.

With entry ticket and tasting glass in hand, I venture inside. Up and down steep, winding streets the ramble begins, stopping at doors or windows open for tasting and buying wine. Taking a sharp left turn

Dancers take part in celebrations to honour the vine, in the Rhône valley.

up rue Raimbaut, a narrow, sun-drenched passage, my first *dégustation* is a wine from Lirac, a small appellation neighbouring the well-known vineyards of Tavel. The soft-spoken *vendeuse* offers a sip of this light red, spritely wine. Next door I try the famous sweet, fruity Beaumes-de-Venise, made a few kilometres south of Vacqueyras. Indeed, the Côte du Rhône region encompasses many different wines. My morning tasting includes elegant reds from Cairanne and sweet whites and fruity reds from Rasteau, as well as deep, supple winter wines from neighbouring Gigondas. All are in the Côtes du Rhône-Villages appellation.

Tasting etiquette follows a strict pattern. First, one sniffs the wine to capture its aroma, then a small sip is taken for tasting. Once its qualities have been considered, the remaining wine is poured into metal or porcelain pots provided on each stall. In the midday Provençal heat, tasting-not-swallowing is, as one Vacqueyras *vigneron* advised, *prudent*, a wise measure. Some tasters are equipped with their own shallow, metal *tastevin* saucers and a holder for the excess wine.

A sleepy tree-shaded street is quickly transformed into an open-air banquet.

At the base of a stone tower, once part of the medieval château, we enter an arched doorway marked *Caveau* and cross the large, crowded dark room. A trim, blonde woman is arranging glasses on a long wooden service bar, ready for the next siege of tasters. Behind her, above a heavy wooden door, an old sign reads: *Salle d'armes du château, XIIIe*, a thirteenth-century armoury. Geneviève Henry, the vivacious proprietor of the *caveau*, has tasteable answers to my questions about the wines, beginning with a fine red from the Domaine La Fourmone, run by the Combes, one of the oldest Provençal winemaking families. Their Cuvée des Ceps d'Or is full, balanced yet not too heavy. Next a splash of their "Sélection Maître de Chais" is poured in our glasses. This red wine has the marvellous depth of colour and plummy, black cherry aftertaste that is characteristic of Vacqueyras. When I ask Mme. Henry if they add pepper, she laughs. "Mourvèdre grapes often give that quality, a slight pepperiness, even blended in a small proportion as this is. Not all winemakers here grow the grape, as it ripens late and is a bit fussy in our climate," she explains. Our

Wine-tasting.

purchase is packed up, I thank her and turn to face a fresh onslaught of tasters.

Beside the tower wall, musicians playing pipes and drums lead a troupe of dancers to the summit of the old town. A crowd gathers near the steps of the simple village church, under strings of bright yellow-and-red-striped Occitan flags fluttering against a cloudless cerulean sky. We hear the voices of a choir concluding the solemn mass. Then a small white-robed *confrère* leads the *Confrérie des Maîtres Vignerons de Vacqueyras* across the square to take their places in the centre of the wide, stage-like steps of the facing château. The scene is set for the *sacrifice rituel de la souche.*

Daube d'agneau aux olives / Lamb stew with olives

Ingredients
56 ml/2 fl oz/ ¼ cup cooking oil
2 kg/4-5 lbs lamb shoulder, boned and
   cubed
2 large yellow onions, thinly sliced
3 carrots, peeled and chopped
3 cloves garlic, chopped
450 ml/16 fl oz/2 cups dry red wine
Bay leaf, fresh thyme, chopped parsley
10 anchovies in oil, drained, chopped
Black olives, as desired, chopped

Serves 5 to 6.

Method
Heat the oil in a large braising pot, and brown the lamb on all sides. When done, transfer to a heated bowl, and cook the vegetables and garlic in the oil, for 5 minutes, stirring.

Return the meat to the pot, and add the wine gradually. Then add the seasonings and anchovies, but no salt. Stir, cover and cook for 2–3 hours over a very low heat. Add the olives.

Leave to cool overnight, then skim off any surface fat, reheat and season to taste, removing the stems of thyme and bay.

Serve with rosy-brown rice from the Camargue and garnish with chopped parsley. Choose a ruby red Vacqueyras as a match for this *daube* in any season.

The scene is set for the "sacrifice rituel de la souche".

An old, gnarled grapevine, the *souche*, is wrapped with yellow-and-red-striped ribbons and rests on a bundle of twigs in the centre of the square. When the moment is right, a match is lit and little by little the fire takes hold, fanned by summer's light gusts of Mistral winds. Dancers in Provençal costumes skip nimbly around the *souche* in a ritual dance that was originally an act of thanksgiving for the vine. Red cummerbund scarves wrapped around the men's waists flash past the crowd. Women's full petticoats swirl under layers of brightly patterned skirts pulled tight at the waist, simple white caps are tied beneath their chins and wide-brimmed straw hats ride on their backs. The parade then re-groups, led by the same elder *confrère* in white, and makes its way to lunch.

Bright pink oleander blossoms edge the cours Strassart where the convivial al fresco banquet, a long lunch for three hundred, will extend through the afternoon. In the dappled light, tricolour French flags flutter overhead, alongside the European Union blue and gold stars. After speeches of welcome, the *confrérie* wishes everyone *bon appétit*, and waiters and waitresses begin serving the eight-course *repas*. Each year's menu varies, but Vacqueyras wines are always featured in sauces and are served during the banquet. Reservations for this wonderfully festive meal are made several days in advance and, at about thirty-five euros, including wine and entertainment, it is a feast fit for poets and kings.

The following day a popular *rallye-découverte* is held, giving keen winelovers the chance to taste more wines, as well as take part in a winetasting competition. Instead, I opt for a *rendez-vous dégustation* (an appointment to taste) so that I can find out more about the Cuvée des Ceps d'Or wine sampled at the *fête*, and in the afternoon we turn into the lavender-lined entrance to Domaine La Fourmone. Mme. Combe and their brisk, petite daughter Aline supervise the tasting, seeing to several customers at once. Roger Combe explains what's behind the stunning red wine that we sampled earlier. "This is made with grapes from fifty-year-old Grenache *ceps* (vines), our oldest, and we age it in oak for the last eighteen months." When I ask about the words

Raço Racéjo on the wine's label, he smiles. "It translates from the Provençal-Occitan as 'The tradition continues.' Now my daughters run our vineyards, our business – they'll maintain the quality, and keep up our traditions." The wines of Vacqueyras will thrive in this millennium: *Raço Racéjo!*

The vines at Vacqueyras hang heavy with fruit.

L'Ail en Fête / Garlic Festival

Beaumont de Lomagne/Tarn-et-Garonne, Gascony

Around every corner, down every narrow street, past corbelled houses leading to the huge covered market that commands the centre of this historic *bastide* town, garlic is in the air. On the last Sunday of July, Beaumont-de-Lomagne celebrates this potent, important crop with *L'Ail en Fête*, a festival that fills our weekend with fun and strong flavours. What would the cassoulets, soups and sausages of the southwest be without garlic? The Lomagne region, north of Toulouse and southwest of Montauban, is the white garlic capital of France, responsible for half of the nation's production, and we've travelled to this rocky northeastern corner of Gascony to taste it in its many forms.

Beaumont-de-Lomagne was one of many "new towns" founded across southwestern France in the thirteenth century. The town's main street, rue Fermat, leads to its vast market hall, whose impressive tiled roof covers 1,500 square metres, the old timbers supported by thirty-eight columns. For *L'Ail en Fête*, *la balle* shelters various activities and the *fête's* noon meal. Surrounding streets are humming with the activity and colour of Beaumont's weekly Saturday market.

The wide entry court of the *Maison de Fermat* is the centre for the festival, and for the *Office de Tourisme*, both busy with visitors. On the second floor of this seventeenth-century town house, once the home of mathematician Pierre de Fermat, an exhibition of garlic's history, properties and influence on the region is worth a visit. There are displays of the tools and processes used to grow and harvest *Blanc de Beaumont* (*Allium sativum*), as well as much lore and legend surrounding one of the most widely used garlics in European cooking. *Blanc de Beaumont* ripens earlier and tends to have larger cloves (*gousses*) and heads (*têtes*) than its close competitor, the pink-tinged *Rose de Lautrec* grown near Albi in the Tarn. This king of condiments has been deeply rooted in the culture and heritage of rural culinary traditions of the Lomagne since the thirteenth century and, through troubled times, wars and drought, has held its place in the diet and folklore of the south. Just one of many local sayings predicts: *"L'ail mince de peau prédit un hiver court et beau."* (Expect a mild winter if the skin on garlic is very thin.)

Many actual as well as imagined benefits have been attributed to garlic over the centuries. The ancients declared that daily doses prolonged life,

The procession is led by two oxen pulling a garlic-laden cart.

which concurs with current use of garlic to treat circulation and heart problems, respiratory illnesses, anaemia and fatigue. A bundle of garlic hung on the door of a house or barn is said to keep bad spirits away, and sheafs are still seen on rural buildings.

Today, garlic finds its way into French cuisine at nearly every turn of the soupspoon or *rôtisserie*. In March, *ail nouveau* are just long green shoots with a slim white bulb at the bottom, used in salads, or just dipped in salt. By April, when each clove is forming and the green tops begin to stiffen, it is used as a mild, easily digestible seasoning. July through September is garlic's peak season, when it is juicy and ready to use in countless dishes; pressed and mixed with salt, mint and yoghurt, perhaps, for summer cucumber soups. Or it can be cooked: first sliced across the top and then baked with chicken or lamb, each clove caramelizing, softening and turning sweet. In the autumn, as the heads firm up, the outer papery shell is easily removed after a quick blow with the side of a large kitchen knife. Garlic is chopped and used to season pumpkin soup and cassoulet with beans, duck and Toulouse sausages, *garbures*, *tourins* and most classic dishes of the southwest.

Back in the market hall my attention is drawn to a table of perfect bundles of garlic tied in a braided handle-like loop and decorated with strawflowers. Mme. Martignan displays not only bundles (*manoques*), but also braids (*tresses*), sheaves (*gerbes*) and wreaths (*couronnes*). Her dark brown hair is pulled straight back from the fine features of her narrow face, and tiny golden loop earrings catch the sunlight as she talks about her team of garlic braiders. "Our garlic harvest is always in June, on or around St-Jean, the twenty-fourth. It is lifted, then dried for a week or ten days. We can't braid it right away. I have seven women peeling, which is very delicate work, taking off the outer dried layers without injuring the bulbs." She takes a bulb of garlic to show me how the firm inner core is cleaned of excess papery covering. "But I have seven extra women doing the braiding for the three weeks before this *fête*". Mme. Martignan agrees with my practice of keeping garlic in a cool, dry and well-ventilated place to prolong its life. A two-kilo braid may last six months, though when hung in a warm, bright kitchen, tiny green shoots soon appear. By January, garlic begins to sprout, and any bitter green *germe* inside can be probed out with a knife tip. With three *manoques* from Martignan's garlic fields tucked into my basket, I thank her and turn to the next events.

A bell rings at the far end of the hall, announcing the *vin d'honneur* and *le pan tintat* to open *L'Ail en Fête*. Moving with the crowd past stalls sporting the season's brown and gold sunflowers, I stop to examine a structure that might be a spaceship, but on closer inspection is a huge Eiffel Tower – built entirely of garlic. Past garlands of braided garlic, cups are set out on the official table next to large chilled bottles of the region's light red St-Sardos wines. Sliced baguettes fill trays, and bowls of both sliced garlic and olive oil are in place for the ritual; drizzling olive oil over bread rubbed with garlic creates the *le pan tintat*, a southwestern variant of Nyons' *l'Alicoque* (see page 30). After the mayor's welcome and speeches, cups of wine and *le pan tintat* are served to all gathered round.

Magret de canard piqué d'ail / Garlic-spiked duck breast

Shorten the cooking time for small *magrets*. Steamed fresh green beans, the pencil-thin *haricots verts* found in July markets, complete a festive *repas*.

Ingredients
4 cloves garlic, sliced in slivers
2 duck breasts
Fine sea salt and freshly ground
  black pepper
28 ml / 1 fl oz/1-2 tbsp of oil (if
  roasting)

Method
Preheat oven to 200°C/400°F/Gas Mark 6.
  With a knife-tip, poke the garlic slices into the duck pieces. Wrap kitchen string around the duck length-wise, then secure it in about 5 evenly spaced points around the *magrets*. Rub seasoning over both sides and let rest for an hour.
  To cook, grill the duck over hot embers for 10 minutes, or sear in a heavy cast-iron frying pan, fat side first, and then roast in the hot oven for 10 minutes.
  Let the magret rest for 5 minutes before slicing on the diagonal to serve.
  A regional red St-Sardos, or a less tannic Côtes de Gascogne, complement the duck's richness.

Appetite-tickling aromas, rustic scents of garlic-spiked duck crackling on the grill – the essence of summer days in Gascony – can be recreated at home. *Magret de canard*, the breast of a fattened duck, is simply seasoned, held in shape with kitchen string, and grilled or seared in a hot pan. The thick, protective layer of outer skin is a deliciously crisp contrast to the tender duck within. One *magret* serves two people, and is always cooked rare or medium-rare, as it becomes tough if cooked longer.

Huge pans of simmering garlic cloves send more marvellous aromas into the air. Women in aprons and long skirts, and men dressed in vests over collarless peasant shirts, turn garlic sausages and chicken on grills under the market hall's vast beams. I choose to begin with a *Tourin* (or *Tourain*), a bowl of garlic soup followed by a plate of garlic sausages, swimming in a pool of preserved garlic and served with crisp garlic

Sausages cooked in garlic

potatoes and slabs of country bread. Lunch is topped off by a thick slice of dark, delicious prune tart, and as we finish, I hear an approaching parade.

The procession is led, slowly but surely, by a pair of two sturdy white oxen pulling a garlic-laden cart and followed by the colourful town band, *Bandas de la Gousse d'Or*, in wild print shirts and lime-green hats. A large woman in a print dress and straw hat carries a long stick in one hand and her handbag in the other. She keeps the oxen on track, talking to them all the way. Students from a circus school in Toulouse follow, juggling on unicycles. Costumed citizens, who appear to be part of a seventeenth-century court, stroll past, nodding and waving to the crowd. On this bright July weekend food and fun are clearly in focus.

In the evening, we turn from the market hall to walk through the sleepy back streets, admiring Beaumont's tall brick bell-tower. Built in 1390 as a copy of the Jacobin's tower in Toulouse, the imposing structure served as a watch-tower when the *bastide* town was fortified. As the light of this summer evening fades I hear voices just a few steps beyond the church. Along rue l'Esplanade, wrought iron street lamps flicker, lighting corners where people sit at their doorways, chatting with neighbours half-hidden in the shadows. The garlic harvest has been hung to dry in open, wooden-timbered rafters behind the homes of farmers and field workers. Now there's time to relax in the cool night air, and to reflect on the day's festivities.

August

Fête de la Moisson / Wheat Harvest Festival

Beaulieu-sur-Oudon/Mayenne, Pays de la Loire

The harvest season, a golden time in northern France, brings us to the Mayenne near the eastern edge of Brittany. In early August, baled hay rolled like spools of flaxen thread dots the fields north of the Loire. To find the farming village of Beaulieu-sur-Oudon, I study the map with a magnifying glass. From Laval we drive west, relieved to find our route marked by small arrows directing us to the village, and the *Fête de la Moisson*. At a sharp curve in the country road, volunteers direct cars to parking spaces in a vast, hummocky pasture below the Beaulieu church. The village is made up of less than four hundred people, and it appears that everyone between the ages of four and ninety-four plays a role, in some way, in celebrating the wheat harvest.

Beaulieu-sur-Oudon, a tiny, tidy village in the breadbasket of France, is clustered around its large grey-granite church. Traffic rushing on the nearby N157 from Rennes to Le Mans seems light years away from this tranquil glen beside the little stream, l'Oudon. For over twenty-five years, on the first Sunday in August, the *Fête de la Moisson* has drawn increasing numbers of visitors. From the inaugural mass at ten-thirty in the morning, until sunset, it is a journey into a rural world of traditions, a taste of times past.

Before the heat of the day sets in, we find a shady spot at the edge of a clearing where people are seated on bales of straw for the *Messe des Moissonneurs*, a mass celebrated in the open air. Vendors and

Voices of villagers ring out above the sound of the noisy old threshing machines.

organizers continue to set up their stalls as the mass is broadcast across adjacent fields. Voices of the village choir alternate with words from the priest and intonation of the liturgy. Behind it all, we hear the commotion of vintage threshing equipment rolling into fields around the village for the afternoon's demonstrations. The occasional whinny of a horse tethered in the birches on the banks of the Oudon joins the choir.

Long open, wooden shelters and tents surround the clearing, all preparing food for the *fête*: pots of pork *rillettes*, a staple in kitchens north of the Loire, are ready to be spread on halved baguettes – the day's sustenance for many visitors and vendors. The ever-present *crêpe* is equally popular, and watching these being flipped and deftly stacked is entertainment in itself. Each cook has his or her own technique of ladling out the batter, quickly spreading it with a long handled *raclette*, watching for tiny bubbles to indicate the time to turn.

Once cooked, the *crêpe* or buckwheat *galette* is then swept through the air to a stack, and batter for the next is poured onto the hot griddle. A ten-year-old boy in an orange baseball cap attentively guides ladled batter across the black iron surface, and I soon realise these young fingers have managed many a *galette*. His mother is intent on her own skilled production, and when I ask about her apprentice, the tall, slender woman wipes one hand on her white apron and responds: "*Oui*, Jean-Paul really likes making them – he began with *crêpes* before he was six!"

As the day grows warmer, a crowd gathers around the *buvettes*, stocked with bottles of juice, water, beer and wine and jugs of cool cider. An old apple press is in operation (with great effort), pressing cider

Above: young fingers turn the crêpes. Below: a raclette guides batter across the griddle.

A morning's load of crusty loaves is ready for the hungry lunchtime crowd.

which is poured into bowls for thirsty customers. Bottles of cold cider and wine are sold with tickets for the *fête's* noon meal, but spring water appears to be most popular with the visitors who have come to watch artisans demonstrate their ancient skills. Hand-crafted leather objects are tapped and tooled by a young man in a leather vest and jeans. A sun-weathered *sabotier* shapes a rough wooden form to the outline of a foot, then files the edges of a large *sabot* on his bench. (Like clogs, *sabots* are still worn by some farmers in the north of France and in the western, marshy *marais* regions.) A small, muscular man in a green T-shirt turns pottery bowls in *grès*, stoneware, on a portable potter's wheel. The traditional ware in his display includes beige pitchers to keep cider or water cool through harvest days, and earth-toned canisters to hold flour and sugar. Woven wheat "talismans", both bundles and flat sprays sprigged with dried flowers, are crafted in the next stall. We see them later, tied onto doors and farm machinery. Nearby, a vendor of *cacabuètes vertes* (green peanuts) from Noirmoutier roasts the nut-like *legumes* on a metal tub.

In a shady glen, we watch as a woman intently weaves a wrapped basket to hold loaves of bread as they rise. "These will be lined with a simple canvas or linen, brushed clean after rising and used

until they wear out – which is a very long time!" explains the *vannier* (basket-maker).

Villagers aged between four and ninety-four enjoy playing a part in the fair.

Nearby, a wooden trough is filling with oval loaves of bread as three bakers work together to re-enact the work of the travelling baker of days gone by, the *boulanger ambulant* who appeared weekly or monthly in Mayenne villages. All morning, they have baked in a grove of trees facing the central clearing. One keeps the fire at a constant heat, another in a white T-shirt, shorts and running shoes kneads the dough in a *pétrissage* trough, while the third shuffles the oval forms through the oven door. As each batch is ready, the loaves are slipped off the paddle into a large basket and carried to a smiling *vendeuse*.

Two menus are posted for the noon meal. One features meaty *jambonneau* (smoked pork hock) grilled over wood fires, with *frites* and sliced melon. The other includes country-style pork *pâté*, sliced tomatoes, a slice of cold roast pork, a wrapped triangle of Camembert and a fresh nectarine. There is a short wait for tickets, but everyone finds a place at the long tables under the tents or in the rooms of the village hall, the *Salle des Fêtes*. Some families bring picnics, finding a spot in a shady pasture, while many are content to munch *crêpes* and sandwiches from vendors near the *buvette* (a sheltered beverage stall).

Pain rustique / Country Bread

In the picnic spirit of this *fête*, I have devised an adaptable bread recipe.

Ingredients
1½ kg/3 lbs/6 to 8 cups light wholemeal flour, or mix white and wholemeal
8 g/½ oz/1 level tbsp dry bakers' yeast
1 tbsp sugar or mild honey
1 tbsp fine sea salt
560 ml/20 fl oz/2½ cups warm water
oil for kneading

Method
Measure 3 cups of flour into a large bowl, mix in the yeast, sugar and salt. Then pour the warm water in gradually, stirring with a wooden spoon. Let the mixture rest for 20 minutes to prove. Surface bubbles should form.

Scrape the sides down and stir in more flour, gradually adding enough for a workable dough that does not stick to the bowl. The amount will vary with the day's humidity and type of flour used.

Coat the palms of your hands with oil and knead the dough, turning and folding it until the dough is smooth and elastic. Form a round ball, oil the surface, cover with cling film and wrap with a kitchen towel to cool-rise overnight or for 8–10 hours.

Preheat the oven to 200°C/400°F/Gas Mark 6. Let the dough rest for 20 minutes at room temperature before punching down the dough and shaping it into oval loaves or rolls. Then let the bread rise for another 20 minutes on the baking tray. Just before baking, make diagonal slashes in the loaves with a sharp blade.

Bake on the lowest oven shelf for 35 minutes until golden. For a crisp crust, place a pan of hot water at the bottom of the oven, or spray-mist while baking. Rub warm loaves with a knob of butter.

The bread's texture is rather fine, making good toast for canapés or with *foie gras* in winter. Alternatively, roll flat and use as the base for an onion tart or *pissaladière* (see page 28).

A clamour of voices announces a *promenade en carriole* (a parade of light carts). This involves a collection of assorted farm wagons, covered buggies and farm workers dressed in white shirts and dark pants or long skirts. Some carry wooden rakes, others haul baskets for the harvesters' lunch. Oxen have been teamed under old yokes, and an ox-boy rides on the broad, spotted back of one of the heavy creatures. One small family carriage carries three generations. All dressed in vests, long skirts and Sunday bonnets, they ride in style in the long, spirited procession. Fiddlers tune up, folkdancers adjust their costumes, and the music intensifies as the carriages are driven faster on the second and third rounds of the fair.

Later in the afternoon, the crowd gathers along a sloping wheat field at the edge of the village, left uncut to "harvest" during the *fête*. At one side of the roped field, watching the wagons, workers and old steam harvesters, I find I'm in the middle of a four-ring rural circus! Next to the threshing field, a rough pasture is ploughed with a powerful team of handsome Percheron workhorses. Harvesters and

threshing equipment of several eras rattle along in full operation, followed by crews cutting and forking wheat into wagons. We watch the threshing, then winnowing, at close range – a team of two separates the kernels of wheat from their sharp golden husks. *Monsieur* thrashes sheaves against a large canvas tarp as *madame* adroitly sorts the winnowed wheat and slips scoops of the golden kernels into a large sack.

Throughout the day, and in many different ways, Beaulieu's *Fête de la Moisson* vividly recreates the harvest season's spirit. Voices of farmers and villagers ring above the clackety sounds of old threshing machines ... and in showers of heat and sparkling wheat straw, the origins of the breads of France are rediscovered.

Bread-rising baskets will be lined – and will be used for years.

August

Foire aux Vins / Wine and Local Produce Fair
Duravel/Lot, Monpezat-en-Quercy & Castelnau-Montratier/Lot, Quercy

Quercy is best kept a secret. Part of the Lot, it is often asso-ciated with Périgord, but it has a markedly different character. Leaving the tidy woodlands of the Dordogne behind, we take back roads into a wilder region to the east. The route slices through grey rock walls, whose crevices cascade with wild flowers in the summer. Flat façades of Romanesque chapels rise on hillsides, and ruined fortresses, the châteaux of power past, appear mirage-like above hardwood forests and craggy cliffs. Apart from pilgrims' paths and tour bus routes to historic Rocamadour, this picturesque strip of the French interior feels unspoiled, undiscovered. But, for how long? Quercy, so long renowned for truffles, *foie gras* and the dark, tannic wine of Cahors, is a treasure trove of other gastronomic riches. With each visit, we uncover more, hidden among its hills.

A simple description for such a jigsaw puzzle of land escapes me. Quercy (pronounced *Kaircee*) is a long region, sliced into four *départe-ments*. Each sector of rugged terrain influences the region's cuisine, an economical style of cooking that features fowl, aromatic truffles and succulent pork or lamb. Rich, sweet prunes, coarse country bread, goats' cheese and flaky walnut-pear pastry appear on menus in all seasons. Fresh-water fish from Quercy's network of fast-flowing streams are abundant, and wine is at hand on every sideboard. The middle of August, the season for *les vacances* and time out, is marked in the winemakers' year as well. On August the fifteenth, Assumption, wine fairs toast last year's *vendange*, the *millésime*, across France's winemaking regions. Two towns capture the spirit of a day of fun in very different *foires*. One, a medieval village, commands a vast panorama of the Lot Valley, while the other is tucked into the hills south of Cahors.

Duravel, a sleepy sandstone village of less than a thousand people, perks up for two days while the *Foire aux Vins et Produits Régionaux* lures visitors to explore its quiet streets. From the eleventh-century church and nearby café, all built of the region's warm beige stone, we find steps leading down to a tree-lined square. Under a canopy of linden trees strung with red and yellow flags, the square is filled with the awnings of over forty vendors' stalls.

Families gather in Duravel's shady square.

The weekend closest to August the fifteenth has been the date for Duravel's *Foire aux Vins* for over twenty years. It is a mixed fair of products from the southwest, attracting vendors from Bergerac and Bordeaux vineyards, and fruit-growers from the nearby Agenais. We have visited many fairs steeped in tradition, but here there are no *confréries*, no *vin d'honneur*, no parades or *défilés* – and no *fête foraine's* blaring music. Duravel's focus shines primarily on the wines of Cahors, bringing these and regional products together for all to enjoy, taste and buy.

VIN DE CAHORS

CAHORS
CHÂTEAU
DE L'EGLANTIER
APPELLATION CAHORS CONTROLEE
Tél. 05 65 30 71 48
Fax 05 65 30 54 46
BENAC ET FILS
PROPRIETAIRE RECOLTANT
COURNOU 46140 LUZECH
MIS EN BOUTEILLE AU CHÂTEAU
Produit de France

Vente - Expédition
Dégustation

The *foire's* centre aisle is "winery row", and I stop to speak with two brothers, young dark-haired men working with their father to make wines at Château Laur. One stays behind the counter, the other approaches me to offer a *dégustation*. "Would you like to taste our '97? The '98 isn't in bottle yet – it is aged for at least two years in wood," ventures the taller brother, as their father arrives with more cases of wine. Tasting young wine without cheese or bread isn't quite fair to the wine, nor to the taster. My reaction is mixed, it is so tannic, rather raspy, to which he admits: "This is natural, the Auxerre or Malbec grape needs time as it is a bit rough in the first years. Merlot in the blend softens it as it ages. We say "patience will be rewarded". Let it age five or ten years." I nod, and let him pack three bottles for our cellar.

My last stop before leaving Duravel is a stall heaped with ripe Marmande tomatoes and Quercy melons. The pert redhead tending the stand cuts us a fresh slice, and asks: "When will you serve it? Today?" No, the day after tomorrow, I reply. So she reaches into a shallow basket of lightly greener, veined melons, and suggests: "Try it with our Quercy *vin de paille!*" Now I must find *vin de paille!*

On a lazy August afternoon, why not pause for a dégustation?

It is a beautiful drive into Quercy across the green valley of the Lot, a rough country where angular grey rock thrusts up into pastures, pierces woodlands and edges vineyards. Wheels of hay glitter in the mid-August sun, and orchards hang heavy with fruit. Suddenly the strange copper-domed church of Castelnau-Montratier comes into sight. We drive to the hilltop, into a town of sun-bleached white stone, and walk straight to the church for a sweeping vista over the Barguelonne Valley.

In alternate years, the bastide towns of Castelnau-Montratier and Montpezat-de-Quercy take turns hosting a fair for the local vintners. It is a fair just for Côteaux de Quercy winemakers to sell wines from the last vintage, and to enjoy a *grand repas* together. The fair is a treat, a colourful jumble of brass bands, truffle stands and the local wines. Even as we approach the town square, the mood is light, a *fête* with a

Cailles à la ventrèche fumé / Quail in bacon blankets

Small birds from Quercy's dense forests or the *basse-cour* (barnyard) are popular fare for special *fêtes*, served as a first course or main dish. To enhance the flavour of the delicate meat, the quails can be stuffed with the season's fruit – peaches or plums, for example – or with fresh herbs. A blanket of bacon protects the tender breast meat. Pigeon meat is darker, and one is an adequate serving; plan on two quail or game hens per diner. Serve them medium-rare.

Ingredients
6 quail or game hens, livers
   retained
Sea salt
Fresh herbs: sage, thyme, bay leaf,
   summer savory
6-8 wide rashers of lean smoked
   bacon
Olive oil and butter to sauté
28 g/1 oz/2 tbsp
   flour
170 ml/6 fl oz/3/4
   cup light red wine
   or stock

Method
Sprinkle the insides of the fowl with sea salt, fill with herbs, wrap strips of bacon around each and tie securely with kitchen string.

In a braising pot or broad, deep sauté pan, sauté the birds in hot oil, turning to brown on all sides. Lift them out onto a warm plate, and set aside.

Add a spoon of butter to the pan, sprinkle in the flour and stir as it bubbles. Slowly add half of the wine to deglaze the pan. Into this sauce, stir the chopped livers (which will "melt" into it).

Return the fowl to the pan and add the remaining wine, making sure all the birds are coated in the sauce. Cover and simmer, or bake at 180°C/350°F/Gas Mark 4, for about 30 minutes. Baste and add a little stock as the liquid reduces. Be careful not to overcook the fowl. Serve with crisply fried garlic potatoes and glasses of Côteaux de Quercy wine.

more festive ambiance than that of Duravel's. The oddly triangular central square is roped off and the usual afternoon games of *boules* postponed. The village is full of vendors, and an expanse of tables is set for hundreds to dine on pit-roasted lamb, Quercy melon with country ham, salad with *chèvre* of Rocamadour, rounded out with rich and flaky *croustade*, coffee – and chilled *vin de pays*.

The purchase of a wine glass once again admits each fair-goer. Winemakers form an outer ring around the square, offering *dégustations* at simple stalls, interspersed with local products in displays decorated with flowers, vines and bright flags. Whether I've ever heard of this

VDQS regional wine or not, this is the place to discover its merits and to *assist*, as the French say, to participate in their celebration.

First I try the wines of the Domaine de la Combarade, run by a local winemaking family. Speaking with congenial Mme. Dieuzaide, I'm convinced that these country wines, ranging from light to deep red in colour, are more versatile than the hefty, tannic, long-lived Cahors we tasted along the Lot. Here Merlot dominates the blend, and the domaine's Clef de St-Pierre wins my vote for an appealing wine with character. Before moving on to taste cheese, I stop to watch a stocky *rôtisseur* tending two entire sheep roasting over a pit of coals, in preparation for the *Repas des Vignerons*, a grand community meal.

Continuing around the stalls, I find creamy *chèvre* from Temple-sur-Lot, small discs of *cabécou* and firmer *tommes* of *chèvre*. There are vendors of snails, lavender and summer truffles. Stop: *summer* truffles? A wiry, animated man from Lalbenque admits: "True, they're not as pungent as truffles in January, but worth a try." My instinct tells me to wait for mid-winter's variety – patience, as the young vintner said, will be rewarded.

This pleasurable weekend rambling through wine towns of Quercy just skimmed the surface of the region's gastronomy and history. We'll return in autumn to taste the famed lamb of Quercy when *cèpes* (mushrooms) and chestnuts are abundant, and brilliant red woodbine clings to secluded village walls.

Vintage scales are used to weigh sweet Chasselas grapes.

Fête du Charolais / Beef Festival

Saulieu/Côte-d'Or, Burgundy

Sirloin or *boeuf bourguignon* ... what better place to enjoy a fine cut of beef and fine red wines than in Burgundy? Prize beef is the star of this fair: the massive, muscled Charolais that dominates the rolling Burgundy pastureland from Auxerre to Roanne. For nearly five decades Saulieu's Livestock Fair, the central event of this August weekend, has attracted farming crowds. But, with its contests, parades, street music and regional produce, it is also entertaining for visitors who are not showing, selling or buying cattle. Menus posted in cafés and restaurants tempt palates of any taste or budget. Saulieu's three-day *fête* merits the honour *National Site of Taste*, one of France's one hundred such showcases of flavour (see page 220).

We approach Saulieu from the north, taking the N6 through a bucolic landscape linking Vézelay and Avallon. Though it's possible to whiz from Paris to Dijon on the A6 *péage*, a route that is sprinkled with many Michelin stars (the gourmet's motorway), a slower journey takes us in a leisurely manner through the rolling pine forests and pastureland of the Morvan.

Saulieu holds a large exposition in May, les *Journées Gourmandes du Grand Morvan*, lining up 150 regional producers – including wine-makers – and drawing about 8,000 visitors for *dégustations*. Saulieu's summer *fête* is more in the tradition of a *Comice Agricole*, an expanded livestock fair. Various events interest a broader audience, beginning

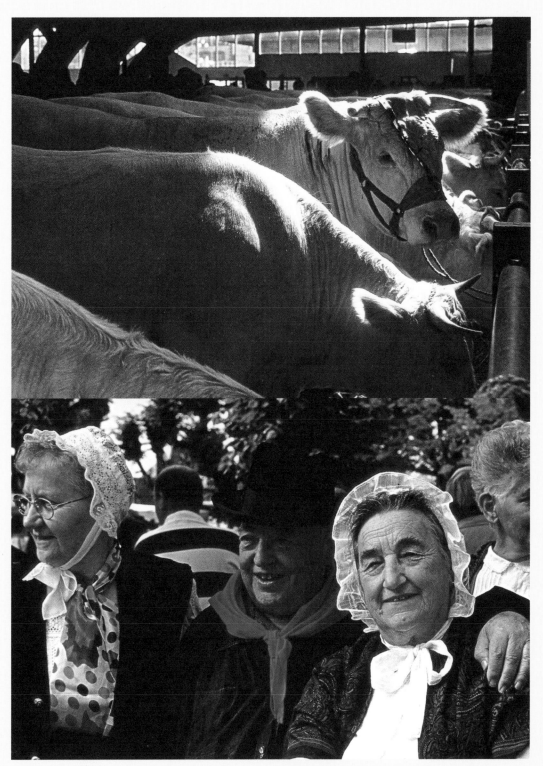

Above: the enormous, muscled Charolais cattle.
Below: folk dancers pause at Saulieu's market.

with Friday's *Journée du Cheval* featuring horses. Work horses are shown in the morning and riding horses in the afternoon, with some ponies remaining for children to ride during Saturday's *Journée Charolaise*, a day that stars the famous Charolais cattle.

On Saturday, Saulieu's market is held on the shaded promenade Monge. The scent of fresh fruit is in the warm morning air, as I admire crates of golden Mirabelle plums, juicy Brugnon and other plump nectarines, mounds of green beans, tomatoes, and stacks of eggs in carton-trays. These eggs, tucked in shoppers' baskets by the dozen, hold the secret of golden Burgundian croissants and flans: their intensely yellow yolks. Small boxes of shiny blackberries, the delicious *mûres* of the Morvan forests, are lined up alongside blackcurrants (the base for the region's famed *crème de cassis*) and redcurrants for *confitures* and jellies, all picked in the cool of the morning and brought straight to market. By eleven o'clock a parade can be heard approaching the market place, led by a spirited brass band in sarapes and sombreros! Pom-pom girls in short yellow skirts prance alongside, soup is offered to visitors by women in local folk costume; everyone is having a good time.

Les mûres sont mûres!
The blackberries are ripe!

Moving on, we return to Saulieu's main street, and on to find the *boeuf*. At the edge of town, an immense exhibition hall houses the livestock show. Once inside, my eyes adjust to the darker space lit only by skylights. Judges are moving slowly down the lines of stalls labelled "Eglantine" (wild rose), and "Padirac, son of Eglantine", and so on, each containing the massive beige back of a farmer's prized Charolais. Steers, cows and calves wait patiently as they are assessed. Men and boys in jackets and high boots tap their long canes to stir any cow that needs to be moved for judging. One young farmer holds the rope attached to a hefty calf, waiting its turn. He has an easy manner, a ready smile and answers my questions about classification. Using his cane as a pointer, he explains: "Bulls, cows and calves are divided into classes by age, by *dents* (teeth). So, for example, this young female calf is a *'génisse, deux dents'*. *Mulots* are male calves, the roundest, most densely muscled." *Mulot* seems to be a local term for a young steer, otherwise it means fieldmouse! I admire his healthy calf's curly ivory coat as he continues: "Charolais have an important quality of early, rapid growth, with a normal weight gain from forty-eight kilos at birth to two hundred and ninety at seven months and close to five hundred kilos at one year." Turning suddenly, he tugs his *mulot* into place as the judge arrives.

In another section of the hall more creatures have come to be judged and admired: sheep take up an entire aisle, and the animals of the *basse-cour*, or farmyard, are in full fur and plumage. Black

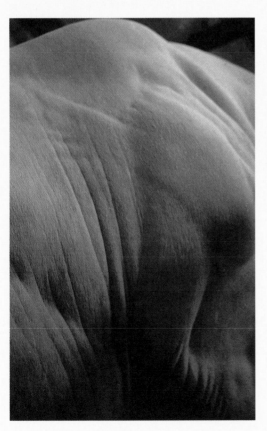

A fine kind of the famous Charolais beef cattle.

hens, copper-feathered roosters, speckled guinea fowl, grey geese and all kinds of pigeons, as well as a few noisy turkeys are on display. Huge, velvety brown *faune de Bourgogne* rabbits, as well as grey, white and black ones, doze through the day. Rabbits are kept by most farmers in Burgundy, and I note in Morvan's calendar of *fêtes* that the village of Pillippeville even has a *Confrérie du Lapin à la Bière*, the Brotherhood of Rabbit cooked in Beer. By sundown, the fun-fair rides begin, vendors of *barbe-à-papa* (candy floss) are busy, and the air fills with toasty scents of roasted peanuts. In the Hôtel de la Poste, l'Auberge du Relais, and la Côte d'Or, tables are laid for dinner.

The region's reputation for hospitality and *la bonne table* is upheld in hotels and restaurants to cater to any traveller's budget. Hôtel de la Poste faces the hotel-heavy intersection on rue Argentine, and this seventeenth-century postal relay, redone as a comfortable stop for travellers, has the ambience of a family hotel. In the dining room, a whiff of *Filet de Boeuf* rises as the dome over a dinner plate is lifted, stirring at least a couple of appetites. The *Filet, sauce Charbon* that initially led us into the room is my husband's choice, while *Sandre au vin rouge*, pike-perch in red wine sauce, is my selection, out of curiosity and hunger. To calm the qualms of those who don't eat meat, this region is heaven for fresh-water fish. The wine list deserves time to study its fine selection of Burgundies, and the waiter suggests a red 1996 Givry-Poncey, Domaine Ragot, made west of Châlon-sur-Saône. Givry is a delicious discovery, intriguingly complex though not as round as the meatier wines of the Côtes de Nuits.

Our coffee arrives with a dainty selection of handmade chocolates and fruit *pâte* sweets. Surrounding tables are cleared as diners finish, and we have a chance to talk with the young chef from the "Poste's" kitchen. The tall young man in white joins us, and through our conversation, Jean-Alain Poitevin's penetrating brown eyes are fixed on us, and on the subject of *qualité*. His approach to selecting beef is simple: "Choose the best beasts, *les bonnes bêtes*. We select our own beef and know how it is aged. Once selected, the meat is aged seven or eight days, then our *faux-filet* will be excellent. The issue of quality also applies to our fish, chicken and free-range eggs." Again the word

I've heard time and again is repeated: "Oui, *traçabilité*, we just want to know where our chickens come from!" We commend his work, and as he strides back to the kitchen, I leave with the sense that the French "kitchen" and its future are in good hands.

On Sunday we stroll through old Saulieu to the stately grey Basilica of St-Androche, a twelfth-century church rebuilt in the eighteenth century. Approaching it, a graceful stone figure on an old well acts as an unofficial roundabout for bicycles and small cars. On the same place du Docteur-Roclore, a mirage appears in a *charcuterie* window's reflection: a tempting tray of *gougère*, made of light, cheesy, cream-puff batter. A few are tucked into my satchel for later, before I amble on to the rue du Marché, where there is time for a coffee behind the

Filet de Charolais aux morilles / Steak with morels

Ingredients
25 g/1 oz/2 tbsp butter
50 g/2 oz/4 tbsp chopped shallots
200 g/7 oz/1 heaped cup morel
  mushrooms, cleaned well and
  sliced
110 ml/4 fl oz/½ cup red wine
1 tbsp parsley, chopped
4 fillet steaks
14 ml/½ fl oz/1 tbsp cooking oil
Sea salt, freshly ground black
  pepper and nutmeg (optional)

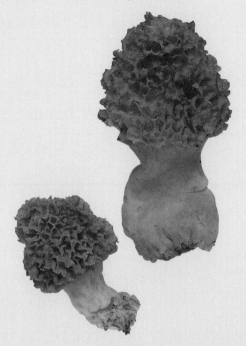

Method
Cook the mushrooms first: in a heavy frying pan heat 1 tablespoon of butter, add the shallots, stir and then add the morels. Cook on a low heat until they give off some juice.

Then add the red wine, turn up the heat for a moment and scrape the pan to heat everything through.

Next add the parsley; at this stage the shallots should be nearly invisible as the sauce reduces. Add the remaining butter.

To prepare the beef: wipe the fillet steaks dry and sear them in hot cooking oil (do not use butter at this point) over a moderately high heat for 2 minutes on each side depending on preference. Pink beads of juice will appear on the fillet's surface when it is medium-done. Lift the meat out onto a hot platter, season with sea salt and pepper, add nutmeg if you like, and cover with the hot morels.

To round out a "repas bourguignon", serve red wines from the Côte de Nuits: a plummy Marsannay, or a well-structured Fixin, decanted earlier, would be an excellent match.

etched windows of Café Parisien. It never seems to change. Inside, there's a sense of arrested time – perhaps new chairs were brought in, years ago. Later in the afternoon, we'll return to see the grand parade, but if truth be told, I'd be content to look through the café's windows, sipping a *petit verre* of Burgundy and nibbling on a cheesy *gougère*.

Fête de la Transhumance et du Munster /
Transhumance and Cheese Festival

Munster/Haut-Rhin, Alsace, Vosges

In early autumn, when cooler weather stirs appetites, two very different *fêtes* in Alsace lure us to a region noted for its hearty cuisine. Where generous portions are a "given", the nip of autumn nights and days of hiking in the Vosges prepare us for special meals ahead. With visions of pungent cheeses and hearty platters of *choucroute garnie* dancing in my mind, I spread out the well-creased map to find which corner of Alsace to explore first. The shape of two *départements*, the northern Bas-Rhin and southern Haut-Rhin, form an arm and fist of diverse border terrain in eastern France that has been inundated by waves of invasions from every direction. Buffeted through times of war and famine, Alsace remains a bilingual region, holding fast to its Alsatian dialects and guarding both French and Alsatian culinary secrets, while sharing its famous *bonne table* with relish and inimitable hospitality.

Preparing the route, I trace this long and complex land from the Ardennes' dark forests and mining towns of eastern France along the Belgian border, then south following the western banks of the Rhine. Here, fields of corn are interspersed with hectares of knobby cabbages spread across the broad Rhine Valley. I follow the river valley to its southern tip at the Swiss border, a hand's length and three fingers' width all the way, edging the evenly rounded silhouettes of mountains, the *ballons* of the Vosges. In recent decades, vineyards have swallowed up more hills and the rich floodplains, where villages are evenly spaced between vines and cabbage fields. This may be the best of all gastronomic worlds, I muse as I pack.

Cowbells and cheese are on our agenda on a bright September Sunday, as clouds gather on the forested horizon of the Vosges. Warm afternoons are nearly over for the spotted Vosgienne dairy

Clockwise from top: Vosgienne cattle en parade; racks of fresh pretzels; an Alsatian night-cap.

herds of central Alsace, whose summer was spent munching sweet wild grasses in open mountain meadows. The Munster Valley, famed for its farm cheeses, celebrates their return each year with the *Fête de la Transhumance et du Munster*. In the town's centre, the all-important brown spotted cows are bedded in straw as they wait their turn in the day's events. The setting is directly in front of Munster's *mairie*, an imposing pink-tinged stone city hall facing a square where today, small wooden cabin-like stalls house cheese vendors. High above all the hustle and

bustle, on the chimneys and rooftop of the town hall, the rough twigs of seven stork nests hold as many pairs of the haughty, beak-clacking creatures.

Elementary demonstrations of cheese-making run through the morning hours of this regional fête. One vendor offers samples of aromatic Munster *Géromé*, made on the Lorraine side of the Vosges. Another has bits of cumin-flecked Munster to taste, aged the requisite three weeks to abide by its AOC regulations. Ripened

Fine dining: foie gras en brioche.

versions, aged for three months, go beyond a creamy nuttiness to pungent, full flavour as the cheeses are washed with salt or white wine.

By noon, vendors on the square have their *assiettes marcaire* prepared. A meek, slim woman in wire-rimmed glasses slices cheese, and offers a creamy sliver off the knife. She smiles and explains: "Every autumn in the Vosges, a *marcaire* – a herdsman – moved from farm to farm, leading the farmers' herds back from high pastures called the *chaumes*. At each farm along his *transhumance* route, he was given a plate of bread and cheese, so we put together this dish – in the *marcaire's* tradition." Savouring a tangy slice and chewing a few bits of cumin, I look for my family and take their orders. Our *assiettes marcaires* comprise a *dégustation* of a cumin-spiced Munster, a tangy-smooth fresh cheese and a slice of a firm old mountain *tomme*, rich and redolent of mountain grasses. A thick slab of country bread sliced from a log-length of *pain de campagne* is laid on top like a lid, protecting the cheese from the drying air. Near the *buvette*, we find a spot at a long crowded table and order draft beers as the sun prevails – for a few more hours at least.

Bibbeleskas / Fresh cheese with herbs

Ingredients
To make about one cup, which
serves four:
1 large garlic clove, chopped
1 tsp fine sea salt
90 g / 3 oz / 1/3 cup double cream
or crème fraîche
14 ml / 1/2 fl oz / 1 tbsp chopped
parsley
Freshly ground white pepper
225 g / 8 oz / 1 cup fromage blanc
(or small-curd creamed cottage
cheese, sieved)
2 white onions (scallions),
finely chopped
1 bunch of chives,
chopped

In Alsace, fresh cheese appears in every course.
For a savoury dish *bibbeleskas* can be melted
over potatoes, or for a sweeter dish try *siaskas*,
fresh cheese blended with kirsch and brown
sugar. Alsatian pastry chefs concoct a wide
range of desserts using fresh cheese – the most
enticing is a cheesecake, *tarte au fromage
blanc*. Other prominent flavours found in
Alsace include garlic, which is used to flavour
dishes from *bibbeleskas* to garlic sausages, and
cumin – a dish of cumin seeds is always served
with the cheese course to sprinkle on slices
of Munster.

Bibbeleskas is easily made at home – we
enjoy this creamy touch on potatoes sautéed or
steamed in their jackets – *en robe des champs*.

Method
Mash the chopped garlic with
a fork, working it into a paste
with the salt in a bowl. Then
beat in the cream, parsley and
white pepper.

Next mix in the fresh cheese
and transfer to a serving bowl.
Chill the *bibbeleskas* for at
least four hours, or overnight.

To serve, chop the white onions,
snip the chives and set these aside
in small bowls.

At the table, each person takes a
spoonful of the chopped onions or
chives onto their plate, then
sprinkles this garnish over their
potatoes and *bibbeleskas*. Serve
with Alsatian beer.

An after-lunch stroll takes me past demonstrations and displays, down side streets, moving towards music. A quintet of long alpine horns serenades the crowd, letting delicate and high harmonies take form slowly, paced as carefully as finding one's footing on a steep mountain path. A different mood prevails in the community centre, Munster's *salle polyvalente*, now buzzing with visitors and displays. Inside the main doors, an old-fashioned kitchen has been created: ladles and whisks hang above old wood stoves, along with hundreds of tins and spoons. Antique *kugelhopf* moulds, sieves and wooden beaters, cocoa tins and items from kitchens and cheesemakers' shops date back to great-grandmother's time.

Outside, clouds hide the sun, thunder rumbles overhead and the cows are noisily lined up for the afternoon's parade. This begins with a clanging of cowbells, and the town's brass band marches smartly ahead of the farmers. Guiding their great brown spotted Vosgienne cows and a few black and white Holsteins, dairymen dressed in skull-caps and leather vests tap flanks with long staffs to keep them in line. Huge bells handpainted with tiny flowers hang under the chins of some cows. More dairymen in costume dance in groups, stepping carefully and circling with their full-skirted partners, many wearing wooden clogs. A light rain begins to dampen awnings, sending people into cafés for cover.

An impromptu stop in an Alsatian café might call for a cool glass of white wine and a slice of Munster, a fine way to conclude the *fête*. Café and restaurant menus often list the cheese course simply as: *Munster et son Gewürztraminer*. Wines that are especially good with Munster include the famous, floral Gewürztraminer or a pale Pinot Gris d'Alsace. When the clouds lift over the Vosges and sunshine returns, the picnic spirit prompts me to prepare for the next day's trip. A Pinot Gris is my choice to slip into our basket, to enjoy with a palm-sized Munster and slices of rich *pâté en croûte* later. Autumn is the season for *tourte du vigneron*, magnificent round meat pastries topped with decorative pastry vine leaves.

Luckily, picnic weather returns as we leave the Munster Valley. From Wintzenheim to Wettolsheim, grape-heavy vines extend across the valley linking villages on the Wine Trail. The *Route des Vins* is something we will explore later in September, well beyond the aromas of mountain cheese, to the subtleties of ... *choucroute* (see page 164).

September

Foire aux Haricots / Bean Fair

Arpajon/Essonne, Ile de France

Begin with the bean, the versatile, basic haricot bean so essential to French country
cooking. It seems such a simple product, but
enough importance is attached to a certain
bean, the *flageolet chevrier*, that for over sixty
years it has been the theme of a September
fair in Arpajon.

Brought in along with potatoes, tomatoes, cocoa and coffee from
the New World, long-podded beans slowly took root in the French
diet during the sixteenth and seventeenth century. Early in the 1870s,
M. Gabriel Chevrier, an agronomist near Arpajon, crossed two varieties of *haricots* to produce a fine, delicately pale green bean, which
bears his name, the *flageolet chevrier*. Once dried (*haricot sec*) and shelled,
the delicious little bean is the classic partner for *gigot d'agneau*, the
roasted leg of lamb sliced onto platters in all corners of France.

Arpajon lies south of Paris, southwest of Orly airport in the Essonne *département*. Our route to the *foire* cuts through the *banlieue*, the suburban towns and industrial zones, past market gardens that supply vendors in the city. Towns along the way, in general, appear grimy and busy, too busy to remove layers of soot and pollution's residue. We pass through Montlhéry, noting signs proclaiming its famous tomatoes, and soon arrive in the centre of Arpajon. A small core of old buildings remain, and we walk under freshly painted shutters, past modern buildings alongside houses left with some patina of the days

gone by. The striking sixteenth-century covered market commands the broad, cobblestoned place du Marché. Dark timbers support the immense, steeply pitched roof of this community landmark that has seen cart-loads of beans and potatoes come and go for centuries.

Green beans in a kitchen garden.

A figure approaching us on this cool September morning has a twenty-kilo (about forty-five pounds) net sack of beans slung over one shoulder. A woollen cap covers his head, a stub of a *Gauloise* is tucked in the corner of his mouth. He walks past the dark hall, toting his sack of *paimpols*, the large and starchy white beans harvested earlier in northern France. This is the first of just two sacks of beans that I will see during the weekend.

Late in August, some *haricots à écosser*, beans for shelling, are sold *demi-sec*, to be cooked fresh, while the bulk of the crop is hung in dark, airy spaces to dry completely. Each region has its own preferred haricots to see them through the winter. Earliest arrivals from

Most of the crop of haricots are hung in the dark to dry.

Brittany (ready late in August) are the *paim-pols*, then the creamy tender *mojettes* of the Charente. Next come *tarbes*, the medium-sized white, uniform beans that form the base of cassoulets in the southwest. In Provence and the Roussillon, we find the flatter, dried *fèves*, delicious served hot, *arrosée* (drizzled) with a thin stream of olive oil. Fresh *fèves* enjoy a short season in the spring, when they are shelled, each bean peeled and dipped in sea salt, *à la croque au sel*. From the north come flat, white *soissons* beans, a large *haricot blanc* favoured by many chefs, which turns up on menus in dishes *à la soissonnaise*.

For this *foire* weekend, Arpajon's market hall has been transformed into a salon for *L'Exposition Gastronomique*. I step inside, just as officials are gathering, the *presse* on their heels. All make the rounds to see creations constructed on the theme of the *haricot*, one aisle using pastry and chocolate as a base, the next using sausages or vegetables.

The contestants' imaginations have been stretched to create amazing things: fantasy bean gardens, a miniature of Rodin's "The Thinker" carved in white chocolate (what does this have to do with beans?), Father Time twirled in spun sugar and bean *dragées*, and an Eiffel Tower made of candy beans. A *château fantaisie* in cubes and spun sugar with a bean *bonbon* roof is the grand prizewinner.

The grey morning air evaporates as sunshine returns for the week-end, though the day remains cool. Adjacent to the market hall, two large white *exposition* tents house furnishings, regional products and wines. Tasting a sticky, sweet acacia honey, then a morsel of the firm *chèvre* from Valençay south of the Loire leads to a wine *dégustation*. We sample a Sauvignon de Touraine from vineyards near Amboise that is nicely dry with characteristic tones of asparagus. This refreshing touch puts us in the mood for lunch, which is roasting on a *rotisserie* outside the Café du Marché.

Haricots en salade au cresson / Bean salad with watercress

In central and eastern France, a salad of *haricots* is often served as an *entrée*. Flageolets *chèvrier* are well suited to salad, as they hold their shape and are not mealy after slow cooking. A variation on this favourite combines the cooked dried beans with fresh watercress or arugula, for a peppery edge. For the basic vinaigrette, use a fine sherry vinegar.

Ingredients

375 g/12 oz/1½ cups small dried beans, chèvrier or flageolets if available

1 bay leaf, sprigs of savory, sage and thyme tied together

Sea salt and freshly ground black pepper

For the vinaigrette:

28 ml/1 fl oz/2 tbsp good wine vinegar

1 tsp sea salt

80 ml/3 fl oz of oils: 3 tbsp hazelnut oil, 2 tbsp olive oil

2 plump shallots, trimmed and finely sliced

8 tbsp/½ cup finely chopped parsley

30 g/1 oz/1 cup cleaned, de-stemmed and shredded watercress or rocket (arugula)

Method

Rinse the dried beans and sort to remove broken beans and stones. Use cold spring water (tap water often contains chemicals and the beans don't soften as well) to soak the *haricots* overnight with herbs, making sure they are completely covered.

Next day, transfer the beans to a large pot, top up with spring water as necessary and simmer with the herbs for 45 to 70 minutes. The cooking time for older beans may be longer than for the current year's crop. When tender, add salt and let the beans cool before draining them.

Make the vinaigrette: in a serving bowl, stir the vinegar and salt together and blend in the oils in a thin stream. Continue to blend the emulsion while stirring in the shallots, parsley and drained beans. Season to taste.

The salad can be made ahead to this point, and the watercress or rocket added just before serving with peppery Coteaux du Vendômois — a suitable wine for this autumn lunch entrée.

Tables at the café are filling fast. The *plat du jour* is *moules-frites*, the waiter announces brusquely, as mountains of fried potatoes and mounded bowls of mussels arrive on surrounding tables. I inquire about *agneau aux chevriers*, and he taps the end of a scratched Biro pen on the menu to indicate that it can be served. While we wait for this classic roast lamb with Arpajon's *chevriers*, and chicken from the *rotisserie*, I contemplate Sunday's displays of regional produce and *salon d'artisanat*, hoping that I will find fresh cress from Méréville and *crosne*, the amusing little twisted vegetable from Crosne, as well as ... perhaps ... a few beans?

An ample serving arrives: soft *haricots chevriers* drizzled with pink meat juices and slices of tender lamb. A thick rectangular *pavé* of *tarte au pomme*, in this prime season for apple tart, and a cup of coffee cap off lunch. Other than the displays we've visited, and a French singer later in the afternoon, it is an open day until the *artisans du goût* arrive on Sunday morning, so I decide to visit to the *potagers*, the kitchen gardens of the Château de St-Jean de Beauregard. In just thirty minutes, I am in the crowd milling through the château's renovated stables for a few hours watching craftsmen and women demonstrating copperwork, pottery and etching. And in the *potager* there are pumpkins, cabbages and leeks, but the beans have been harvested, and are now stored in the château's cellars.

The following morning, the streets of Arpajon are lined with an assortment of stalls selling anything from roasted peanuts to nougat from Montélimar, and fresh watercress from nearby Méréville to soap and dried flowers.

But I am still simply looking for ... beans. On a small table at the end of the gauntlet of vendors, I eventually spy a basket of pale green *haricots*, the *flageolet chevrier d'Arpajon*. The blonde *vendeuse* has shelled beans in paper bags, or scoops them out to sell by the kilo, and advises me on cooking them. "No, you don't need an overnight soaking – that's only for beans that were picked last year. This *millésime* is tender and will cook in an hour or two. Tuck in a bay leaf and some *sarriette* (savory) while they cook, but wait to add sea salt before serving." The kind *vendeuse* tucks a freshly cut branch of bay leaves into my pack of shelled *flageolet chevrier*. Finally, beans have been found, and all is not lost. Otherwise, the old French expression would sum it up:

"C'est la fin des haricots."

It's the ultimate catastrophe, all is lost ... It's the end of the beans!

Fête de la Choucroute / Sauerkraut Festival

Krautergersheim/Bas-Rhin, Alsace

Memories of my first visit to Alsace were coloured by its decorative details: in the carved balconies, dated keystones over arched door-ways and scrolled metalwork on every door handle. Then, at the table, I remember juicy sausages and mounds of potatoes, stuffed cabbage, dumplings and butter-rich *tortes*. With an eye on the map to chart our next trip, I began to see Alsace as a land knitted with trails: the Wine Trail, the Kirsch Route, the Cheese Road and, of course, a Sauerkraut Trail. Driving north towards Strasbourg along the *Route des Vins d'Alsace* begins an eye-opening ramble into a land of revelations. My old preconceptions of a heavy, greasy or starchy cuisine are dispelled and instead, I find unexpected delicacy.

Red-roofed villages dot the road from Colmar and Sélestat, winding north through slopes cross-hatched with vineyards rising to the edge of the forests blanketing the Vosges mountains. From these gentle eastern foothills, the broad, flat Rhine Valley's fields of corn and cabbage stretch north towards the edges of Strasbourg. Small patches of tall, evenly staked vines are tidily clipped, their leaves lifted with each breeze to reveal plump green-golden grapes. The *vendange*, the harvest, has begun, starting with ripe Sylvaner grapes, touched with the amber tint of maturity.

South of Strasbourg, the first fields of grey-blue cabbage are cut late in August. The round, heavy heads are piled onto trucks in the fields, leaving in their wake a scattered detritus of stems and coarsely cut, once-enveloping leaves. This is cabbage country, an association of towns whose crops are devoted to Alsace's *choucroute* cravings. But late in September the *récolte*, the cabbage harvest, comes to a (tempo-rary) halt. The cabbage cut in August has been shredded, brined and

Top: A bounty of cabbages.
Bottom: vineyards along the Wine Trail.

is ready for tasting – at the annual *fête* that for thirty years has attracted as many as seven thousand visitors.

Krautergersheim's church tower appears pink from a distance, rising above the surrounding red-tiled roofs. From a parking area near the village hall, we approach the church, which I find is actually a cream-beige stucco, not pink at all. It appeared to be an Alsatian mirage – the red rooftops

Smoked sausages for a choucroute royale.

bathed in sunshine create this magical pink effect in many villages. If our early September weekend in the Alsacian Vosges was a bit damp for Munster's *fête*, the day in Krautergersheim is just the opposite: sunny and dry. Along rue du Maréchal-Foch and rue Centrale, we pass houses with freshly painted stucco: blue or yellow, dusty orange or pink, outlined by dark, exposed timbers. Enamel plaques and small hand-painted street numbers personalize many gates, and on several door-posts, dates are carved: 1751, 1860, 1950. Inside each entry courtyard, clusters of golden corn are hung over dark wooden balconies to dry in the sun.

On this *fête* Sunday, streets are bustling. Beer from Kronenbourg's breweries in nearby Obernai stocks colourful kiosks, grills are lit for sausages, to be topped with fried onions or fresh *choucroute*, and samples of *cornichons* are ready. Fifty assorted speciality stalls sheltering under a large white tent, *le chapiteau*, are waiting for tasters. The church rings with singing voices to conclude a special harvest mass.

"The house of cabbage" would be one translation of the town's name, as I learned from an elderly woman who pronounced it *"Kraut ER gesheim"*. In the shadow of the church, a number of vendors are eager to offer tastings. A small woman is intent on fixing the last decorative touches on her *dégustation* stall; tasting spoons and dishes of *choucroute* are set in a row. Her dark brown eyes are curious and she listens intently as I ask about the seasoning in each bowl of finely shredded *choux*. The samples are surprisingly delicate, not at all like the acidic prepared, packaged *sauerkraut*. "Our *choucroute* can be seasoned to your taste," she explains. "This is freshly brined so you can add the *aromatiques* herbs and spices you like best, depending on the *garniture*, what you are serving it with (ham, sausages, game or fish)." Do you use juniper berries, peppercorns or allspice? Bay leaf and cumin? Should I add salt? When do I add white wine, and how much? My litany of questions comes to a pause, she laughs and suggests I talk to her husband, who makes the *choucroute* and is a trained chef.

A broad-shouldered man in a striped rugby shirt turns, and with an easy smile he talks about his town, *choucroute*, and eventually, seasonings. I ask about the work of a *choucroutier*, a subject Eric Rieffel knows very well, and he explains: "The *chou* has been fermenting for three weeks now – if the temperatures drop it can take up to ten weeks! We brine it in salt, adding no water, no bacteria to speed up the process. The salting is a key step and these days it is hard to find an experienced 'salter'. Then it goes into *cuves*, stoneware tubs sunk into the ground, which are covered and weighted down with a stone. It's an old method, but we find the result is finer." I'm offered a taste of *chou* freshly brined, then a *choucroute* seasoned with juniper berries, nicely spicy but subtle, and I ask how long Rieffel et Fils has been making *choucroute* and *cornichons* (as the sign over their gate announces).

"My brother, Francis, and I run it. We grew up in my father's business, but I studied in Strasbourg at *l'école hôtelière* and worked as a chef

A giant sauerkraut at a chef's conference in Strasbourg.

La Choucroute Géante

until thirteen years ago when I came back to work at home. There are nine *choucroutiers* in the village now; there were thirteen here during the 1990s. Our competitors live next door and we all went to school together – it's better that way."

Eric continues: "We find that our clients in northern countries prefer it a bit briny, with more acidity. My interest is in more delicate flavours, so it marries with *garniture* other than the traditional smoked ham hock and sausage – with game or fowl, even with fish. During the 1960s, an Alsatian chef in Paris served a *choucroute aux poissons* – quite a break with tradition! Now it is popular, but the *chou* must be delicate." He agrees that *choucroute* can be marvellous with game, so long as it is not cooked over a high heat, or for too long, and recommends a balance of spices (juniper berries, thyme and peppercorns are best). Many chefs stir in bacon and a little lard to *choucroute*, others swear by goose fat, some mix in onion cooked in butter – it's all a matter of taste. "In my opinion," says Eric, "the finest flavour comes after the cabbage has had a light frost, so it is cut in November. Then we'll have the best of flavours with the *Oie de Noël*, the Christmas goose!"

Finally he gives me a short, classic *choucroute* recipe: for six people, take a kilo (about two pounds) of *choucroute*, drained and layered in a casserole with salt pork and spices (a teaspoon each of bay leaf, juniper berries, cumin or allspice and peppercorns). Pour over this a cup of white wine, and one of chicken or veal stock, let it simmer for about two hours and another two after adding smoked sausages.

Corn is hung out to dry on balconies in the courtyards.

A late afternoon parade of decorated floats (*chars*) rolls through the village, children waving from their cabbage-shaped seats. Fiddlers and accordion players follow, setting the pace for five groups of folkdancers. Many women wear the traditional Alsatian tall black head-pieces, which appear to be a cross between wide, starched ribbons and a cloth cloak caught in a stiff wind. Their skirts are covered with aprons embroidered with pastel wildflowers, and all step lightly in white handknit stockings. The men's white shirts are closed at the neck with black string ties, their red vests sport silver buttons in vertical rows. They grin under black-brimmed hats, circling in pairs with their lacy-gloved partners, moving in step along rue du Maréchal-Foch past the church. A brassy fanfare follows – the "oohm-paa" tradition is not neglected in Krautergersheim's *fête*. At day's end, the last rays of sun cast a pink light across the valley and along Krautergersheim's back streets, where aromas of dinner escape – simmering scents of Alsace.

Sandre sur choucroute / Pike with sauerkraut

Delicacy is the word that surfaces with each bite of *Sandre sur choucroute*, fine white-fleshed pike-perch on a neat bed of perfectly balanced *choucroute*.

Ingredients
80 g / 3 oz / 4 tbsp butter
900 g / 2 lbs sauerkraut, rinsed and drained
Salt and freshly ground black pepper
6 fillets of pike-perch
1 ripe tomato, peeled, seeded and chopped, or 6 stems of fresh redcurrants
For the sauce:
25 g / 1 oz / 1 tbsp butter
2 shallots, peeled and chopped
4 slices smoked bacon, chopped
80 ml / 3 fl oz / ⅓ cup dry white wine
500 ml / 18 fl oz / 2¼ cups court-bouillon or fish stock
340 g / 12 oz / 1½ cups crème fraîche or sour cream

Method
First, make the sauce: melt the butter in a heavy saucepan, add the shallots and sweat them (under a round of waxed paper) for 5 minutes.

Add the wine and reduce over a low heat, then add the fish stock and reduce again by a third.

Next add the crème fraîche and smoked bacon, and season. Simmer on a low heat for half an hour.

In another pan, melt 50g/2 tablespoons of butter and stir in the drained sauerkraut, heat through and add a twist of pepper.

In a frying pan, heat the rest of the butter and sauté the fish fillets, to brown both sides.

Pour the sauerkraut onto a heated serving plate (or plates), top with the fish and pour the sauce (having removed the bacon) over all. Garnish with the diced tomato or redcurrants, and serve.

A brisk, aromatic Riesling is the traditional wine partner for *choucroute*. A floral Klaevener de Heiligenstein, "ancestor" of Gewürztraminer, is our choice, one of myriad and marvellous Alsatian wines.

October

BioFoire / Organic Products Fair
Montauban/Tarn-et-Garonne, Midi-Pyrénées

Is it good for me? Is it good for the balance of nature? These concerns so central to the interest in organic products have increased dramatically through the last decades, and bring us to a mellow brick town on the Tarn. Montauban's successful *BioFoire* is a signal that organic farming is burgeoning, that respect for the environment is conscientiously coupled with producing quality products in southwest France. Participants increase yearly, recently numbering about one hundred producers. Fruits, vegetables, herbs, nuts, wheat products and honey, all organically grown, are spread from one end of Montauban's long marketplace to the other. Vendors of crafts and services related to preserving the environment also gather to sell their products, as well as promoting a forum for exchange of *biologique* information. Autumn's bounty in the Midi-Pyrénées region is celebrated with harvest fairs of many kinds, but the focus in Montauban's annual *BioFoire* clearly has a serious side.

The brick cities of this region, Toulouse, Albi and Montauban, hold within their old walls stories stretching back through ages of faith, power and persecution. Montauban was the earliest of *bastide* towns, built in 1144 by the Count of Toulouse in liason with the abbot of the monastery of St-Théobard. Under the brick arcades of place Nationale, surrounded by the weather-worn seventeeth-century façades that overlook the weekly winter *foie gras* markets, I sense the push-pull of history that has kept Montauban thriving. From here, it

Fruits, nuts and a wide variety of green vegetables are all organically grown.

is a short walk downhill towards the sound of braying donkeys on the place Prax-Paris, today the setting for October's annual organic fair.

This is a day for all the family, so everyone is involved and amused, from tastings of fruits and cakes to donkey rides for the children. A child-care area is provided so that parents can attend the lectures or explore the fair's many subjects, but there are *dégustations* for the children, too. The dark, curly head of a tall man intent on his apple press is the first thing I see over the crowd. The air carries the sweet scent of freshly pressed apple juice. By the time the crowd parts, he is serving the juice in paper cups to a row of children who have been watching the entire cranking process. His helper, a lanky, tanned, rasta-braided blond man, is taking a break from the apple press and munching on sesame-fig cakes out of a paper sack. In amiable conversation, he grins and turns the sack my direction: *"S'il vous plaît*, help youself, *c'est bon, eh?"* Oui! When I ask if he is the apple-grower's partner, they both laugh. The apple-presser retorts: "Not him – he doesn't like to work!" But I notice they're both filling the press for another round of juice.

Crates of popular, sweet golden apples and firm Reine des reinettes are labelled with a hand-lettered sign: organically grown.

It's peak season for pears, as the early, blushing Poire William gives way to the round, juicy Beurré Hardy variety. A petite brown-haired woman unloads flat trays loaded with enormous loaves of wholewheat bread. She is one

Montauban's Biofoire is a short walk from this arcaded square.

of a number of producers who qualify for the *Nature et Progrès* label, indicating that they use no artificial fertilizers or chemical sprays to treat products during or after harvest. She explains: "The bread must be baked from grain grown in soils where no chemicals, either pesticides or fertilizers, have been used. Each batch of flour is marked, as is each baking of bread, so *traçability* is marked at all stages. Maybe it's complicated, but it protects us all." And with this to think about, I turn from apples, pears and breads to almonds.

Almonds, in this climate? Well, yes. M. Alphonse Jurba and his son display filberts and almonds grown using biodynamic methods on their stand. "We're among the few growing almonds this far north, but its going well, most years, using *lutte raisonnée*," the elderly man explains. This is a term used in vineyards and fruit production meaning the minimum use of chemicals in the struggle against insects and plant diseases. "We spray with filtered nettle mash against disease and keep a close eye on the nut groves," M. Jurba continues as his son lifts heavy baskets of fruit and sacks of nuts. It appears their almond grove is thriving in the hills north of the Garonne river, a fruit-intensive *terroir* that depends as much on favourable microclimates as it relies on well-drained hillsides.

Lectures by health specialists, *conférences* and meetings on themes for both amateurs and professionals are held in the adjacent tourist offices, each for a small entry fee. Subjects addressed are different each year, as are the craftsmen and artists showing their work there. The crowd becomes denser and more diverse as we walk along the aisles. A display of water-purifying filters to protect home drinking water attracts a few clients, and I stop to watch a potter throwing dark red earthenware baking dishes from local clay. Natural skincare items using essential oils of aromatic plants are lined up on a large, central stand. Next to their bottles and sachets hang natural cream and beige jackets for both men and women, matched with long skirts, knit tops and 100 per cent organically grown cotton T-shirts. To the touch, they are soft-as-down, not inexpensive, but so comfortable.

We stroll past baskets and dried pastel floral bouquets, and stop to talk at the next table with Bernard Vidal, an apiarist whose honeys are rather unusual. He explains the progression for his sixty hives in four settings: "We follow the blooming sequence, with rosemary and acacia in May, then mixed flowers and wild heather on the upland pastures until the chestnut trees bloom first, about July, and then the sunflowers." This softly spoken producer sounds more like a scientist, passionate about the bee's role in pollination and the cycle of the seasons. He has kept bees near Montauban for over ten years. His concern about pollution is evident, as he explains that his colleagues in the mountains, at higher altitudes, need to use fewer preparations against parasites and that the honey from mountain apiaries will be purer. Against parasites in the hives, he uses thymol (made with

Salade composée tarnaise / Composed salad

A version of this southwestern *entrée* or lunch salad is good, with or without chicken livers. Use organically grown greens, radishes, onions and farm-smoked bacon.

Ingredients
4 slices smoked bacon, thinly
  sliced and cut in small chunks
1 sweet onion, cut in thin slices
28 ml / 1 fl oz / 2 tbsp oil or fat
1 bundle fresh radishes, trimmed,
  scrubbed, sliced in half
8 free-range chicken livers
  (optional), trimmed, sliced
  horizontally if large
Salad greens and/or spinach,
  cleaned, dried and torn
40 g / 1½ oz / ½ cup freshly shelled,
  toasted walnuts
For the dressing:
14 ml / ½ fl oz / 1 tablespoon
  raspberry vinegar
40 ml / 1½ fl oz / 3 tbsp good extra
    virgin olive oil
    1 tsp salt

Method
Sauté the bacon and onion in the oil until the onions are transparent.

Add the radishes and stir in the chicken livers (if used) to brown. Sweat this mixture under waxed paper on a low heat for 8 minutes.

Meanwhile make the vinaigrette dressing, by simply mixing the dressing ingredients, and toss this with the greens.

Arrange the warm bacon and radish mixture on top, sprinkle on the walnuts and serve with a glass of red *vin de pays*.

thyme), and for cleansing, essential oil of cinnamon. "Never anti-biotics – that throws all the systems off!" he explains before launching into the subject of *OGMs*, or genetically modified seeds and plants. "We really don't know what the secondary effects are or will be when genetic modification is practised, on a small or large scale. This is really frightening, and worrying for the next generation." With the purchase of honey, candles and honey vinegar, we turn from this serious apiarist to a lighter feature of the weekend: lunch.

The idea of lunch on the Tarn is as appealing as a walk through Montauban's old centre, paved with glossy granite. Crossing the old brick bridge to the restaurant Ventadour, I look back at the placid river reflecting the Pont Vieux's seven brick arches. It is a deceptively tranquil scene, considering the battering the fourteenth-century bridge has withstood. In flood season the river can rise suddenly, as it did in the fifteenth century, to wash over the sides. We follow the quay road to the Ventadour and walk upstairs into the dark, brick-vaulted dining room that served as a dye-works in the seventeenth century.

A *blanc sec perlé*, a spritely Gaillac *vin blanc* Manoir d'Emmaillé 1996, takes us from a survey of the menu through a savoury *salade composée*. In Albi, Montauban and other towns in the Tarn I've been pleasantly surprised to find radishes served warm.

After a tiny china cup of strong coffee, our route back to the *foire* leads past a stately brick palace on the river Tarn, now a museum dedicated to Montauban's famous son, the nineteenth-century portrait painter Jean-Auguste-Dominique Ingres. The museum holds a strangely diverse collection that includes Ingres' drawings, items of ancient civilizations, and sculpture by Antoine Bourdelle, also a Montauban native.

During the *BioFoire*'s afternoon of music and folkdancers, I encounter an enterprising couple (ex-teachers) whose products revolve around fresh eggs, and a display of well-crafted fruit *tartes* and quiches. "When our chickens were laying more than we could sell fresh, we added the *tartes* and quiches to our egg-stall and now we can't keep up with the orders!" His brown wavy hair is brushed back, wire-rimmed glasses are set on his narrow nose, and his enthusiastic air is slightly startled. "All of our ingredients are organically grown, and of course the chickens are free-range. We've begun selling fresh eggs to bakers and restaurants, and our quiches and *tartes* are sold in markets." His wife adds: "It's been quite a surprise to us, but more people are willing to pay a little more for free-range eggs and organic products. I grow all of the vegetables and herbs for the quiches." I am listening: there is a demand for more biodynamic products that respect nature's cycles, and I sense that this is not just in French markets and fairs but throughout Europe, and beyond.

October

Fête de la Châtaigne et du Cèpe / Chestnut and Mushroom Festival

Villefranche-du-Périgord/Dordogne, Périgord

Rambling in autumn woods is one of the season's great pleasures, wherever there are trees turning colour. Any excuse to shuffle through October's falling leaves is welcome, especially on the forested slopes of *Périgord noir*, the eastern edge of the Dordogne *département*, when chestnuts and mushrooms are ready to be gathered. The first signs of autumn here actually appear in September, when cars are discreetly pulled under low-hanging boughs of chestnut trees, and white panel-trucks hide in overgrown logging trails: the hunters have arrived. Searching the fern-carpeted forest floor, they furtively fill baskets, trugs and canvas bags with the first mushrooms or chestnuts. By mid-October the season is in full swing, as flats and sacks of chestnuts are sold in markets and monthly fairs across central and southern France. Monpazier's afternoon mushroom markets begin and end with the supply of *cèpes* (ceps), the *boletus*, which in a good year flourishes for weeks. But in dry, poor years, none can be found.

Whether there are heaps of *cèpes* or not, Villefranche-du-Périgord always salutes the season for both chestnuts and mushrooms on a festive October Sunday. The *bastide* village bustles with drop banners, events and activities, and restaurant menus feature both chestnuts and meaty *cèpes*. Cars and buses arrive for the day from Bergerac, Villefranche-sur-Lot and Cahors. Early on Sunday morning, under clear blue skies, we allow some time to poke around the back streets of this honey-toned village before the *Fête de la Châtaigne* begins.

Villefranche-du-Périgord salutes the chestnut season with festivities.

176

The monumental, flat beige façade of the church rises on Villefranche's sloping square, dominating the scene like the

Chestnuts are slowly roasted and turned to prevent burning.

backdrop of an opera stage set. Since the village charter was signed in 1270, this *bastide* has been an important market centre in the woodlands of southern Périgord and northern Agenais. Its markets and fairs mark the seasons for prunes, vegetables, mushrooms, walnuts and the chestnuts of today's festivities. Round metal measuring bins for grain and chestnuts, used for centuries, still stand on the western edge of the hall, itself an interesting study in architecture. The hall's stout stone pillars are replacements, built in the nineteenth century, but vestiges of the original thirteenth-century "French town" *bastide* remain in part of the massive *halle*, the arcades across the square and the *bastide* town's grid plan.

Walking uphill towards the square, my notions of a small market of chestnut and mushroom vendors vanish in an instant. Large white trucks, not small workmen's vans, are backed up to the hall. Chestnuts by the sackful are being hefted high and shaken out into wide, wooden trays. These are lifted, one man on each corner, and quickly hauled into the open truck, then stacked so that the doors can just be closed. This morning it is clearly a *marché en gros*, selling in volume, to be followed by vendors selling smaller amounts in the afternoon.

Seeing so many chestnuts prompts me to imagine the diverse ways in which they will be used, from sweetened *crème de marrons* for desserts, to purée for enriching simple soups, and side dishes. Will they be vacuum-sealed, pre-cooked to toss with green beans or to enrich holiday fowl stuffing?

My questions multiply as I do a quickstep around sacks of chestnuts and burly bag-handlers. I tap the broad shoulder of a stocky gentleman as he gestures toward a white truck and ask: "Are these *all* your chestnuts?" From a broad, craggy face, gentle grey eyes smile as he answers: "*Oui, madame,* I sold ten tons of chestnuts this morning! These will go to pastry and dessert manufacturers – they're very pleased with the quality. Our chestnuts in this corner of Périgord are renowned." The more questions I ask, the more curious he becomes, and waving away the driver of the chestnut truck, he wonders if we would like to see where these chestnuts grow. In the afternoon after lunch, it is agreed that we will drive to the Simesak farm, using a map he sketches in my notebook. With "*à bientôt*", he turns and hurries away. The day is becoming more interesting by the minute. Now there is time for lunch, a long Sunday lunch.

Under the *bastide* arcades, I study the Hôtel du Commerce *fête* menu, featuring chestnuts in all courses. After being shown to a corner table in the rather dark but tidy restaurant, an *apéritif à la châtaigne* soon

appears. The deep bronzy colour and sweetness of the wine-based elixir have a remarkable appetite-stimulating effect, a very French taste. A delicate *Velouté de Châtaigne* soup is followed by *Salade de Gésiers*, a gizzard salad with slices of chestnut *boudin* (sausage). Next, a delicious south-western classic arrives, *Confit de cuisse de Canard*, a preserved duck leg and thigh, its texture mellowed and infused with a peppery flavour. A medium-bodied red Bergerac wine suits both salad and *confit*. For dessert, I choose the baker's apple tart, slightly lighter than the whipped chestnut cream mousse. Any dream I had of *cèpes* for lunch disappears, as I remember hearing moans in the morning market about the early season, *trop précoce* this year. "After all, that's nature," someone quipped. Outside in the square, vendors' stalls are spread with vegetables, nuts, dark willow baskets, boxes of shiny apples and just-dug onions.

There is time before afternoon folkdancing begins to visit the Simesak *châtaigneraie*. Following M. Simesak's scrawled map, we turn onto country roads just wide enough for one small van, and finally pull up before a stuccoed beige farmhouse. The stocky figure of M. Simesak emerges, and with a warm greeting the tour of his farm begins. Past apple orchards, he leads us into deeper woods, thick with leaves. "Our chestnut season runs from mid-September to mid-December," he begins, and waves to a team of women gathering chestnuts into wooden trugs, working a slope that drops from the road. Amber light slants through towering trees ahead of us, an arresting moment, bringing us to the subject of land. "We have thirty hectares now in chestnuts. Many are very old, and we've planted one hundred young trees, the cultivated variety for *marrons*. I've lost some to disease already," he says. His smile disappears with a shrug of the shoulders, as a perplexed, lost look flickers in his grey eyes. "Many of our trees are old varieties, good stock of *cassagne* and *montagne*, but these new varieties are supposed to be more disease-resistant." I hear the sounds of "thud-plop", as spiny-cased chestnuts drop around us, and ask if helmets are necessary. "A hat is enough," Simesak chuckles and we turn back to the house.

M. Simesak has devised a system of tubs and conveyor belts to sort *châtaignes* from the largest *marrons*. "The native *châtaignes* have two lobes, are a bit smaller and are sold for *confiture*, chestnut paste and *brisées*, the broken ones are used in desserts," he explains. "The cultivated *marrons* will go to *pâtissiers* and be preserved whole, many for glazed sweets. Have you tasted *marrons glacés*?" I confess this is one of my favourite luxuries. With a glance at my watch, I see it is time to leave, and thank this hospitable man whose vision into future crops is grounded firmly in today's events.

Soufflé aux marrons / Chestnut soufflé

For a lighter twist on chestnut richness, try individual soufflées in ceramic cups.

Ingredients
500 g/16 oz/2 cups puréed, sweetened chestnuts, Crème de Marrons
2 egg yolks
250 ml/9 fl oz/1 cup plus 2 tbsp thick cream
28 ml/1 fl oz/2 tbsp rum or brandy (or strong coffee for a mocha option)
4 egg whites
Icing sugar to decorate
Optional: freshly grated nutmeg or finely ground cardamom

Method
Preheat oven to 240°C/475°F/Gas Mark 9.

Butter the inner bottom of 6 or 8 individual cups or a 20 cm x 8 cm/8 in x 3 in straight-sided baking dish.

Mix the chestnut *crème* with the egg yolks and cream, then blend in the rum.

Beat the egg whites until they form soft glossy peaks and then fold them carefully into the chestnut mixture as quickly as possible – it should not take more than 2 minutes.

Fill the cups or dish two-thirds full, and place them on a large baking sheet. Set this on the lowest shelf of the hot oven.

When the soufflés begin to puff up (after 5 minutes, usually), lower the oven temperature to 180°C/350°F/Gas Mark 4, for 10 minutes more (30 minutes for a large dish) until the soufflés are well-risen and golden.

Sprinkle them with icing sugar and nutmeg or cardamom if wanted, and serve immediately, with whipped cream on the side.

An elegant white Saussignac wine has the velvety fullness to match this rich chestnut finale.

Back in Villefranche, I work my way past vendors, tempting bakeries and displays along rue Notre Dame to the *Maison du Châtaignier et du Champignon*, a dusty but charming little museum devoted to chestnuts and mushrooms. For centuries, energy-rich chestnuts were the peasant's basic diet, survival food that fuelled families through bleak times of famine, wars and drought. The dried husks served as kindling, and as fuel in the hearth.

The directions given for preparing fresh chestnuts are useful. The display suggests that they rest on a cloth (not plastic) in a cool place for a week so that they are easier to peel. Take a large enamel pot, lined with clean fig or grape leaves, and fill it with chestnuts. Cover them with cold water, bring this to a simmer and cook for twenty minutes, checking after ten minutes for tenderness. If cooked too long, chestnuts crumble, so the pot should be taken off the heat, and a few chestnuts shelled at a time while they're hot. To remove the thin layers of peel, make a quick slit along the flat side, prying off the hot shell and the inner membrane, which, with practice, lifts right off. The chestnuts can then be simmered in herbed stock, milk or water for ten to twenty minutes.

Experts judge the quality of the chestnuts.

A *défilé* of folkdancers moves through the village, a spirited parade of six ensembles from surrounding regions, all dressed in their own traditional costumes. Women with bright scarves wrapped around their heads and men in collarless smocks all dance past us in a blur of movement, leading everyone to the shelter of the old market hall. Watching the festivities, I review the day's events and plan what to do with a sack of M. Simesak's glossy chestnuts. They will be shelled, simmered, then sautéd with minced garlic, sprinkled with sea salt and served alongside a rolled pork roast flavoured with prunes from Agen. Best of all, spiced *Soufflées aux Marrons* will conclude an autumn harvest *fête* at home, recalling a fine day in Villefranche-du-Périgord.

October

Foire aux Piments / Pepper Fair
Espelette/Pyrénées-Atlantiques, Pays Basque

Pepper-sellers offer tips on storing and using piments.

Strings of lipstick red peppers, festooned across balconies and under the eaves of Basque farmhouses, have become synonymous with Espelette, putting this mountain village on the gastronomic map of France. Less than two thousand people are counted on the village records, and about twenty are pepper-growers, but their rosy product has become a hot item in *épiceries* and gourmet shops around the world. The annual October *Foire aux Piments* began as a village celebration of the harvest, with a mass and village fair. But now, not only has the pepper been exported from the Pays Basque, but word of the festival has also spread to cities on the coast, inland to Pau and north to Bordeaux. The press arrive in numbers, sending reports across Europe and abroad. So popular is it today that the town is closed to through traffic during the *foire*, as it attracts more than 20,000 visitors per day. At the centre of it all are the famous Espelette peppers, which have been harvested, dried, strung and stored. The villagers have prepared for the winter ahead, and are eager to celebrate their harvest.

Once settled in Hôtel Euskadi, there is time to talk about the local trade with proprietor André Darraïdou. The tall, genteel gentleman

183

has served as Espelette's mayor for several decades. At the same time, he was cooking and managing the hotel with his wife as their family grew up. He begins with a story, a local legend: "A few centuries ago, a vagabond came through the village, asking for shelter for the night, which he was given with courtesy. The fire in the hearth of the small room wouldn't catch, and the host apologized. 'Oh, don't worry, this will warm your soup, and your heart,' the traveller assured him, and pulled out a little pouch full of seeds. The next day, he left some of these strange seeds in appreciation for the hospitality. That's a little pepper story for you," smiles the reserved Darraïdou, as he leans

Sheep graze in Espelette's green pastures.

against the polished wood reception desk. There may be a fine line between the tale of the mysterious traveller and the actual history of Espelette.

It could be true, given Espelette's position high in the French foothills of the Pyrénées on the inland route from the frontier town of St-Jean-Pied-de-Port to the harbour cities of Biarritz and St-Jean-de-Luz. Peppers and cocoa beans were brought from the Americas to Spain in the sixteenth century, and found their way north into the agriculture and commerce of the Pays Basque. But what is it about this long, brilliant red pepper that makes it so desirable? My first encounter with *piment d'Espelette* was in its fresh form, green, stirred into the classic Basque veal dish called *Axoa* (pronounced *ahshowah*) in a café in Bayonne. I was ready for heat, but instead the dish was just pleasantly spicy, with a warming sensation at the finish. The peppers of Espelette are best known, though, in their dried form. The *salaisonneurs* that we met in Bayonne assured me that as a seasoning to preserve hams and sausages they have long been prized. Chefs choose this *piment* to add snap to marinades and to *pipérades*. It is a pepper with subtlety, known not for its fire, but for its warming accent.

We travel to Espelette from Biarritz, noting signs along the way warning: "Cattle crossing". In this meat-loving region, long-simmered *ragoûts* (with curious names like *Xamango*) and beef or mountain lamb grilled over glowing embers are local favourites. Flocks of the native black-faced sheep and fleecy white *manech à tête rousse* nibble mountain grasses on rocky pastures too steep for cattle. In the morning's gauzy valley fog, our route circles through Cambo-les-Bains, then on to Espelette on a straight but undulating road.

Parking is managed by young men in long herders' jackets, swinging poles to direct cars in rows across hummocky pastures. The mist is lifting, skies are clearing, and we have a kilometre to walk into Espelette. Broad, flattened rooftops of farms are nestled into the hillsides, and on their south façades bright strings of peppers still dry in the sun. As we climb a hill into the village, the aromas of grilled ham and bacon fill the air.

The day's ramble through Espelette's *foire* begins with a little snack. Under the word *Taloa*, on a sign printed in typical Basque thick, red lettering, I watch a greying, bearded vendor intent on turning the region's version of a maize pancake. He looks up at me with his dark brown eyes under thick brows and queries: "Do you like a slice of side-bacon or peppered sausage in your *taloa*?" One of each is the order, and is soon ready. Another *taloa* (or *talua*) stand demonstrates the entire process with a maize grinder, wood-fired griddle, and a large, pink-cheeked woman energetically kneading the yellow dough in a wooden trough. Three *taloa*-patters surround the griddle, shawls tied over their shoulders and aprons covering dark print dresses. Each ball of dough is patted flat into a smooth disc, ready to be cooked on the griddle and rolled around a meaty filling. I add maize to the growing list of products brought from the Americas, now firmly rooted in the cuisine of southwestern France.

A father and daughter taloa team.

Several pepper sellers are on hand to explain just what goes into the little jar of *piment d'Espelette*. A brown-haired woman with two small children at her side tells me about the pepper-growers' year. "We sow the peppers in March, plant them out in May and the harvest runs from late August to the first frost which can be as late as November." As she explains the farming and the labelling of the pepper products, I can't begin to calculate the hours involved in producing each batch of rosy spice. The jar we take home is numbered, labelled stating that at least twenty dried peppers went into the jar, has a use-by date and is sealed with a striped sticker noting the *millésime*, the year of harvest. The powdered pepper is pinkish, not brown or dark red, a sweet-hot pepper that will season many *pipérades*, and casseroles of *poulet Basquaise*. A string of partially dried peppers is added to jars of *piment*, in my growing collection of Basque flavours.

As well as the stalls, I explore the shops of Espelette for special condiments. One of the two butcher's at the tight junction of main streets in the village, the Accoceberry family shop, stocks salty, tempting foods, including delicate, almost sweet, pickled fingers of peppers called *guindillas*, as well as piquant *sauce Basque*. Those with a sweet tooth must try the region's dark, jammy *cerises noires* — whole preserved black cherries to serve with a slice of aged *brebis* cheese. The classic regional dessert is a wedge of *gâteau Basque*, a special, flaky pastry with either black cherry or almond filling.

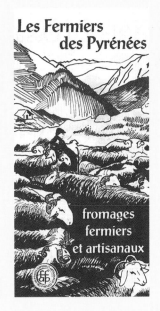

Cheese, too, dominates the stalls, including a wealth of ewes' milk (*brebis*) cheeses such as *Ardi-Gasna* from the steep pastures of the Soule. There is also *Laruns'* firm and nutty *tomme*, *Iraty* cheeses from the Ossou Valley and *chèvre*. The only problem today is getting close enough to the stalls to be able to sample and buy the stuff – the crowds are dense. Cheese and bread from the Dordogne, duck breasts and *foie gras* from the Gers, and wines from the greater southwest are also sold during this weekend of many delicacies. Autumn heather and mountain flower honeys from apiaries in the Landes and Pays Basque are up for tasting, and to season cups of winter tea.

Espelette's *chocolatier* Antton on the square is open today for tours and, of course, shoppers. I join the throng to follow the "transformation" of cocoa from beans to *bonbons*. The last step, dipping *ganache* or nuts into the final glossy coating, is demonstrated with great flair outside the shop, where the sweets are plunged for an instant into a huge copper cauldron of dark, shiny chocolate. Cocoa for baking and dusting over *truffes en chocolate* is among Antton's temptations.

A festive procession marches to the Mass – and the blessing of the pepper seeds.

The town's imposing riverside church plays a central role in the festivities. Sunday's mass for the *Foire aux Piments* is an orchestrated celebration, a great ceremonial *mélange* of participants who dance, sing with the *chorale*, and listen as the pepper seeds for next year's crop are blessed by the priest. I arrive early to find a place, and watch the long procession of *confréries* from across the region. Holding high their banners emblazoned with insignias of leaping salmon, Bayonne ham, wines of Tursan and Jurançon and plump pigs, they arrive in colourful robes to honour and celebrate the famous pepper of Espelette.

Thon aux piments d'Espelette / Tuna with peppers

In this recipe the *piment*'s fiery notes are subdued by using just a pinch with fresh tuna from St-Jean-de-Luz.

Ingredients
3 cloves garlic, 2 finely chopped, 1 halved
2 tsp ground piment d'Espelette
4 thick slices fresh tuna or firm sea fish
40 ml / 1½ fl oz / 3 tbsp olive oil
Sea salt, freshly ground black pepper
2 peppers, green or red, seeded and sliced into strips
75 ml / 3 fl oz / 5 tbsp white wine

Method
Some 2 hours before cooking, rub the halved garlic and piment over the tuna slices and sprinkle them with oil and salt.

Heat the remaining oil in a broad frying pan, and sauté the sliced peppers and garlic for 10 minutes. Stir and reserve on a hot plate.

Add another spoonful of oil (if necessary) to the pan and sauté the spiced tuna, for approximately 5 minutes on the first side, and 3 minutes on the second (depending on the thickness).

Cover the tuna with the sautéd peppers, add the wine and let it all simmer for 2 minutes. Then turn onto a hot serving platter.

Serve with steamed saffron rice and glasses of crisp, white Jurançon Sec.

November

Foire aux Dindes / Turkey Fair
Varaignes/Dordogne, Périgord

In the rolling hills of the southern Charente and northwestern Périgord, church steeples poke through November's mantle of grey ground fog obscuring the pantiled rooftops of Varaignes. The filigree figure on the weathervane is barely visible: but it's a turkey! From the main street, I scan the wooded edge of the village, and before they can be seen, I hear a chorus of deep, persistent ... "gobble gobble" ("*glou-glou*" in French). The parade opening this one-day *foire* comes around a bend in the road, a *défilé* of turkeys, *confréries* in dark smocks and red neckscarves, folkdancers and local dignitaries, all led by a small brass band moving towards Varaigne's central square. Rain or shine, this animated *fête* for the strange fowl – originally called *poule d'Inde* – has attracted increasing numbers of visitors from the neighbouring *départements* of the Charente, Limousin and Gironde.

On Armistice Day and the feast day of St-Martin, this unusual, rustic *foire* always begins with a turkey parade. Varaignes is an important centre of turkey production in the southwest, so this proud fowl is always the *foire's* featured "guest". When the flapping, gobbling black turkeys have been shown their way to the village park, they strut into cages under bare plane trees. The brass band sounds a last fanfare before the musicians break ranks to warm their hands over broad coal braziers lit for today's grilled turkey sausages. By mid-morning, *vin chaud* (mulled wine), heated in the château kitchen, is served to all who want to step inside for a few moments out of the chilly air to warm themselves. Nearby, on this eleventh of November, Armistice Day memorial services are observed in Varaignes as they are in towns across the land, the serious side of an otherwise light-hearted day.

Above: local turkeys. Below: visiting confrérie.

The grey stone château is the anchor in this tight little community of four hundred souls, a village that has one main street, one bakery, one tavern and no cash machine. Taking a few steps up into the château, we leave the turkeys behind and enter a tiled reception room where the village's special events are held. An old stone stairway leads to a series of rooms that for decades were devoted to *pantoufle* production. These soft, warm slippers are still popular in the southwest and today visitors can watch them being made.

In a courtyard dating from the fifteenth century at the back of the château, chestnuts are roasting on flat screens over glowing coals. A man in a blue sweater lazily turns and pushes them with an old, long-handled tool. Children gather round to watch, jostling for a sample. In a dark corner, I notice light coming through a crack in the door, and investigate. It creaks open on rusty hinges, to reveal a room, lit by a single, suspended light bulb. In the middle, a trestle-table heaped with chestnuts is surrounded by men in black berets and cloth caps, talking in low voices as they slit and open the glossy shells. It is a freeze-frame scene, a timeless gathering to get a job done. This vignette could take place anywhere in Périgord, in any decade, but only in this season.

But back to the turkeys, which are the focus of this winter fair. Since they were brought from the Americas in the

Dindon noir, the black turkey, thrives in the bushy, rocky terrain typical of northern Périgord.

The band relaxes, warming up for the next fanfare.

sixteenth century, several breeds have established themselves in French barnyards. The black turkey, *dindon noir*, common to the southwest, does well in the rocky terrain and bushy woodlands of northern Périgord, while the *rouge d'Ardennes* adapts better to the harsher climate of the forests and fields near the Belgian border. These European fowl are smaller than their American counterparts, the brassy-plumed *bronzé d'Amérique*, and are better suited to less capacious European ovens, one cook confided. Today, I hope to clarify for myself the differences between the *dindon*, *dinde* and the *dindonneau* raised in France.

Cages of turkeys fill Varaignes' square, where the band is relaxing from the last performance and warming themselves for the next. All the musicians sport black bowler hats, and each wears a different coloured neck-tie as they juggle a sausage roll in one hand and a cup of wine in the other. Also gathering at the wine kiosks are the satin-robed *confrères* from Licques, a region in northern France well known for turkey production. (Licques' *Fête de la Dinde* is held in December.) Featured in the square today, though, are the turkey farmers' finest birds, ready to sell. Some visitors will take home a turkey to fatten for December feasts, while others might take a pair for their *basse-cour* (farmyard) collection of fowl.

Above the noisy *"glou-glou"*, I speak with a producer. He tips his black hat, *"Bonjour"*, as I ask about the *dindons*. "The *dindon* is the male, larger, and somewhat less tender than the *dinde* – but it has wonderful flavour!" he explains. "This is our traditional feast fowl, roasted and stuffed with chestnuts or *cèpes* for Christmas dinner... or stuffed with truffles if it is a good *saison des truffes*. In some areas, a young turkey, a *dindonneau*, is prepared

Ferme de la Bouyssonnie

Le respect de la Tradition

Volailles élevées au grain et en liberté

05 53 24 35 05 ou 06 81 60 81 10
24240 Rouffignac de Sigoulès

for *les fêtes*, but at our house, we're traditional: *toujours un dindon!*" To my questions about *blanc de dinde*, turkey breast that is available fresh in butcher shops year round, he replies: "*Ah oui*, there are more *dinde* than *dindon* in the flock, so the tender leg and breast meat is in good supply." Thus, I see the seasonal role of the *dindon*, fattened on corn through November until the *Noël* feast is prepared. Year round, when recipes call for *blanc de volaille*, chicken or turkey breast work equally well, seared with shallots and green peppercorns ... or in a chilled terrine with mushrooms.

The fowl/mushroom partnership in this region is legendary, and autumn is prime season for both. Baskets of *cèpes* appear on stalls in Varaignes, a pleasant surprise as I thought the season was over. But these mushrooms are occasionally known to make a comeback in oak and chestnut forests through the month of November. The thick *boletus* on a mushroom stall are darker as they are late-season varieties. The *vendeuse* has one sliced in half to show its white interior, and I ask for cooking tips. The small, solid woman, whose worn hands tell the story of many seasons collecting *cèpes* and walnuts, has a hearty laugh. "Oh, there's not much to tell," she insists. "They'll need trimming and brushing – wipe them, but don't wash them in water. The early ones in September are better for drying, but they must be perfect to dry well. It's better to cook these *cèpes* right up, they'll be good with game – or with turkey! Heat some duck fat and cook the mushrooms with garlic, add a handful, a *poignée*, of chopped parsley and a spoon of *verjus* (juice made from grapes still green at harvest time) before you eat them." With *cèpes* and *franquette* walnuts in my increasingly heavy basket, a menu takes form, using turkey and mushrooms.

Turkey sausages and pork loin grilled over *sarment* (grapevine embers) sizzle as noon approaches and appetites mount. Tastings include creamy local goats' cheese – *chèvre* in logs or little discs called *cabécou* in Périgord (*chabichou* in Charente). Then I sample *Pineau des Charentes*, the region's sweet apéritif of grape juice blended with Cognac. Next I am tempted by an onion vendor with garlic strung across his stall, as well as dangling braids of white or red

Blanc de dinde aux cèpes / Turkey breast with cèpe mushrooms

Ingredients

56 ml / 2 fl oz / ¼ cup cooking oil

4 turkey breast "steaks" (boneless, skinless breasts)

1 tbsp paprika

2 shallots, sliced in rings

2 cloves garlic, finely chopped

500 g / 18 oz / 2¼ cups cèpes, trimmed and cleaned (drained if soaked to rehydrate). Caps can be sliced, stems finely chopped

50 g / 2 oz / ¼ cup flat-leafed parsley, finely chopped – retain 4 sprigs for garnish

170 ml / 6 fl oz / ¼ cup verjus or dry white wine to deglaze the pan

Method

Heat half of the oil in a broad frying pan. Pat the turkey pieces dry and sear in the oil to brown on both sides. Sprinkle them with paprika and reserve on a warm plate.

In the remaining oil, sauté the shallots and garlic until transparent, stir in the cèpes and sweat (under a circle of waxed paper) for 5 minutes. Add the parsley and continue to cook for 5 minutes, stirring.

Slip the turkey breasts back into the pan, under the mushrooms, pour the verjus or wine over, bring to a simmer and cover until cooked – about 10 minutes on a low heat. Test to make sure the meat doesn't dry out – add more verjus or wine if necessary.

Serve with sliced *pain de campagne*, follow with a salad of *mâche*, lamb's lettuce, and pour a medium-bodied *Côtes de Bergerac* red from the region.

onions and net sacks of shallots, all grown in local fields. My basket grows even heavier ...

Hot turkey sausages on crusty, fresh half-baguettes in hand, we find a place on a low sandstone wall near the château to enjoy our movable feast. Sunshine breaks through the clouds as I scan the orange and red pumpkins, green melons and bright squash on one stall, leather vests and belts on the next. This is, without doubt, a diverse *foire*. Later in the afternoon, mime performances, a *pantoufle* tossing competition and a gobbling contest are entertaining bonuses during this shopping excursion – at the *Foire aux Dindes*.

Foire aux Harengs / Herring Fair

Dieppe/Seine-Maritime, Coastal Normandy

In a season of grey days, it is time for a weekend away for many city dwellers. And where better than the *Foire aux Harengs* in Dieppe? Driving through northern Normandy towards the Channel coast, brambly hedges and the *bocage Normand* of lush pastures flash past. Anticipation *en route* to any *foire* is half the fun, and my imagination crowds with images and memories of coastal towns, fishing boats riding low on the water as the herring catch is brought in. Will fishermen be docked, selling herring preserved in salt, herbs, or mustard from their boats? A change of scene always stirs a sense of anticipation.

I look beyond the harbour to Dieppe's solitary church, which is set like a watchtower on the distant cliff, as if surveying history passing from decade to decade in the busy fishing port. Then I notice that Dieppe's fishing boats are secured in their moorings, apparently empty through the weekend; the catch is already in. Cafés and brasseries along the quayside have bought their fresh herring for the grill, filling the November afternoon with smoky fish smells – an altogether different interpretation of a Herring Fair than I had imagined. A fun-fair dominates the Quai Henri IV with carnival music thumping from speakers. Vendors of Peruvian sweaters and stalls selling shiny yellow sailing jackets are interspersed between games, rides and sausage stalls. But we are here to find fish, shellfish and other savoury treasures from Channel waters. The search begins for a good *marmite dieppoise* as well as herring on the quay. The quest will be easy, *n'est-ce pas?*

We arrive in time for the lively Saturday market, a wide-ranging sprawl of vendors around the church of St-Jacques in Dieppe's old

Above: Dieppe's busy marina

Below: whole herring and scallop brochettes crowd harbour grills.

centre. Leather belts and bags are sold alongside leeks, cabbages and poultry. Flower vendors sell onion and cardoon sets for winter potagers, and bright jackets and boots wave from corners of an all-weather gear stall. A corner fish shop with an impressive range displays iced, delicate white sole, shimmering skate and large violet-skinned cod. Blue-pink-silver slippery fish fill the *poissonniers'* baskets, as do sparkling herring in heaps. We're closing in on our goal – a good fish lunch can't be far away.

Tempting aromas of Normandy's famous *crêpes* fill my nostrils, as I pass a stack of paper-thin pancakes with great willpower. Moving along, sizzling fowl roasting on portable spits quicken my step with appetite-teasing scents in the chilly air as we edge into a restaurant near the church on bustling place St-Jacques. At the *Grand Duquesne*, there is a wait for our table as the busy staff serve and clear, so we review the morning's impressions over a glass of flowery, golden *Muscat de la Loire*.

This popular restaurant's hubbub is the perfect ambience for a market day lunch, and we go straight to the seafood menu. Their speciality, a *Soupière de St-Jacques* (or *marmite dieppoise*), arrives in traditional footed white porcelain bowls, topped with a light, flaky pastry crust. I gently pierce the lid to let the steaming cream-infused aromas of scallops and salmon escape – ah, an excellent choice – and concentrate on twirling thin strips of carrot and endive around a forkful of delicate scallop. An Alsatian Gewürztraminer, made near Pfaffenheim, is the perfect accompaniment with its spicy, floral tones complementing the *fruits de mer*. It is clear that a portion of this mission is not impossible: a *marmite* has been tasted.

Sunday morning dawns grey, but not as foggy as I feared. By eight o'clock, fires in braziers brighten the *quai*-side road as café and brasserie owners prepare long shallow grills, allowing time for the flames to create glowing embers. Some work in teams, wearing goggles over the heavy smoke of their braziers, deftly turning herring or rolling over brochettes of scallops and peppers to feed the coming onslaught of fish-lovers. Inexpensive herring greatly outnumber the scallops on

most grills, as the fair's thirty years of experience has taught the cooks how to please the crowd. Several vendors of crisp, white Sancerre wines, another crowd-pleaser, are ready to provide a sip or a case of wine to visitors. A *pression*, or draught beer, is more popular.

We duck into a brasserie for breakfast, chatting with the couple drying glasses behind the counter as they prepare for the midday crowd. I ask what fish besides herring and scallops are caught in Dieppe's waters. The proprietor listens, moving quickly as he speaks with us. Between his manner and movement, he has a perpetually surprised look, with high, arched eyebrows under a shock of brown hair levelled in a crew-cut. Reaching for his denim jacket, he says: "*Oui*, I'll find Monsieur TT for you," and dashes out. As the door closes, his wife quips: "We've all called him M. TT for so long I don't know his real name!" Soon he returns and introductions are made. M. Héroud, the local *grossiste*, is a seafood wholesaler supplying most of the restaurants and cafés along Dieppe's busy *quai*. He sits down for a few minutes to express his concerns about fish and his region's future. For thirty years, he has been on the wharves, an active participant in the economy of local fishing. This small, clean-cut man, dressed in a checked shirt under a navy V-necked sweater, is not happy about the way things are going.

"My concern is for the future," he begins, leaning forward to make his point. "In ten years it will be so much harder for young fishermen to make a living. To put it simply, there are fewer fish in the Channel today. Thirty years ago when I began working on the *quai*, the daily catch here was about four hundred tons. Today eight tons is a good day. For years there have been warnings about over-fishing the Channel waters, but it was only a few years ago that they began insisting on wider gauge nets, allowing smaller fish to remain in the sea. In the past they did not throw back the little fish. Listen, it takes three years for a good cod, a *cabillaud*, to reach maturity!" Holding up his index fingers to indicate the small to large gauge, I sensed that this experienced caliper had measured many a cod, a flounder, a sole, and herring, many *petits poissons*. "It is the same," he continues, "for shellfish. The harvesting claws used in the past for scallops scraped the ocean floor, bringing up everything – small and large shellfish – so a more selective fishing claw is now required. But these changes in fishing regulations took time, and are not always enforced; natural supplies of shellfish have diminished."

He waves away a cup of coffee, anxious to return to preparations on the *quai*. But his voice rises: "Tastes are changing, too – you know, people don't want fish with bones any more! The old folks still like their fish fresh, grilled or sautéd whole, but a large portion of my market wants fish without bones, *sans arêtes*. Have you tasted fish *merguez* (sausage)?! Processed fish takes new forms every month ... " He shakes his head. I quickly draw a square on my notebook, showing him what a city child drew in an art class when our subject was fish and sea creatures. He glances at it and quips: "It's not just city children now, many don't know what a fish looks like – eating square fish everywhere, I guess. Time to go, excuse me." The trim, earnest man stands and waves *"Salut!"* to the woman behind the bar. She comments: "M. TT is kind and fair, we can trust him," as the door closes with a draught of damp November air.

By eleven, the fish aficionados arrive for their appetizers, equipped with pen-knives and appetites sharpened by the misty chill. I marvel at the dexterity of one herring enthusiast as he quickly slits the grilled fish to neatly pull out the backbone, places the fish in a crusty slab of baguette and bites in. The knife is then wiped 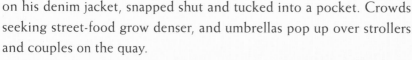 on his denim jacket, snapped shut and tucked into a pocket. Crowds seeking street-food grow denser, and umbrellas pop up over strollers and couples on the quay.

More *brochettes* of scallops, threaded on skewers with strips of onion or green pepper, appear on the grills on Sunday morning. I stop to watch a young chef in his white toque, carefully turning the delicate white kebabs over the grill. When asked whether they are *pétoncles* (a smaller variety of scallops) or *Coquilles Saint-Jacques* (scallops), he glances at me through his horn-rimmed glasses and confirms: "These are nice plump scallops – they need to be thick for grilling. We use *pétoncles* in salads and *escabèche* (raw in a thick citrus marinade) or creamed dishes, and some in *marmite dieppoise*." Normandy is responsible for two-thirds of French scallop fishing, so this is the place to enjoy

St-Jacques au poivre vert / Scallops with green peppercorns

Fresh scallops are easily stirred up for a special lunch – *un vrai régal* – a Sunday treat. For a quick, spicy approach, try this.

Ingredients
24 Channel sea scallops, washed and each slit in 3 parts, just to one edge
Sea salt, white pepper
2 cloves garlic, finely chopped
60 g / 2 oz / ¼ cup green peppercorns, drained
140 g / 5 oz / 1 cup shallots, peeled, finely chopped
100 g / 3½ oz / 5 tbsp fine breadcrumbs
100 g / 3¼ oz / 5 tbsp butter, cut into pieces

Method
Heat the oven to 200°C/400°F/Gas Mark 6.
   Slice the scallops, season with salt and pepper and sprinkle with garlic, peppercorns and shallots before coating each with breadcrumbs.

Arrange each scallop in a fan shape on a scallop dish or shell. Distribute the butter over each and bake for 20 minutes.
   Once they are cooked, take them out from the oven and brown them quickly under a hot grill.
   Serve with a casserole of creamed leeks and endives, and pour *flûtes* of sparkling Vouvray from the Loire.

them fresh from October to May. We can't resist *brochettes de Saint-Jacques* to nibble on, walking along the quay facing the fishing boats in *Bassin Ango.* The smoky overtone of the grill gives each scallop a nuance that creeps into its smooth, hint-of-the-sea richness.

   Herring is still lined up on grills late in the afternoon when it is time for our return to Paris. Along the undulating back roads of the Pays de Caux night is gathering in the shadows, darkness seeping through the woodlands and trim hedges. The day was interesting and I reflect on how the coast is changing, glad to have tasted fresh herring and scallops – while there are still fish in Channel waters.

Gastronomades / Rambling Gourmet Festival

Angoulême/Charente, Poitou-Charente

Some festivals just get better every year. When quizzed to define Angoulême's annual November gastronomic wonderland, my response can only be that this ever-expanding, changing, lively and informative event is simply about good food. It is an exceptional weekend that has drawn international attention since its inception in the early 1990s. This is not a country *foire*, not a grass-roots *fête* with a few stalls and folkdancers. The farmers are here, with the honey-vendors and bread-bakers alongside cheesemakers, but the organization has set this event apart as a *vitrine*, a showcase for the products of the *départements* of the Charente and its coastal sister, Charente-Maritime. For many travellers, western France is only a verdant blur seen from autoroutes or windows of the TGV from Tours and Poitiers to Bordeaux. Some *voyageurs*, *gastronomades*, know better.

Gastronomades offers a concerted extravaganza to give small producers broader exposure to their public, alongside the renowned houses of Cognac. The seat of power for this gastronomic salon is the gothic-Renaissance city hall, reconstructed in the nineteenth century. Its towering white stone turrets are visible from a great distance, shimmering like a white Camelot above the rich farmlands and vineyards of the southern Charente. For medieval kings, the counts of Poitiers and Angoulême and powerful clergy, the tenth and eleventh

Above: colourful heather and cyclamen in the market.
Below: samples are prepared, ready for eager tasters.

centuries were golden, expansive eras. Eleanor of Aquitaine and Marie-Thèrese of Angoulême are among the city's renowned historical figures.

But now, how do we approach *Gastronomades'* vast buffet, an initiation for novice tastebuds? A good place to start seems to be the Saturday morning market, where the day's first *dégustations* can also be found. Angoulême's monumental market hall is perched on the edge of a hill surveying the Charente Valley and is worth the trip just for the panorama. The interior, too, is stunning, with its exemplary *belle époque* iron gridwork, while the market itself is one of the most interesting in France. This bountiful region, not far from the Atlantic's oyster beds and fishing trawlers, is in the middle of truffle-oak woods, surrounded by pastures dotted with pigs and cattle. No wonder a *fête* inviting gastronomic tourism and culinary journalism is such a success in Angoulême!

A long white marquee next to the freshly renovated *halle* is the winners' tent, devoted to the best of everything. Competitors for the prized medals given to the finest Cognac, best *Pineau des Charentes apéritif* wine, finest *chèvre*, best *foie gras*, richest cake, *Gâteau d'Angoulême*, and best wines are all gathered here.

I stop to taste an award-winning Pineau. Producer Alain Jousseaume explains: "Lots of people know our region as the land of Cognac, but we make other wines, too. Our Pineau des Charentes is made of grape juice – the same varieties used for Cognac – blended with *eau-de-vie de moût de raisin*. Then, for at least one year (we hold ours for two) the Pineau is kept in oak barrels. After ageing, it is ready when it measures between sixteen and twenty-two degrees alcohol." He pours a *dégustation* of his prizewinning white Pineau, exemplary of the wine's fullness and almost-sweet quality. A sliver of creamy *chèvre* cheese, the only winner in the dairy category of the contest, is the ideal match. Mme. Jousseaume, whose thick, short brown hair seems to increase her height, wraps up our cheese and Pineau, with an invitation to visit their farm (and their 300 goats). I'm finding more reasons to return to Angoulême, and through the day discover more uses for Pineau des Charentes.

Jousseaume's white Pineau is one of two types produced in the region, the other being a rosé

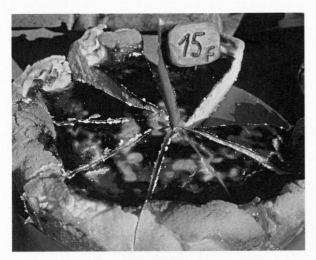

Tempting cheesecake is made with fresh chèvre.

made from Cabernet Franc, Merlot and Cabernet Sauvignon grapes. After one year in the barrel, this is a lightly pink *apéritif*, but when aged for a few years, the colour turns a burnished brown similar to that of an aged sherry, and its sweetness mellows. Both white and sweeter rosé Pineau are delicious with summer's bounty of Charentais melons. Or they can be mixed with peaches, fresh cherries and raspberries for a quick dessert. Steam mussels with a splash of Pineau, or use it in winter cakes and puddings to macerate dried fruits – in fact Pineau can begin or end a meal in any season.

Cognac, the region's most famous product, is the star attraction in the courtyard of the magnificent city hall. Outside the Cognac marquee, a pair of coopers heat and bend staves, forming the barrels so essential for the mellowing time *en tonneau*. These *tonneliers* work over a brazier of embers to heat the staves while water is splashed over them, thus making them pliable. The staves are then rapidly slipped into place within metal rings to form another new oak barrel. On Sunday, we watch a team of Cognac barrel-rollers running a unique slalom race, rolling barrels in and out of the trees along a boulevard – quite a sport!

Inside the brightly lit tent, the polished copper of an alambic distillery is to the left. A large bar is front and centre, and on the right, people are gathered around a table concentrating on something intriguing: a "sniff workshop". Step right up and test your olfactory talents: identify aromas of vanilla, tree bark, citrus, coffee, aromatic herbs and flowers. Can you distinguish between jasmine and honeysuckle? This gets very specific, but the point of the exercise is to refine one's capacity to sort out one aroma from the other. Using strips of paper dipped in essential oils, we tick the boxes on a worksheet as each is sniffed. One old Cognac might have the nose of one aroma, an aftertaste of another, but the same could apply to a fine

Poires aux Pineau / Pears poached in wine

A light dessert made with fruit from local orchards is spiced with star anise to ease the digestion of rich festive meals.

Ingredients

4 firm autumn pears, such as Duchesse d'Angoulême or Conférence

Juice of one lemon to keep fruit from browning

For the syrup:

340 ml/12 fl oz/1½ cups water

250ml/8fl oz/1 cup sugar

Spices: 1 cinnamon stick, ½ vanilla pod, 4 star anise

110 ml/4 fl oz / ½ cup Pineau de Charente (or Madeira)

1 lemon: zest peeled as spirals

Method

First make the syrup (this is best done a day ahead so that the spices infuse the syrup thoroughly): cook the water, sugar and spices together for 20 minutes, add the Pineau and simmer for 10 minutes more.

Halve, seed and peel pears and sprinkle with lemon juice to stop them turning brown. Poach the pears in the hot syrup for 10 to 15 minutes. Test with a knife; the pears should still be firm.

When done, lift the pears out carefully, cool them, then partially cover them with syrup and chill.

To serve, dish 2 pear halves (depending on their size) onto each plate and add a lemon spiral as garnish. Serve with a Pineau rosé.

chocolate or, of course, a wine. Moving along from this sensory-challenging activity, we skirt the Cognac bar with its impressive rack of suspended bottles and posters promoting *les apéros de cognac*: on ice, with mixers, fruit, juice, decorated with paper parasols.

Outside again we wander over to an area where two men are working steadily, shuffling flat white loaves in and out of domed bakers' ovens. A crowd is gathering to watch, to sample, and to buy hot *fouées*, soft puffed discs of bread that resemble large pitta rounds. The flour used in these hot puffed snacks can be bought from a nearby stand. We move on, discovering the region's staples. First, *mojette* beans, white and tender, are delicious just with parsley, sea salt and the Charente's fresh butter. Then, the butter itself, *beurre de Charente*, shipped to chefs across Europe, is sold by the kilo here, sliced off a *motte*, a tower of butter. Finally, fresh *tourteau fromagé*, a regional delicacy that is at its best here. The crusty, blackened (intentionally) dome hides a soft cake made with fresh goats' milk cheese and the *vendeuse* explains its name. "Its shape is like a crab although each area makes it a bit differently. Around Poitou or La Rochelle, it might be drier or crustier, for example." Standing on tip-toe, she hands me the packet of *tourteaux* over their display case, with a *"Bonne Journée"*.

The long, tree-lined boulevard of place New York links the city hall with Angoulême's ramparts. Stalls, grills roasting pork and lamb, and a menagerie of farm animals kept in wooden shelters stretch towards the other side of the city. Looking out from the *promenade des Remparts* over the neat, rolling fields, orchards and vineyards that contribute to the richesse of the Charente, I understand why the lords of times past battled to control this land, the *Angoumois*.

For chefs at their grills, vendors cutting samples and tasters trying to sort out multiple aromas, "discovery" sums up the movable feast *Gastronomades*. Five long tents in open squares and boulevards near the city hall make it a compact, walkable progression of *dégustations*. What will my nose discover next year? Scottish salmon, fruits from Trinidad or curries served by men in turbans may be in the international tent. But, on home ground, future gastronomic exploration could delve into the coastal riches of this rich western *terroir*. High season for *moules*, oysters and crab offers another gamut of flavours, in a region whose gastronomy appeals to *gastronomades* willing to sample the best of both land ... and sea.

Fête de St-Nicolas / St-Nicolas Fair

St-Nicolas de Port and Nancy/Meuse and Moselle, Lorraine

In a glittering city known for its sweets, *la saison des fêtes*, the holiday season opens in Lorraine on the Sunday closest to the sixth of December. The tradition of paying tribute to Saint Nicolas on the saint's feast day is a colourful event for children of all ages. Two cities share the celebration of this, the patron saint of Lorraine (as well as of school children and sailors), and each has its own special *fête*.

December's first *fête* is held in a port on the river Meurthe south of Nancy. The elegantly curved, slate-roofed twin spires of St-Nicolas-de-Port punctuate the dim December skyline over this small city. They have long served as a landmark for pilgrims. Through medieval times, pilgrimages to the reliquary of St-Nicolas, and fairs, attracted throngs to the city, which in the fifteenth century was larger than the nearby town of Nancy.

Entering St-Nicolas-de-Port, we pass a large, brick brewery that now houses the *Musée Français de la Brasserie*, a brewery museum. Then the streets become narrower, all leading to the distinctive white basilica. Today the church courtyard is filled with figures in peasant dress, hovering around a cauldron of hot cider. The mood is medieval and jocular: a juggler, an ever-moving figure in a velvet-patched harlequin suit keeps oranges whirling in the air. Women in long skirts (and braids as long as their skirts) and children in bright vests all add to the jumble of colour and motion that spills out into the street. A stout blonde woman, padded in layers of skirts, sweaters and shawls, ladles cups of hot cider for children gathering round a huge copper cauldron.

An arched passage across from the church is marked by flaming torches; inside, a small courtyard is filled to overflowing with artisans selling their wares. *Confitures*, including the preserved redcurrants

Clockwise from top left: the twin spires of St. Nicolas-de-Port; a typical restaurant in Nancy; place Stanislas, the symbol of Nancy.

called *Bar-le-Duc, mirabelle* golden plum preserves and other delicacies of Lorraine line the table of a *vendeuse* who is eager to talk. Her long brown hair is tucked under a red stocking cap, her animated manner that of one of Saint-Nick's elves. "Our *pain d'épice* made with *mirabelles* isn't really traditional, a true *pain d'épice* is made purely of honey and spices, an eggless cake. But, the *madeleines* **are** made with eggs," and she offers a sample of the rich oval cake that held Marcel Proust under its spell, the true *madeleine de Commercy*. The *pain d'épice* is moist, and I purchase loaves for gifts and *madeleines* "for the road", hoping that her perky spirit will be sustained through an afternoon that is rapidly turning wet. Sputtering flames of torches brighten the dim afternoon light as more arrows direct us into a long room lined with stalls of crafts. There are painted silk scarves, calligraphed poems, watercolours and stone sculptures, as well as wooden chess sets. The entire event would be brightened by a sunbeam, but the patient vendors are cheerful as customers pour in out of the misty afternoon.

Carved ridges line the portal of the church, the doorway into a vast, vaulted white space that seems brighter than the reality of the afternoon. I study the slender windows that stretch upward, ending in a rounded point under vaulted bays, each composed of a row of lancettes, sections of panes with a spear-pointed top form. Overhead, suspended by red ribbons over the centre aisle, a huge horizontal wreath of fir and holly wrapped in red velvet ribbon elegantly announces the advent season. Before we leave this luminous sanctuary, I catch a glimpse of the legendary golden hand reliquary before it is placed back in a dark, carved cabinet.

The large and small fairs that begin the parade of Christmas traditions are the icing on the cake of a weekend in Lorraine. The second *fête* we visit is in the larger city of Nancy. Here the shop windows are a treat in themselves at this time of year: *pâtisseries, confiseries, boulangeries*, even *charcutiers* display innumerable temptations. Once inside a *salon-de-thé*, it is easy to sample a forkful of golden plum tart (*tarte aux mirabelles*) or caramel cream puffs (*choux-au-caramel*) with a cup of tea or a *tisane*. Among the many attractions of this city is its festive approach to a season of sweets. *Bergamote de Nancy*, the leading lady in a cast of sweets, is a transparent golden square with a lightly citrus taste that sets it apart. Made only in Nancy, formed on a slab of marble, its unique ingredient is the essential oil of a citrus, the hard-skinned

Gâteau aux fruits et mirabelles / Festive fruit cake

This dried fruitcake can be made using the dried *mirabelles* and pears found in Nancy's *Marché du Noël*.

Ingredients

125 g/4 oz dried mirabelle plums (or dried cherries), pitted and quartered

125 g/4 oz dried pears, sliced in strips

125 g/4 oz sultanas, chopped

100 g/3½ oz whole almonds or filberts, toasted and chopped

80 ml/3 oz/5 tbsp rum or eau de vie

125 g/4 oz/ ½ cup butter

100 g/3½ oz/5 tbsp sugar

4 eggs

250 g/9 oz/1 cup plus 2 tbsp flour, sifted with 5g/1½ tsp baking powder

5ml/1 tsp nutmeg

Method

Soak the dried fruit in the rum overnight.

Preheat the oven to 180°C/350°F/Gas Mark 4.

Line a 28 cm x 13 cm/11 in x 5 in loaf tin with greaseproof paper, and grease the base, or use a buttered 25 cm/10 in bundt cake mould.

In a large bowl, cream the butter and sugar, then add the eggs one by one, mixing all the time. Fold in the flour, nutmeg, dried fruits and nuts.

Bake for about 45 minutes, until the top is springy to touch and a knife comes out clean. (Cover with cooking foil if it turns too dark while cooking.)

Let the cake cool on a rack, unmould, then wrap in foil. Douse with rum if desired at this stage.

This cake improves with time, so make it a week before you need it, and serve in thin slices with a glass of demi-sec Champagne or sparkling wine.

bergamote. Arguments over the origins of Bergamote de Nancy vary. Some say that they can be traced back to the time when the Dukes of Lorraine were also Dukes of Sicily (where the bergamot tree grows wild). Others suggest that a certain immigrant *confisier* began making them in the middle of the nineteenth century. Whatever the origin of this golden square, the people of Lorraine have long been known for having a sweet tooth: *bergamote* remains in their *patrimoine du goût*.

The symbol of Nancy, place Stanislas, was an eighteenth-century extravaganza of grandeur, dotted with balconies and refreshed by fountains. The genius behind this grand square, Stanislas the Magnificent, was the brother-in-law of King Louis XV. The Polish nobleman's taste left its mark on the city's architecture and parks, his public legacy. Place Stanislas glitters with a gigantic Christmas tree, brightly lit for St-Nicolas. We wait in the crowd for the evening's parade amidst children carried aloft on broad shoulders. Some are little over two years old, bundled up with caps tied tight against the cold night air. Finally the parade arrives, a *Grand Défilé* of brass bands, floats, a parade-within-a-parade of vintage cars, musicians and clowns. It is such an extensive production that it has re-runs in seven outlying towns during the following week. When the last *char* draws near, it is a glass bubble holding St Nicolas himself, a tall red *mitre* on his head, waving a white-gloved hand while his elves toss sweets to the crowd.

But it is not over. Brass bands lead on, circling the statuesque Christmas tree. Suddenly a fanfare is sounded, and as if by magic, the patron saint of Lorraine appears above the crowd, waving from a golden balcony. After the parade, we stop for a cup of hot chocolate in any of Nancy's many cafés and *salons-de-thé*, all decorated with festive boughs and berries. From the street, through frosty windows, I see pink cheeks and little chins dabbed with the hot chocolate that they have been waiting for, as sweet traditions continue.

Nancy's old iron-framed market hall is surrounded by rows of wooden stalls for the *Marché de Noël*. Inside, I'm lucky to find a vendor of dried fruit supplying dried *mirabelles*, the plum that looks more like a cherry. The *petite vendeuse* gives me lots of tips, pointing out that the perfect, dried halves of pears will go into the Alsatian holiday bread called *Berawecka*.

A pause for roasted chestnuts on the corner of splendid place Stanislas brings us back to the towering Christmas tree. Holding a cone of warm chestnuts as I review our *fête* and new flavours found in St-Nicolas-de-Port and Nancy, I see these events as variations on the many gastronomic themes we've explored across France. The specialities of Lorraine and the season are so much a part of the weekend's pleasures. There have been *dégustations* of jam made of golden *mirabelle* plums and *madeleines*. I'll bring home *Bar-le-Duc* preserves to garnish game and duck in winter meals. I've bitten into sugary *gaufre*, been instructed about *Berawecka* and *pain d'épice*, sampled leek tarts and *bergamotes* – a plenitude of delicacies. The Christmas season begins deliciously in Nancy, a city where one's fancy can easily be sweet.

Les Glorieuses / Fine Fowl of Bresse Fest

Louhans/Saône-et-Loire, eastern Burgundy

A morning at Louhan's fowl market attracts all ages.

A sunny field in the Bresse appears to be paradise for chickens. The fine fowl, prized by Europe's connoisseurs and chefs, is, essentially, a chicken allowed time and space to grow naturally. In this pastoral stretch of eastern France, they refer to "happy chickens", content fowl raised in the open air. The result of producers' great efforts is a stress-free fowl, and the ultimate flavour is delicious. *Les Glorieuses*, Bresse poultry for Christmas tables, are celebrated with a series of competitions and local festivities.

Before venturing to east-central France, some points on the map need to be circled to define just what and where the Bresse is. The long, narrow wooded and rocky wedge of eastern Burgundy that lies between the Jura mountains and the mighty river Saône is the northern portion of the Bresse. Its name is derived from a tenth-century reference to the humid region, *saltus Brexius*. Louhans (pronounced *Loo-ahn*) lies in the easternmost farmlands of *la Bresse bourguignonne*, forty kilometres north of the larger city, Bourg, which is the centre of the *Bresse savoyarde*. The entire region is threaded with an interlace of rivers that run mills and water farms from north to south, a region well suited to raising fowl. Bourg is the best-known city for poultry, but a number of other regional towns also raise chickens, turkeys, geese, and guinea fowl for *bonnes tables* around the world. What, then, sets Bresse fowl apart?

First, a choice must be made: three or four towns host the week of competitions, so one will be our focus. Bourg-en-Bresse lies at the southern point in the *Bresse savoyarde*, Montrevel is just northwest of Bourg, and Pont-de-Vaux lies above Mâcon closer to the river Saône. The capital of *Bresse bourguignonne*, Louhans, is at the northern tip of the triangle of towns involved in the annual festivities. Its Monday morning poultry market has drawn the attention of the National Culinary Institute, which awarded Louhans a *National Site of Taste* citation. The surrounding pastures and rough woodlands are typical of the rural Bresse landscape, renowned for its fowl, so this should be an exemplary *fête*, and it is our choice.

Rolling into this *terroir* east of Tournus, we pass flocks of white fowl strutting in open fields, and I notice that they all have dark feet – steely grey-blue feet that iden-

The glazed tiles of Louhan's church glisten in the sun.

tify the only breed of chicken that qualifies for the AOC label, *Poulet de Bresse*. The region is not a land of vast fields and rich soil – the small farms built of timber and brick are modest, and grand châteaux are rare. But, since 1862 when the first competition of fine fowl was held, concentration on raising fine poultry has been a success story. Now, about four hundred registered producers abide by the strict rules for *elevage* of *Poulet de Bresse*, celebrated for five days each December with the *Semaine des Glorieuses*, the week of glorious fowl.

Monday morning's weekly market in Louhans crowds the old streets with stalls and old friends meeting on street corners. The December air is still damp as I walk along the curving Grande Rue, a street of 157 arcades dating from the late-Middle Ages. Off to one side I notice the patterned tiles of the church rooftops, like a colourful cross-stitch of yellow, red and brown, shining in the morning sun. The market is a riot of winter hues and forms – the church square is packed with leafy vegetables, wonderful Burgundian cheeses, savoury Jura sausages, apples and pears. Leaving the stalls, I cross an avenue where *gendarmes* are directing traffic, and find myself in a very special-ized section of the market, for a morning among … fowl.

Louhans' *Marché aux Volailles* is held in a long open field bordered by tall trees, which on Mondays becomes an avenue of feathered crea-tures of all sorts and colours, destined for the cooking pot or chicken coop. In the spring, this *marché* resounds with peeping chicks and crowing roosters as farmers stock their flocks. Now, in December, fowl have been fattened and are ready for *les fêtes*. Elegant geese and plump ducks wait in tall wooden cages, poking their beaks out through dowel-bars that confine them on market day. There are spot-ted guinea fowl and a long row of rabbits, tables of eggs of all sizes with ivory or speckled shells, and turkeys – both white and black. Other than the Alsatian tradition of the Christmas goose, the turkey appears most often on French dinner tables at this time of year. Running a close second is the *chapon*, a very tender fowl that is avail-able only during the Christmas season in most regions. The *chapon*, a capon, is a rooster castrated at four months, raised free-range for eight months before ten weeks of "being lazy" as one producer described it – in confinement. A grain-fattened hen, a *poularde*, is also popular. The fowl are never overfed, as the distribution of the fat must be even.

I stop at a stall stocked with freshly dressed fowl, each enveloped in a white finely knit "sweater" to protect the delicate meat. My queries about these chickens with the blue feet bring a quick response from a busy *vendeuse*, who points to a plump example of the *race gauloise*. She explains: "They must be *race gauloise*, white with blue-grey feet, and the space calculated for each chicken on our farm must be no less than ten square metres, giving the birds lots of room to forage. Twice a day they're fed a mixture of wheat and maize; sometimes we mix it with milk, so after four months these *poulets* are ready for the table." Customers are pressing in, so she wraps up a fine, plump *poularde*, turns to me and adds: "This little beauty took six months

– a *chapon* takes eight!" The white knit covers that protect the dressed fowl are but one sign that they are authentic Bresse products. Each has a band on the left leg with the farmer's name and details, and a tricolour seal naming the slaughtering company and shipper. A sticker of the *Comité Interprofessionel de la Volaille de Bresse* is also required under these AOC regulations. At noon, wooden crates are slid into vans, doors slam shut and vendors pack up all traces of this *National Site of Taste* – until next Monday.

In Louhans, producers line their best fowl up with hundreds of others entered in the contest, in the *Concours de Volaille*. This is a high point of the poultry year: at 2.30pm the doors open and long tables in the cold *Halle de la Grenette* are covered with rows of white-cossetted fowl. Chefs from the region's *Logis de France* hotels, all in their white toques, preside at one end of the hall. They work over hotplates heating copper frying pans to prepare their specialities with a flourish: in a great whoosh of flames, a chicken is flambéed and the sauce is ladled over samples for the crowd. *Dégustations* range from *poulet* with a touch of tarragon or morel mushrooms, to chicken with crayfish or in a salt crust. I glance around, and realize I'm the only *non-producteur* sampling the little speared samples. By five o'clock the town is buzzing, the winners have been announced, and preparations for the *fête* dinner are under way.

The town's community centre on the *river* Seille is the setting for dinner, an evening specially prepared for Louhans' fowl producers by the regional chefs I watched earlier. Our table overlooks the stage, and soon a retired couple is seated with us. During dinner, the quality of Bresse fowl is again the subject and the veteran farmer expands on the theme: "The extra space and time allowed for a *Poulet de Bresse* to grow is well worth the effort. The secret," he almost whispers, "is in the subsoil, which gives nourishment and basic elements of flavour. They are healthy and strong, flavourful fowl ... *les poulets heureux* ..." Yes, happy chickens.

Following a tangy serving of a caper-layered *terrine de volaille au capres*, plates of delicious "little muffs", chicken wings in a wine sauce, arrive. To someone not familiar with the sleeve, *manchon*, the meaty upper wing of a duck or chicken, it is a tender mouthful with a distinctive texture. The band begins, and as we finish the delicate *manchon*, glasses of Beaujolais *primeur* are lifted for a toast ... to the *Poulet de Bresse*!

Suprême de volaille au safran / Chicken breasts in saffron sauce

Burgundy's rich variations on elegant fowl inspired this dish.

Ingredients

3 tbsp olive oil

4 plump chicken breasts, with their skin intact

For the sauce:

3 shallots, trimmed and sliced

3 carrots, peeled and cubed

1 medium leek, rinsed, trimmed, cut in 2.5cm/1in diagonal slices

Butter for cooking

250 ml/8 fl oz/1 cup dry white wine

250 ml/8 fl oz/1 cup white port

Sea salt, pepper, bay leaf, saffron to taste (1 tsp if fresh)

250 ml/8 fl oz/1 cup chicken stock

2 tsp cornflour in 1 tablespoon water

225 ml/7 oz/1 scant cup thick cream

To serve: 1 fresh tomato, peeled, seeded and diced

Method

Soften the vegetables, excluding 1 tbsp of shallots, in 1 tablespoon of butter, then add half of the white wine, the port, bay leaf and chicken stock and simmer for 1 hour.

Strain this stock into a saucepan, add the saffron threads and cook for a few minutes before thickening the liquid with the cornflour. Add salt or extra saffron to taste.

Finally, add 80ml/3fl oz/5 tablespoons of the cream, adjust the seasonings, and let it rest.

Preheat the oven to 200°C/400°F/Gas Mark 6.

Heat the oil in a frying pan and sear the chicken breasts until golden. Transfer to a baking dish, and season each with salt and pepper.

Sprinkle the reserved 1 tablespoon of shallots, the rest of the wine and 3 small knobs of butter on each. Cover with foil and bake for 20 minutes, basting occasionally.

Remove the chicken breasts and keep them warm while you warm up the sauce gently over a low heat. Whisk in 1 tablespoon butter, correct the seasoning and add the remaining cream at the last minute.

To serve, place the warm chicken breasts on hot plates, ladle the saffron sauce over and top with the diced tomato. Serve with steamed broccoli.

A fine white Pouilly-Fuissé is a fitting complement.

Across France
A summary of taste and terroir

When it is time to conclude this *tour de France* of gastronomic *fêtes*, and return home to the hills of Périgord, there are a number of lasting impressions to note and share with my fellow travellers and *gastrono-mades*. *Fêtes* and *foires* in all regions of France have been in turn amusing, puzzling and delightful. For the most part, the encounters and adventures have been positive, and surprise forays into sheepdog trials or chestnut groves were unexpected bonuses. From the heavy winter scent of truffles to the nuances of flavour in a *Poulet de Bresse*, I have explored the aromas and flavours that lovers of French cuisine hold dear. It has been a personal quest for the authentic, inevitably leading to the *terroir*, the all-encompassing combination of soil, seed, air, water, nourishment and climate.

Artisans du goût, French cheesemakers, biscuit bakers and salt rakers have been of one voice in their concern about their *terroir*, echoing this triad: best flavour, distinct aromas, purest quality. These themes are heard across the *hexagone* in exchanges with producers in all corners of France. I hope that the honey vendor in Montauban will pursue his efforts to make pure honey, and that the cheese and wine producers in Angoulême will continue to produce their award-winning *chabichou* and Pineau de Charentes. Prize medallions of gold, silver or bronze on their bottles of wine or tins of *foie gras* point to these producers' consistent efforts, both in competition and in bring-ing their region's best flavours to markets and fairs.

Traçabilité, a word linked to quality, is a word that reverberates in conversations at many *foires*. There is concern about tracking a batch of cheese in the Loire, a bottle of wine in Vacqueyras or a chicken in the Bresse: trackability. Its relevance is clear at both ends of the

spectrum, as the wine is made and each *cuve* is coded, the wine blended, aged, the trackable bottles corked (corks must be trackable, too), labelled with their number and/or code. The bottle arrives at our table for dinner, and if it is sent back the restaurant must trace it to the vintner, the year, the barrel, the cork-source and the bottle factory. The young chef in Burgundy who said, "We want to know where our chickens come from," summed up *traçabilité*. This signal goes back to the chicken farmer we spoke with in the Bresse market. It is a circle intent on quality in all phases, and obviously involves the diner. In the same exchange, the subject of appreciation was voiced: "If we go to great lengths to assure quality at the table, does the diner appreciate it? I sometimes wonder, and would like to know when they do!" Feedback on quality, to the chef or producer, is clearly encouraging.

The national passion for flavour is in revival. *La Patrimoine du Goût*, the heritage of taste, is being given more attention in schools and in the French press. What signs are flashing in the kitchens and markets of this taste-conscious land that flavour is worth working for, worth paying for? First, the re-sensitizing of tastebuds — not an easy task — is one goal of the annual *Semaine du Goût*. For one week in mid-October, a nationwide campaign focuses on flavour. This effort has spread rapidly since its inception in 1990 near Paris. Coordinated programmes in school lunches introduce new flavours and concentrate on discoveries as well as discriminating tastes and scents.

Tastings offered in bakeries and *épiceries* involve entire communities. One example of a successful adaptation of the *Semaine du Goût* theme has been organized in the Provence-Alpes Côtes d'Azur. A *Centre Régional du Goût et des Terroirs* coordinates programmes with the co-operation of regional groups of culinary professionals. Cooking classes, tasting workshops, special exhibitions and meet-the-artisan sessions are lined up in all parts of France. Chefs' involvement rises out of professional interest as well as real concern: 65 per cent of the French population didn't know what mayonnaise was made of, according to a poll taken before one *Semaine du Goût* in the mid-1990s. It is not so shocking when we remember our conversation with the worried fish merchant in Dieppe who said: "Children don't know what a fish looks like any more!"

Site Remarquable du Goût, a round seal or sign in red with a blue border, is a symbol created by the *Conseil National des Arts Culinaires*

(CNAC). There are now over one hundred such markers on sites that produce everything from beer to beef, and from oysters to watercress. Choices are made by a council formed by the ministries of Agriculture, Education and Health, with input also from the Tourism and Culture ministries. Founded in 1989, the *CNAC* is involved in scientific, cultural and economic aspects of French gastronomy. Markets and fairs, such as Louhans' fowl market and Saulieu's *Fête du Charolais*, are in the council's listings for Remarkable Sites of Taste.

Reviewing *fêtes* and *foires*, there are some with a serious nature, but most have been lighthearted affairs. Local *confréries* clearly play an important part in these dynamics, as they have in supporting their trade and community through the ages, for a successful event that all will enjoy. The accompanying cast of volunteers often numbers into the hundreds for the smallest fair, and their spirit is contagious, drawing in more to participate.

Over the decades, some fairs lose their focus. The original product is left on the fringe while unrelated activities prevail. This appeared to be the case in Arpajon's Bean Fair, which seemed to keep the local *haricot* bean only as the fair's symbol. Apart from an agricultural exhibition, the event now has little to do with this staple of French cuisine. When an event grows too large, success carries its own hazards in problems with managing crowds and parking at a distance. Shuttle buses are arranged and parking areas are enlarged. As hundreds of thousands of visitors arrive, the *foire* loses a degree of identity as a local festivity about a special product.

The list of food and wine *fêtes* and *foires* grows each year, with every season and time of harvest. Whether it is a small village *kermesse*, like the Black Cherry Fête in Ixtassou, or a grand salon attracting thousands to Colmar's *Festiga* in February, each has its own set of delights. Young *fêtes*, such as Aurillac's Snack Fest, will grow, and more innovative and amusing *foires* will follow. There will be more olives to be tasted in the Midi, variations on autumn *pâtés* to be tried with the *millésime's* white wine in Alsatian *foires*, cheeses in new shapes, and sweets revived from great-grandmother's day, all to be sampled in the ambience of celebration. The flavours of regional traditions will flourish through the new millennium, shaped and brought to the *fête* with pride, for the pleasure of tasting.

Map of France

ENGLISH CHANNEL

Dieppe

PARIS

Coulommiers

Nancy STRASBOURG

Arpajon

Krautergersheim

...lieu-sur-Oudon

Seine

Munster

Loire

DIJON

...TES

Saulieu

Louhans

St·Pourçain

LYON

Angoulême

Varaignes

MASSIF

Rhône

Pauillac

Aubazine

CENTRAL

ALPES

Brive-la-Gaillarde

Aurillac

Beaulieu-sur-Dordogne

...RDEAUX

Le Buisson

Villefranche-du-Périgord

Nyons

Duravel/Castelnau-

St·Paul·Trois·Châteaux

Vacqueyras

Montratier

NICE

...gues-sur-Ourbise

Montauban

Uzès

Banon

Beaumont-de-Lomagne

NÎMES

Cavaillon

Valbonne

Bayonne

TOULOUSE

Espelette

PYRÉNÉES

Céret

MEDITERRANEAN SEA

Gazetteer

When the curious gastronome takes to the road, the following pointers will help find selected *fêtes* and *foires*. Use general map Michelin 989, and regional Michelin maps. Use up-to-date road maps, as new roads are completed each year and journey lengths are constantly becoming shorter. The closest large town is given in bold to assist the map-reader in "Getting there".

The author cannot guarantee quality of services or products listed. Owners, chefs and telephone numbers may change. Consult the Office de Tourisme in the nearest town for up-to-date information. It is advisable to make reservations at the hotels and restaurants. To telephone from outside France, drop the first zero and replace with access code 33.

JANUARY

BRIVE-LA-GAILLARDE/FOIRE DES ROIS

Getting there
Michelin map 75

Take highway D60 from **Sarlat** or the N89 from Clermont-Ferrand, following the road around Brive and into Brive centre, where underground parking is available near the market place and city centre. Brive is a major rail centre, so train connections are available from Clermont-Ferrand.

Where to stay

Le Chapon Fin, 1 pl. de Lattre de Tassigny. Tel: 05 57 74 23 40.

Where to eat

Lunch in the unique ambiance of **Chez Francis** offers a chance to catch one's breath after the hustle and bustle of market place crowds. Originality and perfection in chef Francis' cuisine are just two reasons to find a table here, seated amidst an amazing collection of posters, paraphernalia and lamps from the early twentieth century. **Chez Francis**, 61 av. de Paris. Tel: 05 55 74 41 72.

Discoveries

Any tools a cook may need can be found at **Bonino**, *quincaillerie par excellence*, a hardware store for serious cooks at 9 av. de Paris, near Brive's market place. For history buffs, a museum of archaeology and popular traditions is found in a fine sixteenth-century palace, the **Musée Labenche**. The museum follows the history of the region and houses a fine collection of costumes, kitchen paraphernalia, farm tools and textile equipment.

Office de Tourisme, pl. du 14-Juillet, 19100 Brive-la-Gaillarde. Tel: 05 55 24 08 80.

UZÈS/JOURNÉE DE LA TRUFFE

Getting there
Michelin map 80

Take the D979 north from **Nîmes**, the D981 southeast from Alès, or the D981 northwest from Avignon.

Where to stay	Facing the Cathedral of St-Théodore in the heart of medieval Uzès, **Hôtel du Général d'Entraigues** welcomes guests into a fifteenth-century home, *un ancien hôtel particulier*, renovated with nineteen antique-furnished rooms. **Hôtel du Général d'Entraigues**, 8 rue de la Calade, pl. de l'Évêché. Tel: 04 66 22 32 68.
Where to eat	The **Jardins de Castille**, an elegantly appointed restaurant in the vaulted entry level of the Hôtel du Général d'Entraigues (see above), offers superb cuisine. On Sunday, a truffle-infused "Tasting Menu" requires advance reservation. There is a good choice of brasseries and restaurants in old Uzès.
	Office de Tourisme, Chapelle des Capucins, 30700 Uzès. Tel: 04 66 22 68 88.

VALBONNE/FÊTE DE ST-BLAISE ET DU RAISIN

Getting there Michelin map 245	North of Cannes, take the N85 route around **Mougins** towards **Grasse** and turn east toward Plascassier, onto the D4 to Valbonne. Be careful as the roads are very winding.
Where to stay	Just 3 kms (2 miles) outside Valbonne, on the route to Grasse, **Relais de Sartoux** is a reasonable and convenient hotel. Tel: 04 93 60 10 57. Alternatively, a discreet, chic hotel in Valbonne's old arcades is **Les Armories**. Tel: 04 93 12 90 90.
Where to eat	Although freshly painted, the old beams and stones are still intact and flavoursome adventures can be found in the elegant, intimate bistrot **Lou Cigalon**, 4 blvd Carnot. Tel: 04 9312 27 07.
Discoveries	Visit **Le Domaine de Manon** for refreshing scents, rose soaps and jasmin sweets from the family of Hubert Biancalana, 36 chemin du Servan, Plascassier, 06130 Grasse. Tel: 04 93 6012 76.
	Office de Tourisme, 11 av. St-Roch, 06560 Valbonne/Sophia Antipolis. Tel: 04 93 12 34 50.

FEBRUARY

NYONS/L'ALICOQUE, FÊTE DE L'HUILE NOUVELLE

Getting there Michelin map 81	Take the D976 off the N7 north of **Orange** and then the D94 to Nyons. Or take the TGV from Paris to Avignon and then a regional bus to Nyons.
Where to stay	Hotels in the Drôme Provençale tend to be expensive, but the **Caravelle** on rue Antignans with access from the *quai* has reasonably priced rooms. Reserve in advance during *l'Alicoque*. Tel: 04 75 26 07 44.
Where to eat	For fine dining in a cosy, historic setting reserve a Provençal table in a tiny restaurant in the oldest corner of Nyons – **Le Petit Caveau**, at 9 rue Victor-Hugo, is set in a renovated fourteenth-century stable. Tel: 04 75 26 20 21.

Discoveries   Market day in Nyons is Thursday (morning only). A visual feast, full of temptations for the cook, the market is a good source of olive-wood bowls, spoons, spatulas and salad servers. Park along the river and walk through old Nyons to the arcaded market place.

Office de Tourisme, pl. Libération, 26110 Nyons.
Tel: 04 75 26 10 35. For information about olive products contact *Comité économique agricole de l'olivier*. Tel: 04 42 23 01 92.

CARESTIEMBLE / ST-BRANDAN/FÊTE DU PAIN CHAUD

Getting there
Michelin map 59   From St-Brieuc, on the Channel coast, take highway D700 south and drive for about 15 kms (10 miles) to Quintin. Continue south from Quintin but on the D7 towards Loudéac. After driving under the D790 overpass, turn right to Carestiemble. **St-Brandan**, southeast of Quintin on the D22, is the closest large village to Carestiemble.

Where to stay   Tiny Carestiemble is close to Quintin – a "Breton City of Character". A reasonable place to stay, and just across an old cobbled street from a bakery, is **Hôtel du Commerce**, 2 rue Rocheronen, 22800 Quintin. Tel: 02 96 74 94 67.

Where to eat   In Quintin, restaurant **La Vallée**, 12 Rue Vallée, tel: 02 96 74 80 99, is popular. **Le Commerce** restaurant (see above) has more formal menus featuring Breton specialities, but is closed on Sunday night and Monday.

Discoveries   A weekend in this rolling, wooded corner of Brittany allows time to discover two of Brittany's "Cities of Character", **Quintin** and **Moncontour**. Within their old stone walls, history and gastronomy go hand in hand. Make sure you taste the local cider: Val de Rance, Cru Breton or Cidre Bouché Brut.

Office du Tourisme, 6 pl. 1830, 22800 Quintin. Tel: 02 96 74 01 51.
Tues.–Sat., 9.00 a.m.–12 noon, 2.00–5.30 p.m. Limited hours in winter.

ST-POURÇAIN-SUR-SIOULE/FOIRE AUX VINS D'ALLIER

Getting there
Michelin map 238   Michelin map 238. From Clermont Ferrand or **Riom**, take the N9 highway. From Montluçon, drive east on the N145/E62 to Montmarault, then on route D6 to St-Pourçain.

Where to stay   **Hôtel Chêne Vert**, blvd Ledru-Rollin, located between the church and the river, is central and reasonable. Tel: 04 70 45 40 65. Try their *Menu du Terroir* to sample specialities of Bourbonnais and Auvergne.

Where to eat   Besides the restaurant **Chêne Vert** (see above), auberge and brasserie meals are good options. For a meal-in-itself try *salade composée* – layers of local hams and cheeses on or under several crunchy winter varieties of lettuce.

Discoveries   A mustard mill with its grindstone, a soap-maker, and a nineteenth-century market hall lie just south of St-Pourçain in the medieval village of **Charroux**.

To see the village museum (open by appointment) contact Mairie de Charroux, 03140. Tel: 04 70 56 81 65.

Office de Tourisme, 13 pl. Maréchal-Foch, 03500 St-Pourçain-sur-Sioule. Tel: 04 70 45 32 73.

MARCH

LE BUISSON/FOIRE DU PRINTEMPS ET AUX BESTIAUX

Getting there
Michelin map 75

Drive east from **Bergerac** towards Sarlat on the D660, cross the Dordogne at Lalinde and continue on the D29 to Le Buisson-de-Cadouin.

Where to stay

Drive through Le Buisson on the route de Siorac, enter the gates of **Manoir de Bellerive**. Relax in this nineteenth-century home, and dine in its restaurant, truly *une bonne table*, 24480 Le Buisson-de-Cadouin. Tel: 05 53 22 16 16.

Where to eat

The cosy restaurant **L'Abbeye** faces Cadouin's historic abbey and serves hearty lunches from 12 noon–1.45 p.m. Tel: 05 53 63 40 93.

Discoveries

Find a well-structured red from winemakers Bruno and Dominique Fauconnier at **Château La Tilleraie** – among the best of the *Pécharmant* in the Bergerac *vignoble*. Tel: 05 53 57 86 42.

Office de Tourisme, pl. General de Gaulle, 24480 Le Buisson-de-Cadouin. Tel: 05 53 22 06 09.

COULOMMIERS/FOIRE INTERNATIONALE AUX FROMAGES ET AUX VINS

Getting there
Michelin map 237

Coulommiers is east of Paris. Take route A4 to exit 16, onto route N34, then drive 17 kms (11 miles) to Coulommiers.

Where to stay

Le Bois Frais is in a large *maison de maître* just as you enter the town; meals can be arranged. **Le Bois Frais**, 32 av. des Alliés, 77320 La Ferté-Gaucher. Tel: 01 64 20 27 24. From Coulommiers, follow route N34 east to La Ferté-Gaucher.

Where to eat

At the fair there are lots of good snacks available, such as cheese *ravioles de Royan*, *crêpes* and cider, cheese pastries and quiches. For dinner, venture out to a *Pays Briard* village. Head northeast to **Bellot**, to **L'Assiette Gourmande**, tel: 01 64 65 90 79, for a taste of the country: beef simmered in cider, and superb desserts served in a setting facing one of the Brie region's loveliest old churches.

Discoveries

Pâtisserie **Thireau**, at 40 rue Bertrand-Flornoy, offers endless temptations and speciality breads to enjoy with a slice of Brie. Look for boulangeries **Fiacre**, 2 rue Formoy, and **Mouilleron**, 8 pl. Marché, for crusty traditional breads. In **Coulommiers**' place du Marché, find **Fromagerie Lauxerrois**, one of the best cheese shops in the Paris region.

Office de Tourisme, 11 rue Général-de-Gaulle, 77120 Coulommiers. Tel: 01 64 03 88 09.

BAYONNE/FOIRE AU JAMBON DE BAYONNE

Getting there
Michelin map 989

From **Bordeaux**, follow route N250 south towards Arcachon, but do not leave at exit 22, instead keep going south (toward Dax) on the N10 and continue to Bayonne, exiting at the sign for "Bayonne centre".

Where to stay

Tulips bloom on the boulevard in front of the **Grand Hôtel**, 21 rue Thiers, 64100 Bayonne. Tel: 05 59 59 62 00.

Where to eat

For a hearty market-day lunch on the spot, stop in at the **Bar du Marché**, 39 rue des Basques, tel: 05 59 59 22 66. For fine dining, reserve a table at the restaurant of chef **François Miura**, who innovates while holding on to Basque traditions, 24 rue Marengo, tel: 05 59 59 49 89.

Discoveries

Bayonne has been a major chocolate centre for centuries. Sample fine cocoa and chocolates in **Chocolatier Daranatz**, 15 arceaux du Port-Neuf. Tel: 05 59 59 03 55.

Office de Tourisme, pl. des Basques, 64100 Bayonne. Tel: 05 59 46 01 46.

APRIL

SARZEAU/FÊTE DE L'HUÎTRE

Getting there
Michelin map 63

Sarzeau is in the middle of the Rhys peninsula on the southern edge of the Gulf of Morbihan. From **Nantes**, take the N165 through Pontchâteau heading northwest. Just past Muzillac take the D20 exit to Sarzeau, a scenic route. Coming from **Vannes**, the centre of the Morbihan *département*, take the N165 heading southeast, before taking the exit to Sarzeau just past St. Léonard onto the D780.

Where to stay

Straight through **Penvins**, out of Sarzeau on the D198, follow the road to the sea, and to **Hôtel Le Mur du Roy** (the hotel is marked from the road), a small family hotel with excellent cuisine. Chef-owner M. Obellianne may divulge some cooking tips! Tel: 02 97 67 34 08.

Where to eat

One of several *crêperies* in **Sarzeau** is the **Rose des Vents**, 5 rue St. Vincent, which is a local favourite for *galettes* with seafood fillings. Tel: 02 97 41 93 77.

Discoveries

Salty sweets? The Bretons love their salted butter, and it even turns up in chocolates! Look out for *"Tas de Sel"*, a small drop of almond paste, *ganache* and caramel, coated in white chocolate and sprinkled with salt crystals, which is a speciality of **Chocolaterie Guisabel**, 49440 Cande. Tel: 02 41 92 74 11.

Office de Tourisme, pl. des Trinitaires, 56370 Sarzeau. Tel: 02 97 41 82 37.

FARGUES-SUR-OURBISE/FÊTE DE L'ASPERGE

Getting there
Michelin map 79

From **Agen** or the A62 Bordeaux-Toulouse tollway, take the D119 and after 31 kms (20 miles), head south at Feugarolles on the D930 through Lavardac.

At Barbaste turn onto the D655 and follow it for 14 km (8 miles) to **Fargues** (towards Casteljaloux).

Where to stay

Closest, and cosy, is the **Auberge des Quatre-Vents** (southeast of Aiguillon), 47190 Lagarrigue. Tel: 05 59 29 92 18.

Where to eat

Within the *foire*, buy a lunch ticket. Sausage sandwiches, apples and pastries are also available.

Discoveries

For asparagus, violet and white, or Buzet wines, red and white, contact M. Cugnière, 47230 Pompiey. For *biologiques*/organic asparagus, north of Fargues off the D20, contact Michel Barat, "Bentémil", 47700 Anzex.
Tel: 05 53 93 04 42.

Mairie, 47700 Fargues-sur-Ourbise, or contact M. Cugnière (see above).

AUBAZINE/FÊTE DE LA CHÈVRE

Getting there
Michelin map 239

Coming from **Tulle** on the N89, take a left turn to Vergonzac and Aubazine, halfway between Tulle and Brive-la-Gaillarde.

Where to stay
and eat

Above Aubazine (on route D48 uphill 2 km [1 mile]), the small family-run restaurant and hotel **Saut de la Bergère** offers hospitable bed and board and is reasonably priced. Menus reflect the *saveurs du terroir* and the seasons. Try the Limousin veal and *Poire charlotte maison*. Tel: 05 55 25 74 09.

Discoveries

M. Charageat's charming bakery, **Au Bon Pain d'Autrefois,** features nut breads, rye and *pain de campagne*. To place orders for bread and for details on the goat fair. Tel: 05 55 25 71 11.

Syndicat d'Initiative, 19190 Aubazine. Tel: 05 55 25 79 93.

MAY

PAUILLAC/FÊTE DE L'AGNEAU

Getting there
Michelin map 71

Pauillac is 50 km (31 miles) north of **Bordeaux.** Coming from Bordeaux take D2 (exit 7 from the A630/E5's northern edge), or take the ferry from **Blaye**. There are two morning ferry crossings. Schedules change, so check times in advance and arrive in good time, as a queue forms an hour before the ferry departs.

Where to stay

Hôtel France & Angleterre, 3 quai A. Pichon, tel: 05 56 59 01 20. Quiet and private, the hotel is centrally located facing the estuary boulevard.

Where to eat

L'Agneau à Table is a meal served under tents during the *fête*. Start with a snappy fish soup garnished with croutons and grated cheese, then the featured tender Pauillac lamb with haricot beans, followed by cheese, and finally a refreshing sorbet in a cup of fruit compote. Several brasseries are other options.

Discoveries

To buy fresh Pauillac lamb visit M. **Bernard Ardouin**'s butcher shop/stall in the market hall, which is open on Sunday morning during the fair. He provides advice along with your choice cut of meat, and will even advise on roasting an entire lamb for a *méchoui*! (Order well in advance.) Tel: 05 56 59 07 16.

Maison du Tourisme, La Verrerie, 33250 Pauillac. Tel: 05 56 59 03 08.

BEAULIEU-SUR-DORDOGNE/FÊTE DE LA FRAISE

Getting there
Michelin map 239

From **Tulle**, take the scenic route south on the D940, or take the D703 from Sarlat.

Where to stay

Reserve a room in the small **Hôtel Le Turenne**, 19120 Beaulieu-sur-Dordogne. Tel: 05 55 91 10 16.

Where to eat

Hôtel Le Turenne, an old abbey on the square, is a fitting place to dine in historic surroundings (see above).

Office de Tourisme, pl. Marbot, 19120 Beaulieu-sur-Dordogne. Tel: 05 55 91 09 94.

CÉRET/FÊTE DE LA CERISE

Getting there
Michelin map 86

Drive south from **Perpignan** on the N9. At Le Boulou take the D115 to Céret.

Where to stay

Hôtel **Les Arcades** is simple, central and clean. Don't miss their collection of vintage, signed twentieth-century posters. 1 pl. Picasso, tel: 04 68 87 12 30.

Where to eat

In the Place des Neuf-Jets it is hard to choose between restaurants. During the weekend why not try all three? Reserve in advance for Saturday evening.

Office de Tourisme, 1 av. Clemenceau, 66400 Céret. Tel: 04 68 87 00 56.

JUNE

ST-PAUL-TROIS-CHÂTEAUX/FÊTE GOURMANDE

Getting there
Michelin map 81

St-Paul-Trois-Châteaux is in the Rhône Valley between **Orange** and **Montélimar**. Take exit 19 to Bollène, north of Orange on the N7 or the A7 motorway. From Bollène, drive north on the D458, turning off to St-Paul on the D71.

Where to stay

The **Ferme St-Michel**, 26130 Solerieux, tel: 04 75 98 10 66, is on the D71 southeast of St-Paul-Trois-Châteaux. This hotel, hidden down a shady lane, is in a grand old manor house and is a lovely refuge whatever the season. The stonework and stairways inside are original; rooms are spacious and well appointed; and there is a cosy bar. Take a dip in the secluded pool before dinner. Weather permitting, breakfasts and dinners are served in the courtyard.

Where to eat	Busy bar-cafés and pizzerias line the streets of town. Excellent Provençal cuisine is served at the **Ferme St-Michel** in the courtyard under the stars.
Discoveries	For Côteaux-du-Tricastin and Côtes-du-Rhône wines visit M. P. Daniel, Château la Croix Chabrière, route St-Restitut, 84500 Bollène. Tel: 04 90 40 00 89.

Office de Tourisme, rue République, 26130 St-Paul-Trois-Châteaux. Tel: 04 75 96 61 29. |

BANON/FÊTE DU FROMAGE

Getting there Michelin map 81	From **Apt** take the D22 then the D51 into Banon and drive 33 kms (21 miles) up into the hills. Montsalier is on this route.
Where to stay	In a hamlet near Banon, travellers find comfortable rooms with private bathrooms in a Bed & Breakfast run by Karolyn Kauntze, a petite, multi-lingual Englishwoman. Reserve well in advance. **Montsalier**, 04150 Banon. Tel: 04 92 73 23 61.
Where to eat	During the cheese fair, the **Hôtel des Voyageurs** composes a delicious menu for Sunday diners featuring *chèvre* cheese in every course. Reserve a table, and a room if you wish to stay in Banon on the square. Tel: 04 92 73 21 02.
Discoveries	A bright red awning facing the centre of Banon announces **Chez Melchio**. In this little *épicerie*, strings of long thin sausages are looped like a bead curtain for an epicurian stage, along with herbs, spices, and many shapes of *chèvre*. Local honey and sweets are stacked alongside basic foods.

Syndicat d'Initiative, pl. de la République, 04150 Banon. Tel: 04 92 73 2102. |

AURILLAC/FESTIVAL DU CASSE-CROÛTE ET DES GOUDOTS GOURMANDS

Getting there Michelin map 239	Take the N120 southeast from **Tulle** through Argentat; or from Figeac in the Lot, follow the N122 northeast.
Where to stay	Close to Aurillac's centre is **Hôtel la Thomasse**, a Logis de France Hotel, 28 rue Docteur-Mallet. Tel: 04 71 48 26 47.
Where to eat	Grilled beef sandwiches with Roquefort sauce, sausages, *aligot* by the plate or tub, savoury and sweet pastries, apple juice, beer and regional wines can all be purchased and enjoyed at the *fête*. If you still have an appetite for dinner, reserve a table at **Reine Margot**, 19 rue Guy de Veyre, tel: 04 71 48 26 46.
Discoveries	Flower vendors fill the *place* in front of Aurillac's imposing Hôtel de Ville (City Hall), lining the walk to an animated Saturday morning market, where plants and products from the region can be found inside the hall. Look for massive boulder-size Cantal and Salers cheeses from *crèmerie* stall of F. Courbouleix.

Office de Tourisme, Le Bourg, 15000 Aurillac. Tel: 04 71 48 46 58. |

JULY

CAVAILLON/FOIRE AUX MELONS

Getting there
Michelin map 81

From **Avignon**, follow the N7 southeast towards Marseille, or take the A7 south from Orange. From Arles, take the scenic back road, the D99, from St-Rémy-de-Provence.

Where to stay

During this country *fête*, explore the sun-washed Luberon from **Le Mas du Souléou**, 5 chemin St-Pierre-des-Essieux, 84300 Cavaillon. Tel: 04 90 71 43 22. Reserve well in advance, as the hosts, Nadine and François Lepaul, have just four rooms. Breakfast is served by the pool.

Where to eat

Walk through the heavy door of the restaurant and up the stairs to enter the elegance of days gone by. **Fin de Siècle** is an ideal *bonne table* to sample Provençal specialities. Next door is their *brasserie* at 46 pl. du Clos. Tel: 04 90 71 12 27.

For fine dining, reserve a table at the exclusive **Restaurant Prévot**, 353 av. de Verdun, tel: 04 90 71 32 43, which is known for its innovative cooking with melons.

Discoveries

For the full gamut of melon delights, the **Hédiard** shop facing pl. du Clos is a shopper's delight. Shelves are lined with melon preserves and jams, delicate and sweet fruit paste, and melon liqueurs.

Office de Tourisme, pl. François-Tourel, 84305 Cavaillon. Tel: 04 90 71 32 01.

VACQUEYRAS/FESTIVAL DES CRUS DE LA VALLÉE DU RHÔNE

Getting there
Michelin map 81

From **Orange**, follow route N7, then the D960 toward Carpentras. At Sarrians turn onto the D52 north to Vacqueyras.

Where to stay

Hôtel Montmirail, 84190 **Vacqueyras**, tel: 04 9065 84 01, is 2 kms (1 mile) out of town towards the Dentelles.

Where to eat

Surrounded by vineyards, the restaurant at **Domaine de la Ponche** (also has rooms), outside Vacqueyras on the Route to Bollène, is a local favourite with wine-makers. Tel: 04 90 65 85 21. For a summer lunch prepared with élan and imagination, a 3 km (2 mile) drive to Gigondas for lunch or dinner at **L'Oustalet** is a pleasure; all desserts and breads are baked in their kitchen. At sundown, the view over the vineyards from the *mairie* on **Gigondas**, pl. Portail, is spectacular. Reserve a table on the terrace, tel: 04 90 65 85 30. If truffles of Provence interest you, ask about their winter cooking class.

Discoveries

To order wines from the region, contact Geneviève Henri, Caveau des Dentelles de Montmirail, pl. de l'Église, 84190 Vacqueyras. Tel: 04 90 65 86 62.

Vacqueyras' *fête* Director, Mme. Bouteiller. Tel: 04 90 65 86 72.

BEAUMONT DE LOMAGNE/L'AIL EN FÊTE

Getting there
Michelin map 235

Take the D928 southwest of **Montauban**, or drive north from **Toulouse** on the D18 from Blagnac to Beaumont-de-Lomagne.

Where to stay

At **L'Arbre d'Or**, 16 rue Despeyrous, 82500 Beaumont-de-Lomagne, an English couple welcome bed and breakfast guests to their seventeenth-century home. Mrs Ellard prepares meals for guests (only), using products in season. Tel: 05 63 65 32 34.

Where to eat

Auberge de la Gimone, on av. du Lac, is a duck specialist.
Tel: 05 63 65 23 09.

Discoveries

For decorated garlic braids and clusters contact Mme Patrick Martignon, on blvd de Verdun. Tel: 05 63 65 31 23.

Office de Tourisme, 3 rue Fermat, 82500 Beaumont-de-Lomagne.
Tel: 05 63 02 42 32.

AUGUST

BEAULIEU-SUR-OUDON/FÊTE DE LA MOISSON

Getting there
Michelin map 232

Halfway between **Laval** and **Vitré,** east of Rennes, take the very straight D32 south to Laval to find **Beaulieu-sur-Oudon,** which is north east of St-Poix. Driving from Laval, take the N157 towards Rennes, but turn south at either St-Berthevin or **Loiron** (on the D124) to the D32, then turn right after Montjean to Beaulieu-sur-Oudon.

Where to stay

The attractive, historic city of **Laval,** on the river Mayenne, about thirty minutes' drive from the Harvest Festival, serves as a good base. Quiet, centrally located **Hôtel de Paris** at 22 rue de la Paix offers city comforts. Tel: 02 43 53 76 20. There are no cafés or hotels in Beaulieu-sur-Oudon.

Where to eat

While in Laval, enjoy one of the finest tables in the north. The **Bistro de Paris** is altitudes above any run-of-the-mill bistro, and is a short walk from the river Mayenne at 67 rue du Val de Mayenne, in Laval's picturesque old quarter. Reserve ahead. Tel: 02 43 56 98 29.

Mairie, 53320 Beaulieu-sur-Oudon, tel: 02 43 02 11 40.
For information on flour mills: *fédération française des amis des moulins,*
5 rue Villiot, 75012 Paris. Minitel: 3615 Moulinsinfo.

DURAVEL/FOIRES AUX VINS

Getting there
Michelin map 79

Follow the Lot river's path along route D911 from **Cahors** west towards **Villeneuve-sur-Lot**, and Duravel is just west of **Puy-l'Évêque**. Drive south from **Sarlat** through Gourdon on scenic route D673 to Montcabrier then turn south onto the D58 to Duravel. Locate **Castelnau-Montratier** following the N20 south of Cahors, then turn south onto the D19 for 12 kms (7 miles).

Where to stay   Southwest of Duravel drive 7 kms (4 miles) on the D911 (turn to **Touzac**) to discover one of the valley's most charming retreats for summer-weary travellers. The medieval **Moulin de Leygues**, restored with great care, houses the very hospitable **Hôtel La Source Bleue** and its restaurant, **La Source Enchantée**. Tel: 05 65 36 52 01.

Where to eat   While in this corner of the Lot, spend an evening dining under the stars. In the village of **St-Médard** near **Catus**, **Le Gindreau** star-chef Alexis Pelissou orchestrates refined traditional cuisine of Quercy in an elegantly restored village school. Tel: 05 65 36 22 27. Located east of Duravel, follow the D911 to the point where it meets the D660, and drive northeast on the D5 towards St Médard for 7 kms (4 miles) from that intersection.

Discoveries   For Cahors wines, visit Château Laur, run by Patrick Laur, 46700 Floressas. Tel: 05 65 31 95 64.

Office de Tourisme, Le Bourg, 46700 Duravel. Tel: 05 65 24 65 50. Castelnau-Montratier *Fête des Vins* chairman: Pierre Belon, 82240 Puylaroque. Tel: 05 63 64 92 52.

SAULIEU/FÊTE DU CHAROLAIS

Getting there
Michelin map 65   Saulieu lies west of **Dijon**. Take route A38 west to **Sombernon**, exit onto the scenic D905 to **Vitteaux** and turn onto the D70 to **Précy-sur-Thil**. Drive through Précy and to the west of it take the D980 south to Saulieu.

Where to stay   In a city with such a reputation for hospitality, there are many good options. One of the most popular, central and comfortable is **Hôtel de la Poste**, 1 rue Grillot, rue d'Argentine, which also has secure parking. Tel: 03 80 64 05 67.

Where to eat   The **Hôtel de la Poste** restaurant has several tempting menus (see above). If beef is not your favourite, try chicken fricassee in a creamy Chablis-chive sauce with fresh *cèpes*.

Office de Tourisme, 24 rue d'Argentine, 21210 Saulieu. Tel:03 80 64 00 21.

SEPTEMBER

MUNSTER/FÊTE DE LA TRANSHUMANCE ET DU MUNSTER

Getting there
Michelin map 242   From **Colmar**, follow the D417 through Wintzenheim for about 20 kms (12 miles) to reach Munster in the Vosges mountains.

Where to stay   The **Hôtel aux Deux Sapins**, 49 rue du 9ième-Zouave, is within walking distance of the centre of Munster and the *fête* activities. Tel: 03 89 77 33 96. **Ferme-Auberge du Crystalesgut**, 68380 Breitenbach, south of Munster, is run by the Dischinger family and offers *gîtes* (with kitchens) or simple rooms at the end of a trail into cheese country. Open from 1 May to 1 November. Tel: 03 89 77 51 11. Also serves rustic, hearty meals.

Where to eat The **Hôtel aux Deux Sapins** dining room is popular with local gourmets (see above). Outside Munster, 6 kms (4 miles) east on the route to Colmar, the **Nouvelle Auberge** is good for Alsatian specialities. Tel: 03 89 71 07 70.

Discoveries Tuesday and Saturday are market days in Munster.

Office de Tourisme, 1 rue du Couvent. Tel: 03 89 77 31 80. Ask for a map of La Route du Fromage.

ARPAJON/FOIRE AUX HARICOTS

Getting there
Michelin map 237 Drive from Paris on the N20 through **Antony** and Arpajon is about an hour south, just past Monthiery. Regional trains, the R.E.R., run south to the Arpajon station. Check timetables and connection points to travel from Paris.

Where to stay There aren't many hotel options in Arpajon, but the **Hôtel Arpège** is close to the centre and to the R.E.R. station, at 23 boulevard Jean-Jaurès. Tel: 01 69 17 10 22. Near Longjumeau, south of Arpajon on the N20, **Relais des Chartreux** at 91160 Saulx les Chartreux, Saulx, tel: 01 69 09 34 31, is a good base for exploring the Essonne.

Where to eat Brasseries facing the Broad Bean Fair tents offer sizzling grilled meat, served with a hearty side of *chevrier d'Arpajon*, and autumn's apple tarts at reasonable prices. Find a table at noon as it gets busy later. For fine *cuisine bourgeoise* in a formal dining room, the **Saint Clément** at 16 av. Hoche is a renowned *bonne table*. Tel: 01 64 90 21 01.

Discoveries *Potager* and grounds of **Domaine de St-Jean de Beauregard**, which hosts three plant fêtes during the year. 91940 St-Jean de Beauregard. Tel: 01 60 12 00 01.

Office de Tourisme, 70 Grande Rue, 91290 Arpajon. Tel: 01 60 83 36 51.

KRAUTERGERSHEIM/OBERNAI/FÊTE DE LA CHOUCROUTE

Getting there
Michelin map 242 **Krautergersheim** is between **Strasbourg** and **Obernai**. Take route N422 and turn east onto the D207 toward Hindisheim.

Where to stay Central, classed historic site – the **Hôtel de la Cloche** faces Obernai's picturesque City Hall, 90 rue du Général-Gouraud, 67210 Obernai. Tel: 03 88 95 52 89.

Where to eat South of **Strasbourg**, 19 kms (12 miles) west of Geipolsheim in Blaesheim, Philippe Schadt, the genial host of **Chez Schadt,** will delight you with Alsatian cuisine. Tel: 03 88 68 86 00. Closed Sunday night and Thursday.

Discoveries Wines and Kirsch – **Au 20 Alsace** is run by Mme Christiane Blanck, 96 rue Général-Gouraud, Obernai. Tel: 03 88 48 32 06. This winemaker's shop near the *mairie* sells their own wines, regional specialities and a good selection of fruit spirits: cherry/Kirsch plus quince, blackberry, blueberry etc. Open Sunday morning.

Gérard Meyer of the *fête* committee, 20 rue de Paris, 67880 Krautergersheim. Tel: 03 08 95 74 01. Not easy to reach; evenings are best. Mairie, tel: 03 88 95 75 18.

OCTOBER

MONTAUBAN/BIOFOIRE

Getting there
Michelin map 989

Montauban is easily located on highway N 20 between **Cahors** and **Toulouse**. Or, take D999 west, about 75 kilometres (47 miles) from Albi. Trains run to Montauban from Toulouse.

Where to stay

In the old centre of Montauban, **Hôtel Mercure** is set in a fine eighteenth-century mansion at 12 rue Notre Dame. Tel: 05 63 63 17 23. Special but expensive.

Where to eat

Dine under the brick vaulting of **Le Ventadour**, facing the River Tarn, at 23 quai Ville-Bourbon, a unique setting and tempting menu. Tel: 05 63 63 34 58.

Discoveries

For honey – even honey vinegar: *vinaigre de miel au serpolet* "Apis Vinaegria" – visit **Marietta & Fournil**, La Borde, 81340 Trébas. Tel: 05 63 55 91 42.

Office de Tourisme, Ancien Collège, pl. Prax, 82000 Montauban. Tel: 05 63 63 60 60.

VILLEFRANCHE-DU-PÉRIGORD/FÊTE DE LA CHÂTAIGNE ET DU CÈPE

Getting there
Michelin map 75

Take route D660 to **Cahors** and Villefranche-du-Périgord is southwest of Sarlat.

Where to stay

In the forest, a small inn, **La Petite Auberge**, Les Peyrouillères, is the closest place to the *fête* to stay. Tel: 05 53 29 91 01. Eight kms (5 miles) northwest of Villefranche-du-Périgord in Mazeyrolles, **La Clé des Champs** is a Logis de France hotel. Tel: 05 53 29 95 94.

Where to eat

Under the arcades, **Hôtel du Commerce**, pl. Halle, has an all-chestnut menu for the *fête*; table reservations can be made the morning of the *fête*. Tel: 05 53 29 90 08.

Sandwiches, grilled sausages, chestnuts and beverages are available during the day.

Discoveries

A complex and fruity white wine, *Clos d'Yvigne Vendanges tardives* is a dessert in itself. Made by *vigneronne* Patricia Atkinson, 24240 Gageac-Rouillac. Tel: 05 53 22 94 40.

Syndicat d'Initiative, 24550 Villefranche-du-Périgord. Tel: 05 53 29 98 37.

ESPELETTE/FOIRE AUX PIMENTS

Getting there
Michelin Map 78

From Bayonne follow signs to **Cambo-les-Bains** on the D932, then turn (direction Ainhoa) onto the D918 to Espelette.

Where to stay

To stay in the centre of Espelette, reserve a room at the **Hôtel Euzkadi**, 64250 Espelette, run by the mayor of Espelette, M. André Darraïdou, and his wife, Michèle. For the *fête*, you need to write to reserve your room one year in advance. Other villages, such as picturesque Ainhoa, tucked into the foothills of the Pyrénées, offer accommodation, but also need to be booked well ahead.

Where to eat

Dine at the **Hôtel Euzkadi** (see above), a Basque experience itself.
Tel: 05 59 93 91 88.

Discoveries

Take a tour of **Chocolats Antton**, pl. de la Poste, 64240 Espelette.
Tel: 05 59 29 18 70.

Syndicat d'Initiative, 64250 Espelette.

NOVEMBER

VARAIGNES/FOIRE AUX DINDES

Getting there
Michelin maps
75 and 72

Drive north from **Périgueux** towards **Brantôme** on the D939, then take the D675 north to Nontron. Alternatively, drive south from **Limoges** on the N21, turning right after Chalus onto the D6 and then taking the D85 to Nontron.

Where to stay

A family-run hotel in the old style, **Grand Hôtel Pélisson**, 24300 Nontron, has clean, comfortable rooms and reasonable rates. Tel: 05 53 56 11 22.

Where to eat

The restaurant of the **Grand Hôtel Pélisson** in Nontron serves excellent food. Its cosy restaurant with copperware also has a grand piano.

Discoveries

Flour and nut oil mills in the area are worth visiting. For more information, call Moulin de la Forge, 161110 Rancogne. Tel: 05 45 23 10 32.

Centre d'Étude du Patrimoine du Haut-Périgord, 24360 Varaignes.
Tel: 05 53 56 23 66. Varaignes Office de Tourisme, tel: 05 53 56 35 76.

DIEPPE/FOIRE AUX HARENGS

Getting there
Michelin map 989

From **Rouen**, take route N27 north. From Le Havre, follow the D925 east.

Where to stay

Between the old quarter and the quays and facing the sea is the quiet **Hôtel Aguado**, 30 blvd Verdun. Tel: 02 35 84 27 00.

Where to eat

On the market place, **Hôtel Grand Duquesne**, 15 pl. St-Jacques, is fun.
Tel: 02 35 84 21 51.

For the catch of the day, try **Marmite Dieppoise**, 8 rue St-Jean,
tel: 02 35 84 24 26 (closed late November).
Dine superbly in a seventeenth-century setting at the restaurant at **Les Hêtres**, on the route from St-Valéry to Fécamp. Tel: 02 35 57 09 30.

Office de Tourisme, pont Jehan-Ango, 76203 Dieppe (on the quay).
Tel: 02 35 84 11 77.

ANGOULÊME/GASTRONOMADES

Getting there
Michelin map 989

From **Poitiers**, take the N10 south.

Where to stay

Facing the Palace of Justice in old Angoulême, the **Hotêl du Palais** at
4 pl. F. Louvel is in a central location, is simple, clean and reasonable if a
little creaky. Tel: 05 45 92 54 11.

Where to eat

Set in two very old houses in Angoulême's old centre, **La Ruelle** offers a
mouth-watering menu and professional service. Charente's finest ingredients
and traditions are interpreted with imagination by Véronique Dauphin.
La Ruelle, 6 rue Trois-Notre-Dame, tel: 05 45 95 15 19. Reserve for Saturday
evening dinner (usually closed Saturday lunch).

Discoveries

For Pineau des Charentes and *chèvre* cheese visit Jousseaume's farm,
16440 Roullet-St-Estèphe (route to Barbezieux). Tel: 05 45 66 33 41.

Office de Tourisme, pl. des Halles,16007 Angoulême. Tel: 05 45 95 16 84

DECEMBER

NANCY AND ST-NICOLAS-DU-PORT/FÊTE DE ST-NICOLAS

Getting there
Michelin map 989

From **Toul**, take route A31 east into Nancy.

Where to stay

Hôtel Crystal is centrally located at 5 rue Chanzy. Tel: 03 83 17 54 00.

Where to eat

Tucked into a square around a gateway from Stanislas Square, at
1 pl. Vaudémont, **Comptoir du Petit Gastrolâtre** is perfect for a special
lunch. For dinner try **Mirabelle** at 24 rue Héré; reservations suggested. Both
restaurants have moderate- to high-priced menus. Sunday brunch is not to
be missed at the glittering **Brasserie Excelsior**, with its classy Art Nouveau
interior, near the train station at 50 rue H. Poincaré.

Discoveries

There are several good shops selling *Bergamote de Nancy*, but **Nathalie Lalonde**
at 32 rue St-Jean & 2 av. Milton, 45000 Nancy, has a superb range of sweets
and pastries. Tel: 03 83 40 23 63.
For good, regional wine try vintner G.Walter, 11 rue des Quartiers, 57630
Marsal, and ask for the Vin Gris de Vic-sur-Seille 1996. Tel: 03 87 01 14 92.

Office de Tourisme, 14 pl. Stanislas, 54000 Nancy. Tel: 03 83 35 22 41.

LOUHANS/LES GLORIEUSES

Getting there Michelin map 989	From **Dijon**, travel south on the A8 through Chalon-sur-Saône, then turn southeast onto the D978 (signed to Lons-le-Saunier) to Louhans.
Where to stay	In a wooded glen on the edge of Louhans, an old mill provides a quiet spot for the night – or for a week. Rooms at the **Hostellerie du Moulin de Bourgchâteau**, route de Chalon, are simple, adequate and modern. Tel: 03 85 75 37 12.
Where to eat	At **La Cotriade**, 4 rue d'Alsace, both fowl and fish are delicious (and don't skip dessert!). Tel: 03 85 75 19 91.
Discoveries	For more about this fascinating rural area (find out why the Bressans are called "yellow bellies"), and a grand setting, visit the Ecomusée de la Bresse Bourguignonne in the Château de Pierre-de-Bresse. North of Louhans, in the direction Dole, this makes a good day trip. Opening hours in winter are 2.00–6.00 p.m.

Office de Tourisme, 1 arcade St-Jean, 71500 Louhans. Tel: 03 85 75 05 22.

Sites Remarquable du Goût / Remarkable Sites of Taste

An assocation of five government offices awards their seal to places (sites) or events (fairs or markets) in all parts of France. Some regions have printed brochures or information on their sites of taste. For example, the Roussillon has published a brochure with maps describing each product and its site. It lists the following: **Bouzigues** for its oysters and fair in August, **St-Hilaire** for an abbey that makes sparkling Limoux wines, **Thuir** for its hall and vats that contain Dubonnet and other apéritifs, **Collioure** for its anchovies, and **Banyuls** for wines. For more information (in French) detailing your area of interest, look at the website: www.sitesremarkabledugout.com

The above address is also the source for details on the October **Semaine du Goût**, as it is one of the sponsoring parties. Each region has a great deal of independence in organizing the programmes, events and publications for the week of focus on flavour. One region that has organized extensive activities is the Provence region's **Centre Régional du Goût des Terroirs**, which has its own website: www.gout-en-provence.asso.fr e-mail: gout.en.provence@wanadoo.fr

Terroir et Patrimoine issues a useful booklet listing regional specialities and restaurants (in many parts of France) participating in their programme. Information in English is available on their programmes, given on their website. Tap into "local heritage" to learn more about the "petite gourmet" menus for children. Contact: Fédération Nationale des Offices de Tourisme et Syndicats d'Initiative 280 blvd St-Germain, 75007 Paris. Tel: 01 44 11 10 30. http://www.tourisme.fr

Bon Appétit!

Popular Festivals and Saints' Days

The church year traditionally sets the year's events, along with patron saints.

6 January, Twelfth night	Les Rois
20 January	St-Sébastien, patron of cider-makers
22 January	St-Vincent, patron of vines and olive trees
2 February	Candlemas, Chandeleur
Shrove Tuesday	Mardi-Gras
Ash Wednesday, beginning of Lent (Carême)	Les Cendres
mid-way through Lent	Mi-Carême
Palm Sunday	Rameaux
Good Friday	Vendredi-Saint
Easter Sunday	Pâques
Easter Monday	Lundi de Pâques
23 April	St-Georges, patron of knights and soldiers
25 April	St-Marc, patron of the vine
1 May	Worker's holiday, May Day
8 May	Victory in Europe Day
40 days after Easter	Ascension
14 May	St-Honoré, patron of bakers
seventh Sunday after Easter	Pentecost, Pentecôte
24 June	St-Jean, St John the Baptist's day
14 July	French National Day, national holiday
15 August	Assumption of the Virgin
29 September	St-Michel, nut harvest begins
9 October	St-Denis, patron of France
18 October	St-Luc, patron of butchers
11 November	St-Martin, also Veterans Day
25 November	St-Catherine, Tree Fairs
30 November	St-André, patron of fishermen
6 December	St-Nicolas, patron of schoolchildren and Lorraine
14 December	St-Odile, patroness of Alsace
24 December, Christmas Eve	Réveillon de Noël
25 December, Christmas Day	Noël
31 December, New Year's Eve	St-Sylvestre

Food Festivals and Fairs by Subject

This list of popular festivals has been compiled during eight years of exploring gastronomic *fêtes*, using regional lists (no central list exists) and local information.
Alphabetical listings indicate early, middle or late in the month.
Address inquiries to the Mairie, with town and postal code.

Place and *département*	*Fête or Foire*	*Time*
Apple and Cider Fairs (*cidre*: cider, *pomme*: apple, *fruits*: fruit, *noix*: nut, *châtaignes*: chestnut)		
Auffay (76720) Seine-Maritime	Foire au Cidre	June
Azay-le-Rideau (37190) Loire	Foire aux Pommes	late October
Beton-Bazoches (77320) Seine-et-Marne	Fête du Cidre	early October
Charolles (71120) Saône-et-Loire	Foire au Cidre	mid-October
Châtillon-en-Diois (26410) Drôme	Foire aux Pommes	October
Le Petit Pressigny (37350) Indre-et-Loire	Foire aux Pommes	mid-October
Neuvy St-Sépulcre (36230) Indre	Journée de la Pomme et Fruits	late October
Objat (19130) Corrèze	Foire aux Pommes	October
Pailhares (07410) Ardèche	Foire aux Pommes, Noix et Châtaignes	early October
Poul-Fétan, Morbihan	Fête du Cidre	late September
Beef and Veal Festivals (*bestiaux*: livestock, *boeufs gras*: beef cattle, *viande*: meat)		
Beaucroissant (38140 Rives) Isère	Foire aux Bestiaux	September
Captieux (33840) Gironde	Fête des Boeufs Gras	early February
Evron (53600) Mayenne	Festival de la Viande	early September
Saulieu (21210) Côte-d'Or	Fête du Charolais	late August
St-Léonard-de-Noblat (87400)	Foire à la Viande Limousine	3rd weekend in August
Bread Fairs (*boulangerie*: bakery; *pain*: bread; *vieux four*: bake oven; *pain chaud*: hot bread)		
Blancafort (18410) Cher	Fête de la Boulangerie	early June
Briantes (36400) Indre	Fête du Pain	early July
Catton-Grammont (70110) Haute-Saône	Fête du Vieux Four	Palm Sunday
Lautrec (81440) Tarn	Fête du Pain	mid-August
Olliergues (63880) Puy-de-Dôme	Foire au Pain	mid-August
St-Brandan* (87400) Côte d'Armor	Fête du Pain Chaud	mid-February
(* Town closest to Carestiemble)		

Cheese Fairs (*fromage*: cheese, *chèvre*: goat's cheese, *comté*: a cow's milk cheese)

Anduze (30140) Gard	Fête du Pelardon (Goat's Cheese)	late April
Antony (92161) Hauts-de-Seine	Foire aux Fromages	mid-September
Banon (04150) Alpes de Haute-Provence	Foire de Banon	early June
Chaource (10210) Aube	Rendez-vous Gourmands	late October
Coulommiers (77120) Seine-et-Marne	Foire aux Fromages	Palm Sunday
Condrieu (69420) Rhône	Fête de la Rigotte et du Vin (Goat's Cheese and wine)	1 May
Dieulefit (26220) Drôme	Fête du Picodon (Goat's Cheese)	June
La Capelle (02260) Aisne	Foire aux Fromages	early September
Laruns (64440) Pyrénées-Atl.	Foire aux Fromages du Béarn	early October
Poligny (39800) Jura	Fête du Comté	late July
Roaix (84110) Vaucluse	Fête du Chèvre	early July
Rocamadour (46500) Lot	Fête du Chèvre	Pentecost weekend
St-Martin-Valmeroux (15140) Cantal	Fête du Fromage de Salers	late September
Ste-Maure (37800) Indre-et-Loire	Fête du Chèvre	June
Sancerre (18300) Cher	Foire aux Crottins de Chavignol (Goat's Cheese)	early May
Taulignan (26770) Drôme	Fête du Picodon	early June

Chocolate or Sweets Fairs (*chocolat*: chocolate, *sucre*: sugar)

Bayonne (64109) Pyrénées-Atl.	Journées du Chocolat	mid-May
Erstein (67150) Bas-Rhin	Fête du Sucre	late August
Guignicourt (02190) Aisne	Fête du Sucre	May

Christmas/Holiday Food Fairs

Albi (81005) Tarn	Foire de Noël	1st Friday in December

Fish and Seafood Fairs (*écrevisse*: crayfish, *harengs*: herrings, *hûitres*: oysters, *poisson*: fish, *Ttoro*: fish soup)

Aigurande (36140) Indre	Festival de l'Écrevisse	3rd week in August
Dieppe (76208) Seine-Maritime	Foire aux Harengs	mid-November
Bouzigues and Sète (34140) Hérault	Fête des Huîtres	August
Gujan-Mestras (33470) Gironde	Fête des Huîtres	August
Lachaussée (55210) Meuse	La Fête du Poisson	late November
Le Tréport (76470) Seine-Maritime	Foire aux Harengs	mid-November
Reuilly (36260) Indre	Fête aux Huîtres	late October
St-Jean-de-Luz (64500) Pyrénées-Atl.	Fête du Ttoro	early September
St-Valéry-en-Caux (76460) Seine-Maritime	Foire aux Harengs	mid-November
Sarzeau (56370) Morbihan	Fête de l'Huître	April

Foie Gras Fairs *(fattened fowl – by département)*

Ariège

Mazères (09270)	Foire au Gras	December
Verniolle (09120)	Foire au Gras	1st Sunday in December

Aude

Belpech (11420)	Foire au Gras	2nd week in December
Castelnaudary (1140)	Foire au Gras	1st Sunday in December
Caunes-Minervois (11160)	Foire au Gras	2nd week in November

Aveyron

Montbazens (12220)	Foire au Gras	3rd Tuesday in December

Corrèze

Brive-la-Gaillarde (19312)	Foire des Rois/au Gras	early January and February
Objat (19130)	Foire au Gras	1 December and 1 January

Dordogne

Issigeac (24560)	Foire au Gras	December
Piegut-Pluviers (24360)	Foire au Gras	January and February
Sarlat (24200)	Foire et Marchés au Gras	December
Thiviers (24800)	Foire au Gras	December
Vergt (24380)	Foire au Gras	1st Friday in February

Gers

Samatan (32130)	Marché au Gras (France's Largest Foie Gras Market)	opens mid-November

Gironde

Loupiac-de-La Réole (33190)	Fête de Loupiac et du Foie Gras	late November
Ludon Médoc (33290)	Foire au Gras	November
Monségur (33580)	Foire au Gras	2nd Sunday in December 2nd Sunday in February

Haute-Pyrénées

Vic-en-Bigorre (65500)	Foire au Gras	early December

Lot

Cahors (4600)	Foire au Gras et aux Truffes	November to March

Tarn

Lavaur (81500)	Concours de Foie Gras	mid-December

Fowl Fairs (foie gras fairs on page 243) (*chapon*: fattened fowl, *dinde*: turkey, *volailles*: poultry, *palombe*: wood pigeon)

Bourg-en-Bresse (01000) Ain	Les Glorieuses	2nd week in December
Grignols (33690) Gironde	Foire aux Chapons	mid-December
La Laupie (26740) Drôme	Foire aux Dindes	late August
Licques (62850) Pas-de-Calais	Fête de la Dinde	early December
Louhans (71500) Saône-et-Loire	Les Glorieuses	mid-December
St-Julia (31540) Haute-Garonne	Foire aux Chapons	mid-December
St-Sever (40500) Landes	Fête des Volailles	late November
Sare (64310) Pyrénées-Atl.	Fêtes de la Palombe	mid-October
Varaignes (24360) Dordogne	Foire aux Dindes	1 November

Fruit fairs (*groseille*: redcurrants, *fraises*: strawberries, *cerises*: cherries, *myrtille*: blueberries, *citron*: lemon, *mirabelles*: plums, *chasselas*: grapes, *pomme*: apples, *abricot*: apricots)

Bar-le-Duc (55012) Meuse	Fête de la Groseille	mid-September
Beaubec-la-Rosière (76440) Seine-Maritime	Foire aux Melons	late August
Beaulieu-sur-Dordogne, Corrèze	Foire aux Fraises	late May
Céret (66400) Pyrénées-Or.	Foire aux Cerises	Pentecost
Chaumeuil (19390) Corrèze	Foire de la Myrtille	late July
Glux-en-Glenne (58370) Nièvre	Fête des Myrtilles	mid-August
Juillac (19350) Corrèze	Foire aux Fruits d'Automne	late October
Menton (06502) Alpes-Maritimes	Fête du Citron	mid-February
Metz (57036) Moselle	Foire aux Mirabelles	late August
Moissac (82200) Tarn-et-Garonne	Fête des Chasselas	September, alternate years
Nozières (07270) Ardèche	Fête des Framboises	1 August
Objat (19130) Corrèze	Fête de la Pomme	mid-October
Quévert (22100) Côtes-d'Armor	Fête de la Pomme	early November
Rivesaltes (66600) Pyrénées-Or.	Fête de l'Abricot	mid-July
St-Georges-des-Côteaux (17810)	Foire aux Melons	August
St-Sauveur-Gouvernet (26110) Drôme	Fête aux Abricots	15 August
Samer (62830) Pas-de-Calais	Fête aux Fraises	late June
Verlinghem (59237) Nord	Fête des Fraises	late June

Garlic Fairs (*l'ail*: garlic, *ail de lomagne*, a white garlic, *l'ail rose*, pink garlic, *basilic*: basil)

Arleux (59151) Nord	Foire à l'Ail	September
Beaumont de Lomagne (Tarn-et-G.)	Ail de Lomagne en Fête	3rd weekend in July
Billom (63160) Puy-de-Dôme	Foire à l'Ail	2nd weekend in August
Bourgueil (37140) Indre-et-Loire	Foire à l'Ail	22 July
Cadours (31480) Haute-Garonne	Foire à l'Ail	late August

Draguignan (83001) Var	Foire à l'Ail	1st Saturday in September
Hyères (83412) Var	Foire à l'Ail	late August
Lautrec (81440) Tarn	Fête de l'Ail Rose	late August
Locon (62400) Pas-de-Calais	Foire à l'Ail	early September
Mauvezin (32120) Gers	Marché à l'Ail	every Thursday
St-Clar (32380) Gers	Foire à l'Ail	late August
Sauzet (26740) Drôme	Foire à l'Ail	late July
Sollies Pont (83210) Var	Foire à l'Ail	2nd Monday in September
Tours (37032) Indre-et-Loire	Foire à l'Ail et au Basilic	late July
Uzès (30700) Gard	Foire à l'Ail	24 June (St-Jean)

Gastronomy Fairs and Salons

Angoulême (16016) Charente	Gastronomades	late November
Arèches-Beaufort (73270) Savoie	Salon des Sites du Goût	11 November
Auch (32007) Gers	Foire Annuelle	September
Chartres (28190) Eure-et-Loire	Les Artisanales	mid-October
Châtillon-sur-Chalaronne (01400) Ain	Foire-Salon Gastronomique	late April
Colmar (68021) Haut-Rhin	Festiga	May
Dijon (21033) Côte-d'Or	Foire Internationale et Gastronomique	early November
Donzère (26290) Drôme	Foire Gourmande	early May
Hendaye (64700) Pyrénées-Atl.	Le Sukalki de Hendaye	24 May
Launois-sur-Vence (08430) Ardennes	Foire Gastronomique	mid-October
Monte-Carlo, Monaco	Monte-Carlo Gastronomie	late November
Montélimar (26207) Drôme	Salon de la Gastronomie	late November
Mulhouse (68062) Haut-Rhin	Journées d'Octobre Alsatian Specialities	early October
Niort (79022) Deux-Sèvres	Concours: Saveurs de Poitou-Charentes	early October
Romorantin-Lathenay (41200)	Journées de Sologne	late October
St-Etienne-de-Baigorry (64430) Pyr.-Atl.	Foire Gastronomique	late August
St-Paul-Trois-Châteaux (26130) Drôme	Fête Gourmande	early June
Toulouse (31040) Haute-Garonne	Village Gourmand des Capitouls	mid-November
Troyes (10026) Aube	Foire Gastronomique	late November
Valaurie (26230) Drôme	Salon Gourmand	11 December

Harvest Fairs (*battage* threshing, *vendange* grape harvest, *moisson* wheat)

Beaulieu-sur-Oudon (53320) Mayenne	Fête de la Moisson	early August
Le Fieu (33230) Gironde	Fête des Vendanges	last Friday in July
Preuilly-la-Ville (36220) Indre	Fête de la Moisson à l'Ancienne	August
Stotzheim (67140) Bas Rhin	Fête des Moissons	late July

Herbal Plants and Seasoning/Floral Fairs (*tilleul*: lime blossom, *lavande*: lavender, *corso*: parade)

Buis-les-Baronies (26170) Drôme	Foire au Tilleul	early July
Ferrassières (26570) Drôme	Fête de la Lavande	early July
Valréas (84600) Vaucluse	Le Corso de la Lavande	early August

Lamb or Mutton Fairs (*mouton*: sheep, *agneau*: lamb, *cotelettes*: chops)

Gournay (36230) Indre	Fête du Mouton	early August
Pauillac (33250) Gironde	Fête de l'Agneau	1st weekend in May
Luz-St-Sauveur (65120)	Fête du Mouton	early August
Hautes-Pyrénées	Foire des Côtelettes	late September

Nuts and Chestnut Fairs (*châtaignes*: chestnuts, *marrons*: chestnuts)

Bedarieux (34600) Hérault	Foire aux Châtaignes	early November
Bocagnano (20136) Cors	Fête de la Châtaigne	early December
Dournazac (87230) Haute-Vienne	Fête de la Châtaigne	late October
Eguzon-Chantome (36270) Indre	Fête de la Châtaigne	early November
Genille (37460) Indre-et-Loire	Foire aux Marrons	late October
Maron (36120) Indre	Fête du Marron	mid-October
Mourjou (15340) Cantal	Foire à la Châtaigne	mid-October
Nantes (44036) Loire-Atlantique	Fête des Châtaignes et du Vin Nouveau	mid-October
Vianne (47230) Lot-et-Garonne	Dégustation de Châtaignes et Vin Nouveau	early October

Olive Fairs

Corconne (30260) Gard	Fête de l'Olive	July
Montegrosso, Corsica	Fête d'Olive et d'Olivier	mid-July
Nyons (26110) Drôme	l'Alicoque	early February
	Fête de l'Olive	mid-July

Organic Products (*miel*: honey)

Aubazine (19190) Corrèze	Foire au Miel et aux Produits Naturels	mid-September
Langon (33210) Gironde	Agro-Bio Foire	early September
Montauban (82013) Tarn-et-Garonne	Foire Biologique	mid-October
Rabastens (81800) Tarn	Foire Biocybèle	mid-May
Targon (33760) Gironde	Agro-Bio Foire	July

Pastry and Cake Fairs (*flammiche*: cheese tart, *mias*: cherry cake, *tourtière*: flaky pastry, *chausson aux pommes*: apple turnovers)

Brive-la-Gaillarde (19312) Corrèze	Foire des Rois	early January
Maroilles (59550) Nord	Fête de la Flammiche	2nd Sunday in August

Orval (18200) Cher	Fête des Mias	mid-June
Samatan (32130) Gers	Fête de la Tourtière	May
St-Calais (72120) Sarthe	Fête du Chausson aux Pommes	early September

Pork Fairs (*cochon*: pork, *tumbera*: pork)

Puichéric (11700) Aude	Foire au Cochon	early January
Renno (20160) Corse-du-Sud	A Tumbera	1st weekend in February
Trie-sur-Baïse (65220) Hautes-Pyrénées	Foire au Cochon	August
Ungersheim (68190) Haut-Rhin	Fête du Cochon	mid May/ Ascension

Sausage and Ham Fairs (*jambon*: ham, *andouillettes*: tripe sausage, *boudin*: blood sausage)

Bayonne (64109) Pyrénées-Atl.	Foire au Jambon	Easter weekend
Bedarieux (34600) Hérault	Foire aux Jambons (since 1529!)	early May
Mennetou-sur-Cher (41320) Loir-et-Cher	Foire aux Andouillettes	early May
Mortagne-au-Perche (61400) Orne	Foire au Boudin	mid-March

Snail and Frog Fairs (*grenouille*: frogs, *lumas*: snails)

Poulaines (36210) Indre	Fête de la Grenouille	mid-July
Uzay-le-Venon (18190) Cher	Fête des Lumas	late May
Vendoeuvres (36500) Indre	Fête de la Grenouille	late July

Transhumance

Allanche (15160) Cantal	Fête de l'Estive (Salers) (Cows)	late May
Die (26150) Drôme	Fête de la Transhumance (Sheep)	early June
St-Chely d'Aubrac (12470) Aveyron	Fête de la Transhumance (Cows)	May
St-Rémy-de-Provence (13210) Bouches-du-Rhône	Transhumance (Sheep)	June

Truffle and Mushroom Fairs (truffles: December into February, depending on season)
(*truffe*: truffle, *marché*: market, *champignons*: mushrooms)

Aups (83630) Var	Journée de la Truffe Noire	late January
Carpentras (84200) Vaucluse	Salon de la Truffe	early February Friday mornings, market (en gros)
Grignan (26230) Drôme	Le Vin et la Truffe en Tricastin	mid-December
Jarnac (16200) Charente	Les Marchés aux Truffes	9:00am Sunday mid-December tp mid-February
Lalbenque (46230) Lot	Marché	2:30pm Tuesday afternoons
Richerenque (84600) Vaucluse	Messe des Truffes	mid-January
Ste-Alvère (24510) Dordogne	Marché	9:00am Mondays
St-Avit Sénieur (24440) Dordogne	Foire aux Truffes	mid-January

St-Bonnet-le-Foid (43290) Haute-Loire	Fête des Champignons	October
Sorges (24420) Dordogne	Foire aux Truffes	mid-January
Uzès (30700) Gard	Journée des Truffes	mid-January

Vegetable Fairs (*asperge*: asparagus, *choucroute*: sauerkraut, *oignon*: onion, *artichaut*: artichoke, *mojette*: bean, *navet*: turnip, *potimarron*, *courges*: squash, *cresson*: watercress, *haricot*: beans)

Aimargues (30470) Gard	Fête de l'Asperge	early May
Brienne-le-Château (10500) Aube	Foire à la Choucroute	mid-September
Brumath (67170) Bas-Rhin	Foire aux Oignons	late September
Canet-en-Roussillon (66140)	Fête de l'Artichaut	1 May
Citou (11160) Aude	Fête des Oignons de Citou	mid-November
Fargues-sur-Ourbise (47700) Lot-et-Garonne	Foire aux Asperges	late April
Herrlisheim (67850) Bas-Rhin	Fête de la Choucroute	late September
Krautergersheim (67880) Bas-Rhin	Fête de la Choucroute	late September
Le Mans (72039) Sarthe	Foire aux Oignons	early September
Le Poiré-sur-Vie (Vendée)	Nuit de la Mojette	mid-August
Lipsheim (67640) Bas-Rhin	Fête du Navet	early November
Losse (40240) Landes	Asperges des Landes	late May
Lunéville (54300) Meurthe-et-Moselle	Fête du Potimarron	mid-September
Méréville (91660) Essonne	Cresson	early April
Mormoiron (84570) Vaucluse	Fête de l'Asperge	April
St-Mathieu (87440) Haute-Vienne	Foire aux Haricots et au Jambon	September
St-Gilles-Croix-de-Vie (85800) Vendée	Foire aux Oignons	late August
Tournon-sur-Rhône (07300) Ardèche	Fête des Oignons Ardèchois	late August
Tranzault (36230) Indre	Foire aux Courges	October

Wine Festivals and Fairs (including spirits)

Andlau (67140) Bas-Rhin	Fête du Vin	early August
Angers (49035) Maine-et-Loire	Salon des Vins de Loire	early February
Avignon (84000) Vaucluse	Fête Primeur des Côtes du Ventoux	17 November
Avize (51190) Marne	Fête de St-Vincent en Champagne	22 January
Bandol (83150) Var	Fête de Bandol	1st Sunday in December
Barr (67140) Bas-Rhin	Fête des Vendanges	1st weekend in October
Beaugency (45190) Loiret	Foire aux Vins et Produits Régionaux	late September
Beaujeu (69430) Rhône	Fête Vins Primeurs (New Wine)	16 November
Beaune (21206) Côte-d'Or	Vente des Vins de l'Hospice (Wine Auction)	mid-November

St-Vincent	Tournante/January 22nd fair	late January/ early February
Cairanne (84290) Vaucluse	Fête des Vins	late July
Castelnau-Montratier (46170) Lot	Foire des Vins de Quercy	mid-August
Condrieu (69420) Rhône	Foire de Condrieu (Rhône wines)	early May
Die (26150) Drôme	Fête de la Clairette	early September
Duras (47120) Lot-et-Garonne	Foire aux Vins	mid-August
Duravel (46700) Lot	Foire aux Vins de Cahors	mid-August
Eauze (32800) Gers	Foire aux Armagnacs	early May
Épernay (51200) Marne	St-Vincent Fête (for vintners)	last weekend in January
Gaillac (81600) Tarn	Fête du Vin Nouveau	mid-November
Gordes (84220) Vaucluse	Fête des Côtes du Ventoux	early August
Ittersxiller (67140) Bas-Rhin	Fête du Vin Nouveau (New Wine)	mid-October
Lalinde (24150) Dordogne	Foire aux Vins	early August
Larnas (07700) Ardèche	Fête des Côtes du Vivarais	mid-July
Marciac (32230) Gers	Fête des Vendanges	mid-October
Molsheim (67120) Bas-Rhin	Fête du Raisin	mid-September
Obernai (67210) Bas-Rhin	Fête des Vendanges	September
Quincy (18120) Cher	Fête du Vin Nouveau	mid-October
Ribeauvillé (68150) Haute-Rhin	Fête des Vins	July
Rivesaltes (66600) Pyrénées-Or.	Fête du Muscat de Rivesaltes	early December
St-Hippolyte (68590) Haut-Rhin	Fête du Vin Nouveau	September
St-Mont (32400) Gers	Vignoble en Fête	late March
Sancerre (18300) Cher	Foire aux Vins de Sancerre	late May
Sigoulès (24240) Dordogne	Foire aux Vins	August
Troyes (1000) Aube	Foire aux Vins	late November/ early December
Tuchan (11350) Aude	Foire aux Vins	May
Tulette (26790) Drôme	Fête du Vin Nouveau	late November
Vacqueyras (84190) Vaucluse	Fête des Côtes du Rhône	mid-July
Valréas (84600) Vaucluse	Fête des Vins et de la Lavande	early August
Visan (84820) Vaucluse	Fête des Vins	early July

Bibliography

Bardiau, Philippe, *Les Gourmandises du Terroir* (series), Didier Richard, Grenoble (1997)

Bentley, James, *Fort Towns of France*, Tauris Parke Books, London (1993)

Brennan, Georgeanne, *Potager: French Kitchen Garden*, Ebury Press, London (1992)

Busselle, Michael, *French Vineyards*, Pavilion Books, London (1992)

Cabon, Alain, *Tables et Saveurs de Bretagne*, Ed. Ouest-France, Tours (1997)

Ellen, Colette, et al., *Marchés Passion*, Londrey's, Paris (1988)

George, Rosemary, *French Country Wines*, Faber & Faber, London (1990)

Goldstein, Joyce and Evan, *Food and Wine Pairing*, Williams-Sonoma/ Time-Life, San Francisco (1999)

Gouvion, Colette, et al., *Terroirs et Gastronomie*, Midi-Pyrénées, Ed. Rouergue, Rodez (1997)

Graham, Peter, *Mourjou: The Life and Food of an Auvergne Village*, Penguin, London (1999)

Hermann-Lewis, Susan, *French Farmhouse Cookbook*, Workman Publishing, New York (1996)

Hesser, Amanda, *The Cook and the Gardener*, W.W. Norton & Co., New York (1999)

Ingram, Christine, *Les Légumes du Marché*, Larousse, Paris (1997)

Ingram, Christine, *The Vegetable Ingredients Cookbook*, Lorenz Books, Paris (1997)

Koffmann, Pierre, *Memories of Gascony*, Van Nostrand/Reinhold, New York (1990)

Lamboley, Philippe, *Saveurs & Terroirs* (series), Hachette Pratique, Paris (1999)

Long, Dixon & Ruthanne, *Markets of Provence*, Harper-Collins Publishers, San Francisco (1996)

Petitrenaud, Jean-Luc, *Guide des Bonnes Maisons* (annual), Editions 1, Paris (1999)

Pudlowski, Gilles, *Les Trésors Gourmands de la France*, Renaissance du Livre, Tournai (Belgium) 2000

Rance, Patrick, *The French Cheese Book*, Macmillan, London (1989)

Rosenblum, Mort, *A Goose in Toulouse*, Hyperion, New York (2000)

Scitivaux, Armelle de, *L'Almanach du Gastronome*, Editions Bottin Gourmand, Paris (1998)

Steingarten, Jeffrey, *The Man Who Ate Everything*, Vintage Books, New York (1998)

Strang, Jeanne, *Goose Fat and Garlic*, Kyle Cathie Ltd, London (1993)

Strang, Paul, *Wines of South-West France*, Kyle Cathie Ltd, London (1996)

Strang, Paul, *Take 200 Eggs: Food from … fairs*, Kyle Cathie Ltd, London (1997)

Tannahill, Reay, *Food in History*, Stein & Day, New York (1973)

Villas, James, *The French Country Kitchen*, Bantam Books, New York (1992)

Wells, Patricia, *Food Lover's Guide to France*, Workman Publishing, New York (1987)

Wells, Patricia, *Simply French*, Hearst Books, New York (1991)

List of Recipes

Index

Acknowledgements

Without the help of many friends and strangers, the pages in the journal that began: *l'Année de la France Gourmande*, would still be empty. From the early stages, friends Sue and Michael Kay, Sue and Paddy Langdown, and my sister, Jane Downing, have offered reading, critique and encouragement. The eleventh-hour input so generously given by Joy and Chris Lyddon was tremendously appreciated, as was the advice of Paul Charpentier in developing recipes.

Thanks go to my friends and family, to "readers" and wine-tasters, as well as to vendors and *vendeuses*, chefs, bakers and vintners who took time to talk about their work. I wish to thank my agent, Teresa Chris, and Vivien James, Nina Sharman and Claire Wedderburn-Maxwell at Pavilion Books, who guided the book's "organic evolution".

My deepest gratitude goes to my husband, Michel, my support system in the car, kitchen and dictionary-searches, as well as in technology-puzzles at odd hours. Thank you ... all.

Picture credits